STAND UP FOR WHAT'S RIGHT! NEVER LET INJUSTICE GO UNCHALLENGED

DO IT WITH KINDNESS

DENNIS DeROCHE

Kindness Rules Publishing

ISBN: 978-0-578-18284-1

Library of Congress Control Number: 2016953094

PRINTED IN THE UNITED STATES OF AMERICA

Foreword

This book is an example of a proactive response to bullying, the modus operandi of lies, threats and intimidation vs. the MO of Peace, Love and Understanding. The latter path can and does win out in my personal story, a story which includes a Rodney King-type beating to within an inch of my life on 6/29/76 by several white officers of the City of Hartford, CT PD in an act of repugnant anti-blackism. I'm white and chose to be with an African American woman and we were leaving a nightclub on that date aboard my motorcycle. I was a Social Worker with the City of Hartford at the time and my career path was abruptly road-blocked as I was convinced by legal representation that I should not stand up for my rights, that a case against the police was "unwinnable." *'A piece of me died forever'* as I say in the book. I was wrong for not standing up to the system then, *convinced that I would spend time in prison for something I didn't do*, but now I have a voice and will not be silenced any longer. We must know that *standing up for what is right* **is required**. And the *Power of Kindness* to prevail for what is good and what is right **is foreordained**.

This story is also about the wrongful arrest perpetrated by two criminal deviants on 7/26/2010 in Hollywood, FL when I was framed with a felony assault as a way to forcefully evict me from a property to avoid the due process of an eviction proceeding. A volcano erupted within me to restore my reputation and bring out the truth at all costs and to show others that there *is* a way to fight back against the bullies of the world – so the lava that flowed from my erupting volcano became the words on the pages of this book. As Elijah Cummings (D-MD) is fond of saying, **"From your pain comes your passion to do your purpose."** -- And mine is to benefit others with my life.

This is also the personal story about the injustices forced upon a family of seven children at the hands of their bipolar father who created an environment of physical and emotional abuse leading to deep depression and hopelessness where too many thoughts were of suicide, resulting in the self-execution of one of us. Mental illness in its various forms affects *at least* 1 out of 6 of all people.

But above all, this is the story of human will, of insisting upon survival mentally and emotionally from all the negative circumstances of life -- to rise above the challenges and ultimately triumph with personal success and freedom, realizing self-empowerment as the way to live -- a path to motivate that can inspire others to <u>stand up for what's right</u> and <u>never let injustice go unchallenged</u>. There is immense power in the adage, *"Where there's a will, there's a way."* And it is attested to in all languages. For me **"will"** is everything. It holds the key to survival and it is limitless; or, it is limited only by one's paying attention to it, one's application of one's energies and focus to achieve a desired goal or end result. In Spanish: *"Más hace el que quiere que el que puede."*
In French: *"Vouloir c'est pouvoir."*
The power of one's will combined with the power of love and kindness is truly monumental. We need to bring these forces together actively at the conscious level, make them part of our way of life, the way that we relate to one another for the good of all.

Finally, this book is about standing up to the injustices that all of us face as citizens of the *National Security State* we are living in (the USA); and *as victims worldwide* at the hands of unconscionable predatory profiteers who would wipe off the face of the earth our Amazon Rainforest and its indigenous tribal cultures- purely for monetary gain from its ores, timber, oil and hydroelectric power. The clock is ticking and time is running out- if we are going to make a difference, the time is NOW! We must take it personally what is happening to *OUR* MOST PRECIOUS PLANETARY TREASURE! For more on this and how *you* can make a difference, go to: www.amazonwatch.org

Preface

This personal and painful memoir is a sober reminder that our justice system can be both flawed and cruel. His unjust incarcerations of 1976 and 2010 frame, like bookends, his nomadic life, his search for meaning and lasting affection, which seldom occurred. What amazed me throughout the reading was his indomitable resilience, a refusal to let adverse circumstances destroy his hope for love, peace, and personal success.

His writing failed at first to draw me into his saga, but gradually I came to understand and value his personal insights expressed in the many quotes drawn from his wide readings of wisdom and Native American (non-Western) literature. Dennis is the archetypal survivor and consummate collector of people and sayings. His many relationships seem a blur of fond or passionate beginnings and nightmarish endings. One is left at the end of the book with deep yearnings for his success in making the memorable moments last, because his painful personal disclosures of his star-crossed existence reveal a deeply caring and sensitive human being caught in the web of mostly unmerited misfortune. How could so many bad things happen to such a nice guy?

His love affair with the BMW motorcycle and his Dodge camper RV *Peace Machine* have given the "journey" of his life an epic quality reminiscent of Dante's *Inferno* and Persig's cult classic *Zen and the Art of Motorcycle Maintenance*, which draw a thematic thread in the book. His early references to life and death paradoxes reminded me of Freud's concept of the "uncanny," (a short study called *Das Unheimliche*), which finds literary expression in Thomas Mann's novel, *The Magic Mountain*, with the contradictory emotions of falling and the thrill of confronting one's annihilation. It comes up indirectly in his brother's suicide, a theme he referred to in other parts of the book.

The short Facebook message in the middle of the book is a telling motto for Dennis' uneven but affirmative life: *"What an awesome trip life is,"* which in Dennis' case is "the ultimate alternative [RV] lifestyle."

Jon D. Green
Professor of Humanities Emeritus
Brigham Young University
May 11, 2011

Inspiration for the title of this book from Jon D. Green email correspondence of Oct 12th 2011:

"I was listening to NPR on my car radio...and heard a fascinating interview with Harry Belafonte. I didn't realize what an avid activist he was for the downtrodden of the world, especially in the civil rights movement. The most touching moment in the interview came at the end when he told of the day his unsinkable mother *(Melvine)* returned from yet another day trying to find a job and failing. She told young Harry: *'Never let injustice go unchallenged.'* When people asked him whether his activism influenced his music, he would answer: *'I was an activist long before I was a musician.'*"

And from the person who set the bar for activism in the United States: *"I'm for truth no matter who tells it. I'm for justice no matter who it is for or against. I'm a human being, first and foremost, and as such I'm for whoever or whatever benefits humanity as a whole."* Malcolm X – a martyr who fought for equal rights and freedoms for African Americans, for ending the vicious American Apartheidism.

I would like to dedicate this personal history and life guide to all those who have been falsely accused, wrongfully arrested and or convicted, and to all those who have found the power within themselves to stand up for what is right no matter how big or small the injustice may have been.

And the words that I hope all readers of this writing would pay attention to most are these from the former Emperor of Ethiopia from 1930 to 1974, *Haile Selassie I*, who was such a great influence on the life and politics of one my heroes in life, Bob Marley.   In a speech he gave at the League of Nations, Selassie I had these words to say *about justice and doing what is right:*

"Throughout history it has been the inaction of those who would have acted,
the indifference of those who should have known better,
the silence of the voice of justice when it mattered most,
that has made it possible for evil to triumph."

Chapter 1: ⑪ *"Chapter 11"* -- Bankrupt Financially & Emotionally

I begin my story *in medias res*, devoting the first two chapters to what I am presently experiencing.

I was born on the 11th day of 1948. The #11 has always been my favorite number but recently that number has defined a very low state of financial insolvency (although not officially bankrupt) as well as a very high level of emotional stress with the loss of 11 days of personal freedom in the county jail. Today is August 20th 2010, three weeks after my arrest on July 26th • **Malicious Monday 72610**. I remain in lockdown status with ankled GPS in the home of my fiancée's family. Thanks to my life-saving sister Lucille, I was bonded out of the Broward County Jail in Fort Lauderdale, Florida on 8/5/10 and released the next day. The fabricated charge, "aggravated battery causing bodily injury," is a very serious felony offense to whomever it may be attached. And to be totally innocent and be deprived of your liberties and treated as a criminal *(because you are not 'innocent till proven guilty,' you are 'guilty till proven innocent' after you have been arrested)* is a terrible fate forced upon the human condition. And if you have lived your entire life on the right side of the law doing what is right and just and good and in the autumn of your years be cast down as a doer of evil committing a violent act upon another person, this has the potential to destroy oneself or at the least cause significant damage or harm to said victim.

"Entering jail is an instantly dehumanizing process. You have a total and absolute loss –immediate loss-of control over your being." [Huffington Post, 7-13-2016, *'Sandra Bland Died One Year Ago Today'*]

I immediately begin to search my brain, the repertoire of all thoughts and emotions, for a survival plan and then a plan of action or response to the situation, because now I am clearly at war to win back my freedom and reputation that have been so viciously violated.

I am reminded of Jim Morrison's words from the movie *The Doors:* "I think I'll go to Paris and write a book, *'Observations Of An American While On Trial In Miami'.*" But I don't have the luxury to travel anywhere as I remain sequestered in the confines of a private home in Miami Gardens, Florida.

What comes to mind first are my 'guideposts'- those who have come before me offering up their wisdom through the ages. The writings of *Friedrich Nietzsche* on 'suffering' as a prerequisite for *the advancement of self* come to mind first, **"That which does not kill us makes us stronger,"** and all those others who have a similar view of man's woes on this earth such as: *"El sufrimiento purifica"* (Milton) *"Suffering purifies,"* *"El dolor es la fuente de la sabiduría"* (John Keats) *"Pain is the source of wisdom,"* and, *"El dolor es el gran maestro de los hombres"* (Anatole France) *"Pain is the great master of men."*

These words of wisdom force me to look at this travesty or miscarriage of justice as something that will eventually 'make me better' or 'enlighten me.' This process of *'self-betterment'* is eagerly confronted.

But trust me, nobody wants to be here, having to defend oneself against the false accusations and contrived fabrications of two perpetrators bent on forcibly evicting me from the property I had been re-siding at for close to 4 months.

And how do I become a victim of such vigilantism? -- *by having a very inexperienced, young female police officer #179 Robinson from the Seminole Police Dept. in Hollywood, FL believe their concocted story of attack upon one of them with a screwdriver.* She could have believed my version of the events that actually transpired, but she deferred to her conviction that one of the perps was a witness and therefore corroborator of the other, no matter that the two of them arrived on the scene together in the same vehicle. None of the glaring facts to the contrary that were pointed out to her made her reconsider an iota of thought in my direction as I was shocked to hear her yell "NO!" to my question to her: *"Can you tell me that you don't have 1% of doubt about their story; that indeed, I am the one who is the victim here of a staged felony assault – all to forcibly rid me from these premises? They came together to do this deed. This was a planned event!"* She had been conned-- hook, line and sinker- *(unless she was a paid accomplice!)* **-- Because her efforts did not pass elementary police investigation-** **Mark Twain**: *"Some of the worst things in my life never happened."*

So now I have two criminal deviants and an official of the Seminole Police Department's *"finest"* saying I did something I did not and now I will be tied up (handcuffed) and begin one by one to have all of my liberties and *ipso facto* all my abilities to defend myself systematically taken away. A phone call to get someone alerted to my predicament (after I had been transported to Ft. Lauderdale's Broward County lock-up) NOT PERMITTED. The so-called 'one free call' is a joke. The system does not allow you to make long distance calls to any # that has not been paid for in advance to a third party vendor for air time. So you will sit in your cell unable to begin to start a defense because no one can be contacted to know of your situation. This is painfully frustrating and only compounded much more by the fact that all of your primary family members live over 1000 miles away. Appearing before the Magistrate to determine bond, I finally have a chance to give the judge my sister's phone #. Have you ever experienced trying to bond someone out of a lockdown facility from outside the State where the incarceration is ongoing? Well, I found out 11 days after the arrest when I was released in shackle (house arrest), and after many attempts by my sister to find a willing bondsman, that it was an almost impossible feat to accomplish and took much more than 10% of the $5000 bond; it took all of 50%. After paying the bondsman and pre-paying for a month in advance at a 'half-way' house that was not used, an additional, non-refundable $750, my family (<u>my</u> sister <u>Lucille</u>) is now $3250 committed to my cause.

"EQUAL JUSTICE UNDER LAW"- These are the words as they appear on the United States Supreme Court building. I visited this monument and to read these great words defining our nation's judicial framework makes an American proud but it's just not the truth. JUSTICE is meted out UNEQUALLY depending upon whether you are one of the HAVES or HAVE NOTS. That is a lot closer to the truth or the reality of it. Now let's say something about those *others* right now, those HAVE NOTS. Give attention to these words from Professor Kirby Farrell of the University of Mass. at Amherst on the subject of *social death*:
"In effect, to be in a state of social death, is to be without money and to be without the ability to have an influence on other people's behavior and in turn be totally vulnerable to the wills of the people around you; and therefore, from my point of view, social death is analogous to and in many ways just as disturbing and terrifying as real death."

Try to think of all the poor 'have-nots' who are totally innocent of the charge or charges against them in any of an infinite number of framed scenarios that would land them in jail but who do not have family or funds to be released, let alone consider competent counsel that could be retained on their behalf – and please don't be so duped to believe the Public Defender's Office will take real good care of those 'who cannot afford a lawyer and one will be appointed for you'. Although it may be possible, It is truly not the norm and the joke is on the poor slob who is already down and out and may be, as well, totally innocent of the charge(s) against him or her. Johnny Cochran had it right ⚙ »» ⚙ »»» ⚙ »»»» ⚙ »»»»»

"THE COLOR OF JUSTICE IS GREEN"   Let's not forget who got away with double homicide, O.J. Simpson. And let's not forget that some have gone to their deaths via capital punishment falsely accused of crimes that were not committed, all in the name of *'justice.'* This would be *double murder*, first of the social self and then of the physical being- *and with each wrongful execution a cancer on our culture spreads further.* [An eye opener that is most revealing, "Researchers: More than 2,000 False Convictions in past 23 Years," by Elizabeth Chuck, msnbc.com US News (5-21-2012). www.ExonerationRegistry.org *Some of the reasons given for wrongful convictions: fabricated crimes, eyewitness mistakes, and misconduct by authorities.* And as of 5/2012, there were 2.4 million people in prison in the US. The US has 5% of the world population- but more than 20% of its prison population, according to the ACLU.]

To date, I must count myself as one of the 'lucky ones' (although I don't believe in 'luck'). Fortunate, I should say, that I am not still in jail deprived of all my liberties awaiting trial, and doubly so that my sister was able to fork over an additional $2500 to retain a criminal defense attorney to defend my innocence. So let's see; my sister is out $5750, I have spent 11 days of my life as an inmate treated as if I am guilty with no rights whatsoever; and, upon bonded release continue to be deprived of my liberty to move freely about under house arrest with ankled GPS. And this is the 'best case scenario' of someone who is not indigent like the 'have-nots' in the street who suffer a far worse fate of abandonment in the dumping ground of the county jail. I owe so much of a debt of gratitude to my angel sister Lucille DesRoches Glemboski. Lucille has always been good to me and a very caring and giving person to all of her family members. Without her, I would have been one of those indigents on the street, my fate radically affected in a very negative way with a very real possibility of doing serious time in prison. To say she had my back is an understatement; she had my whole life in her hands and has given me the strength and hope to fight this phony felony assault to the finish. Thanks so much Lue for every little and big thing you have always been there for. I am blessed. My life has always been about doing what is right for my fellow man and I never stopped doing 'social work' or human advocacy after my official work in those capacities was over. So now I am questioning the **Law of Karma** wondering how this could all be happening as we wait for the investigative agency to provide their findings to see how much more *justice* I can win back in my life. *My rationalization is that I needed the true victim experience in order to positively relate and be able to write empathetically about all those under similar circumstances.*

Today is Tuesday, August 24, 2010, and I just received a call from the Broward County Sheriff's Office Pretrial Services Program to appear tomorrow for a random drug test to be taken at my expense. I begin to feel the layers of liberty being further peeled away one by one from the onion that was once my Whole Person. The loss of freedom starts with the arrest and then booking and further humiliation, then incarceration and now continues with house arrest and the stripping away of any other liberties that one might still be hanging on to. The only bright light shining upon me now is that my house arrest is at the residence of my fiancée's family, *a family full of love and compassion*, not at a public facility devoid of same. *I am forever grateful to the family of Zoraida and Alejandro Mercedes.*

Collateral damage as a result of being taken into custody amounts to over $2400 in personal possessions and over $500 in UC benefits. A brand new JVC Everio HDD camcorder purchased to record my upcoming wedding day was taken out of my gym bag as it was being transferred to my car right under the nose of a police officer who was also 'helping' to transfer my items from my room to my car. A $1500 commercial grade VCR was never removed from the room I was renting nor were the 30 or so VHS tapes, edited documentaries and products from my former business, *Studio D Video & Photo*. A new 8' aluminum ladder I had just purchased to paint the mobile home I had been living in was also left behind. What appears as irony was a planned action of Mary and her son Billy Fisher to evict me from their home just as soon as I had completely repaired the roof and painted their home and storage shed. Now they have a freshly painted home and shed, a fixed roof and over $2400 worth of my possessions hijacked from my person. *And so far they have gotten away with all of it!* My immediate reaction was to go as soon as possible to the Seminole Police Department and file a theft report to try to get some of my things back. But my attorney advised me that now would not be a good time to initiate this action as it might complicate the ongoing case we are involved in. I defer to his recommendation.

Upon sharing my frustration with my attorney Paul Molle *("Mo-Lay")* of the Legal Justice Center in Ft. Lauderdale, FL, he had these words of encouragement for me: *"Dennis, I understand your frustration and it is certainly justified. The justice system is a slow turning wheel. Please continue to be patient and trust in the process."* So I wait. I have confidence in my attorney whom I feel is doing a fair job as my advocate and I continue to be patient.

My freedom has been unjustly taken away from me and for that *a legal 'injustice' has been committed*. The outcome could have been a lot worse if I had not the assistance of my sister Lucille. As well, there could have been serious bodily injury or death in the confrontation that took place on that Malicious Monday, July 26th 2010. But as it turned out, **there was no physical contact by anybody in this case**. **None**. We haven't come all that far from 1969 when *Easy Rider* came out. Remembering the dialogue Jack Nicholson's character had with Dennis Hopper's before they and Peter Fonda's were all savagely beaten by a bunch of lawless rednecks with Nicholson's character dying as a result is valuable for the redeeming social significance that must be shared and to ask the question, *"What is freedom?"*

*Keep these words in mind from one of my favorite authors, Johann Wolfgang von Goethe: *"None are more helplessly enslaved than those who falsely believe they are free."* From the movie *Easy Rider*:

N: "Ya know, this used to be a helluva good country. I can't understand what's going on with it."

H: "Man, everyone got chicken, that's what happened to it. Hey, we can't even get a second rate hotel or motel. They think we're gonna cut their throat or something. They're scared, man."

N: **"Oh, they're not scared of you. They're scared of what you represent to them."**

H: "Hey, man, all we represent to them is somebody who needs a haircut."

N: "Oh, no, **what you represent to them is freedom**." [Parallel: ***Tragic Tuesday 62976***, Chapter 13]

H: "Whata hell is wrong with freedom; that's what it's all about."

N: "Oh, yeah, that's what it's all about, alright. But talking about it and doing it, that's two different things. I mean, it's real hard to be free when you're bought and sold in the marketplace. Of course, don't ever tell anybody that they're not free or they're going to get real busy killing and maiming to prove to you that they are. Oh, yeah, they are going to talk to you and talk to you and talk to you about individual freedom, but **they see a free individual – it's going to scare them**."

H: "It don't make them running scared." *(The true culprits in my case saw a free man, a longhair, and*

N: **"No, it makes them dangerous."** *thought they had an easy target; then they acted*

H: (Acknowledges with a nod of his head) *dangerously, perjuring themselves.)*

This dialogue represents the heart and soul of that 'landmark American film' as it's been called. And we can all look introspectively as to where we fit on this *freedom scale:*

Slave---------------------"I think I'm free" (disillusionment) -----------"I know I'm free & it feels great!"

(No freedom)   (a member of Sheople – still a slave)   (I do not follow blindly; I keep the fires of freedom burning)

*If you insist upon reading Chapter 2, I apologize for your trip into ennui. I felt it was important to include the six months loss of freedom and the legal process of my case and to have a record of events that occurred. If you would like to jump *back* to the events that led up to my arrest, go to Chapter 23: *A Very Ugly Chapter In My Life That Caused Me To Write This Book/Anatomy of A Frame*: pp. 103-105

Chapter 2: *Case Progress: State v. Dennis DeRoche 10-013532-CF10A   Re: 7-26-2010*
"Strength does not come from physical capacity. It comes from indomitable will."

Jawaharlal Nehru

September 15, 2010. Bad news. I had been expecting a call from my attorney by Monday the 13th after his conversation with the prosecutor of this case, the ASA (Assistant State's Attorney). We both believed the case would be thrown out and that there was no "good faith basis" to officially file this case. We were wrong. The case is now officially filed and it looks like we're headed for a jury trial. I have a hard time accepting this decision but still have a lot of faith in my attorney and he also believes in me; he knows that I am innocent of these charges. So now we will request a hearing to have the GPS ankle monitor taken off. It will probably be in two weeks. The only good news is that now my attorney can depose these actual criminals one on one and begin to poke holes into their thickly woven web of lies.

September 20, 2010. My attorney's office has notified my sister and I that another $2500 installment is due at this time. Lucille agreed to pay half of the $2500 tab bringing her total to $7000 paid by her. I am paying the $1250 balance in three payments from my social security funds. If the case goes to trial, a third installment of $2500 will become due and I will be responsible for it in total.

September 24, 2010. I'm informed by my lawyer's paralegal, Zelda Harrell, that the charge has been dropped to *"assault with a deadly weapon;"* that I need to go to the bondsman, Easy O.Z. Bail Bonds, and get an affidavit "to remain on bond" that I must take with me to my arraignment on October 13th at 8:00 AM in front of Judge Cynthia G. Imperato. *The judge in this case performed beyond reproach.*

September 27, 2010. I received a phone call from Pre-Trial. Unbelievable! Nicola Tyndale is my caseworker. Her supervisor called me about 12 PM and read me the *riot act*! She was about to have me pulled back into the custody of the jailhouse for electronic surveillance issues. My understanding was that the main GPS unit should be centrally located in the home (It was even stated as such in the instructional hand-out): *"The device shall be placed in a central location in the residence approximately 3 feet off the ground and away from large metal objects or mirrors."* So I took a long time in the bathroom a couple of days ago and I got a call that said I was out of range. I couldn't believe it. I was in the house taking care of business and now they're threatening to toss me back in the can! (the *other* can!) *It is extremely difficult trying to adjust to the total control of the GPS monitoring system.* It doesn't matter that you have tried to follow to the letter of the law their requirements; you live in constant anxiety that your ass is theirs and that they can take you back into custody for the slightest irregularity, real or contrived. When you try to honestly explain yourself, they shut you down and make you listen to them, threatening the next electronic aberration will be your ticket back to their house. ✱✱

It's all about total control of the individual, of every moment of every hour and day; this leads to an overwhelming sense of powerlessness, sending any otherwise healthy ego into a state of dangerous vulnerability. It seems like a system designed to make you fail, not to promote a healthy adaptive response. It is a dangerous game of mind control, tempting and encouraging an individual to seek control of his or her life at any cost, yet knowing that their total control of you back behind bars could be the result of your trying to regain any of that personal control. The power trip that these *"Supervision Specialists"* of the *Department of Community Control* are on defies description; they are extremely condescending, not permitting you to enter into conversation; rather, forcing you into one-way dialogue where they are your master and you are their slave. It is a system that further perpetuates victimization of the individual (defendant). I see little difference between the threats and intimidation of these community control junkies and those of the actual criminal deviants they claim to be administering to in their custody. This system needs to be overhauled and manned by competent personnel. I can only hope that the above would be taken seriously by the justice system. My sense is that it will be dismissed in favor of doing nothing to change the status quo. If my personal experience is any indication, however, there is much evidence for vast improvement. I can only hope my input is taken seriously.

September 28, 2010. Received call from Zelda Harrell. Another hearing I must attend on October 6th to remove GPS monitor. I hope there's no problem with this one. I've finished writing the first draft of the book; it's just over 56,000 words in length. Now I'll tweak it and add to it as I see fit to produce the best effort I can. [At press time, as of August, 2016, the revised edition is just over 84,000 in length.]

September 29, 2010. Today I received a phone call from **William Fisher, the main perpetrator** of this whole nightmare *(after my attorney's call to him).* Believing that the conversation could be taped, I keep a lid on my pent-up emotional fury, not wanting to upset the apple cart of progress in this case: "I found a camera and a VCR that belong to you. (Yeah, right, *stolen* from me by you is more like it *to myself*) Can you come pick them up?" I answer him that I'm on ankle monitor, that I do not have freedom of movement; that I have a hearing on the 6th to remove this monitor **and** can call him then. Then he tells me his friend **David Zeuner, the co-conspirator** in this case, wants to drop the contrived charge against me; that he's decided not to go through with this hoax. I guess he was watching that a legal defense had been mounted. I immediately called my lawyer. He advised me to send to his office an e-mail repeating what I had just told him and not to talk to Fisher again; that this could be a set-up; that I should refer any future calls from Fisher to himself. Paul Molle also said he had made arrangements to receive my things at his office. This could be a huge turn of events.

October 2, 2010. Received a large box in the mail today. Lucille, ever attentive to all the needs of my case, sent me a brand new suit, shirt and shoes and a bunch of toiletries to make sure I would be presentable in court. This is one special person! *Now you see why I call her my "angel sister Lucille."*

October 6, 2010. Finally got the ankle monitor off! Partial freedom at last! All conditions of Pre-Trial Division are finally out the window. Next court date set for Nov. 5th -- monitor on from 8/06 – 10/06, 62 days, for a total of 73 days' loss of freedom (including the 11 days in Broward county jail). [Because I brought the *affidavit to remain on bond* on this date instead of the 13th - next week's court date was eliminated, a nice surprise.]

November 5, 2010. Today is a day to celebrate. The ASA informs my lawyer that David Zeuner has contacted the Prosecutor's Office to drop the charge against me. The perp will now be sent a waiver to sign to that effect and if that happens, this case can come to an end. Next court date, Dec. 3, 2010.

December 3, 2010. Waiver not received back as of yet. Continuance set for January 7, 2011.

December 10, 2010. I selected and my sister Lucille DesRoches Glemboski retained the services of Attorney Paul Molle of the Criminal Justice Center in Ft. Lauderdale, FL (www.mollelaw.com). Paul Molle's background began with his desire to follow in the footsteps of his father who had dedicated his life as a police officer. At the end of his criminal justice education, he went for a police "ride-along" and saw many things that made him think twice about law school as perhaps the best way he could make a difference and contribute to the good of society. He had invaluable experience and was very successful both as a prosecuting attorney and public defender, finally electing to go into criminal law where he established himself as a premier criminal defense attorney, counselor and advocate. Molle had these words about my case: *"One function of the criminal justice system is to punish those who violate the law. Another function of the criminal justice system is to protect those individuals who are wrongfully accused. Dennis DeRoche is a man wrongfully accused and this pending case is 'testing' the system. I hope the system 'passes' the test and that Dennis is exonerated soon."*
In my first or second meeting with Paul Molle, I asked him how he could do the job that he does and he answered, *"In the vast majority of cases I get, there is something wrong that the person is guilty of and I am defending that person knowing of his/her guilt. It is therefore very rewarding to defend that small*

percentage of cases that come before me when I know the person is totally innocent and I can feel that I have done a good thing bringing justice to that person."

January 7, 2011. Paul Molle: *"In exchange for a 'no contest' plea, the prosecutor offered to reduce the charge from an Aggravated Assault to a Misdemeanor Assault. The sentence would have been a withholding of adjudication (no criminal conviction), minimal court costs, no fine, and no probation. After consideration, Dennis declined the above offer and the matter has now been reset for January 26. I will continue to try and get the case dismissed and will advise as things develop."*

February 3, 2011 • <u>Final</u> <u>entry</u> and music to my ears*: ✳ "Enclosed please find a copy of the Nolle Prosequi/Memorandum, the State of Florida declined to prosecute the case."* Finally, some justice is served. However, I still have an arrest record and must come up with another $1000 if I wish to have the case sealed, an expense that should not be incurred by the true victim- and with all the money I owe at this time in my life, it's obvious that this action must be relegated to back burner consideration. I will enjoy the partial justice meted out until my life situation improves. Sometimes you take what you can get and be satisfied. But when it comes to one's principles, you cannot stop fighting for what is right. The fight is not over. I hope to live to see it finished, with this case sealed and this book published.

Author's Note

* (I will try to challenge as many of the injustices that I can — including the violated personal rights of all of us.)
The following pages comprise my memoirs. Beyond the facts of my life, I have tried to incorporate several themes, most importantly the one defined by the title of this book. Hopefully, a philosophical perspective will emerge and due consideration to psychological analyses will become apparent as well. My firsthand account of mental illness within the family environment and the tragic ramifications for each family member are for all to benefit by, be you victim of or victimized by same. From the website www.bringchange2mind.org *"Mental illness is a disorder of the brain and 1 in 6 adults lives with a brain-related illness including depression, bipolar disorder, PTSD and schizophrenia."* Finally, I try to observe myself and mankind within the sociological framework of our 21st century here and now experience as we continually threaten the very existence of our species*. We have not come very far from all the ages before us as we continue to rely upon WAR to solve our problems.* The FUTILE death of my cousin George Lescarbeau in Viet Nam has continued to plague my soul. He was born 4 months after me and his life was blown away before he was 20.
And he didn't need to die in a manufactured war!* *USA Deaths – 58,193* ☕ *Wounded – 303,644*
<u>--and millions more from the Vietnamese who were not our enemy but our fellow human brothers</u> ☕
The evil Richard M. Nixon caused the War to be extended for **5 extra years: 68-72 - his treason to be president!*
http://www.commondreams.org/views/2014/08/12/george-will-confirms-nixons-vietnam-treason?utm_campaign=shareaholic&utm_medium=facebook&utm_source=socialnetwork
I am deeply indebted to all those who have touched my heart and soul in this my life's journey. We should all try to contribute something good or positive while we are here. This bio is my humble attempt to reach as many as possible with the crystallized end product of my trials and tribulations. I hope it is taken seriously and enjoyed as well for any entertainment value encountered along the way. We stand upon those before us and we offer ourselves as foundation for those who follow. We are fortunate to have the opportunity to live in this world and to experience all the wondrous joys and beauty that abound. *We must not allow the negative or unfortunate happenings of our sojourns undermine and undertake us. We must never let die our open-armed appreciation for others or for other experiences new and inviting that might promote our mental, emotional and spiritual health and well-being. Life is for the living. Let us live life to the fullest!*

Dennis DeRoche   dennisderoche@gmail.com   @RockDenn

Chapter 3: *The Early Years*

My earliest memory in life was almost my death, and because of that my appreciation of *living* took on a whole new meaning. I was to have a lot of these 'near misses' as the years went by but this first 'close call' is still the most memorable. I was about 2 or 3 years old playing with my sister Lorraine 14 months older in the driveway close to or inside the garage of our Dad's parents. Our grandfather Wilbrod returned home driving his car up the driveway and over the top of the both of us -- a very traumatic experience that shook us up for some time. Visibility forward on those big old cars of yesteryear was just not like it is today. A few scrapes and bruises and we were none the worse for wear.

My mother Therese and father Leonard had eight children, each separated in age by a year or two. After Lorraine and I came Richard, Lucille, Paul, Michael, Thomas and Mark. Our mother was plagued with the *Rh factor*, a blood incompatibility problem. *"The Rh blood group system is a relevant cause of the hemolytic disease of the newborn."* Her last four births were affected in this way with each successive birth presenting a more serious problem to the child than the one before, requiring blood transfusions at minimum to sustain life. In addition to this, Mark suffered from a cyanotic heart defect also known as the *blue baby syndrome* and was unable to survive more than two weeks.

During the early years of life together as a large family living in West Hartford, CT, I would like to say that we enjoyed many healthy memories. Many visits to our cousins' homes strengthened intra-familial ties and gave us a broad base to experience the world outside of our immediate family. Who among us does not (and I would say this to all my brothers and sisters) remember with great fondness all those trips to Uncle Marcel and Aunt Yvette. They owned *Pine Grove Farm* in Dayville, CT, a dairy farm of about forty Holstein cows. We brothers alternated a couple of weeks at a time spending our summer vacations there, learning the ways of farm life with our cousin Gerrod. I remember shoveling manure into the spreader as it moved its way down through the center of the barn, troughs on either side, full of that precious waste commodity that worked so well to fertilize the farm's fields. I remember hooking up the milk machines to the cows and carrying two 5 gallon stainless steel pails heavily laden with all of this calves' nutrition down to the constantly churning milk vat at the end of the barn, being ever so careful not to spill a drop of that liquid currency for fear of our uncle's dismay. There were many other farm duties I can recall but what I most appreciated about these visits was when the day's work was done and everybody had partaken of Aunt Yvette's down home country cooking and then Uncle Marcel would get out his banjo ukulele and start playing and singing his songs. And if that wasn't enough, he would make molasses toffee that was to die for. Those were the best of times.

Our Dad, Leonard Joseph DesRoches, [name changed by him to *DeRoche* because English-speaking people could not pronounce the name correctly- the name means *of* or *from Rock(s)*], aka *Leo the Lip* (just as his namesake before him, Leo Durocher, was nicknamed) and *The Hangman* was born June 17, 1925, in Hartford, CT. I would be remiss if I did not give due credit to him for several positive pathways I chose in life via his example, instruction and tutelage. But first, his aka's. He was often called *Leo the Lip* by his contemporaries both for his protruding lower lip (that I managed to inherit as well) and because he was such a talker and always had something to say about everything *(like Leo Durocher as manager of the Brooklyn Dodgers to so many umpires [1939-1946])*.

He was very intelligent, often times referred to as an artistic genius, had a very engaging personality, was very altruistic with a heart of gold, and was the hardest worker I have ever known in my life – which brings us to why he was known as *The Hangman*. I think the only way I can say it is this: if hanging wallpaper were an Olympic event, Lenny would have received at least four gold medals. He was a perfectionist first and foremost. Have you ever tried to hang wallpaper and been able to say to yourself, *"What a good job I did!"* It's not easy to come out perfect. But Lenny not only wanted every job he did to come out perfect, he insisted on doing a whole house in one day whenever humanly possible.

Think of it. Several different styles of paper or foil or grass cloth that will be covering a two or three room home complete with bathrooms, hallway, living room, dining room and the *extras* as he called them. Dad's trademark was leaving something more behind, something that was a statement of himself on each job he went to. It might be doing small repairs needed in the home or it might be papering the inside of a bathroom cabinet where no one expects to see anything, along with a press-on silver or gold sticker with *LJD Enterprises* on it. He worked himself till his knees could no longer bear his weight upon them, a position all too common in his chosen trade, as if paying homage to the god of Supplication. And what was most impressive of all was when he utilized his artistic abilities and painted with black ink on white canvas. I went with him on many jobs and one day I saw him create a work of art on someone's bathroom canvas, complete with fishermen at sea, their nets and their catch, all executed with such skill and beauty. So now you know the *pathway of work ethic* that he instilled in me and the rest of us kids. <u>One had to conclude that he worked too hard and suffered terribly for it</u>, eventually affecting his health and welfare and then that of his entire family as well.

I must credit my father for introducing me to the *pathway of photography*. My whole adult life has been dedicated to the pursuit of artistic photography and anyone who knows me knows how central photography has played a part in who I am. I have Dad to thank for that. I was most impressed growing up as a kid being absolutely fascinated when he would dim the lights, set up a reflective screen, turn on a 35mm slide projector and wow us with hundreds and hundreds of images he had taken of his courtship with our mother, his life with the two of them and all the people related to us whom we did or didn't know. I was hooked. I knew what I wanted to do with my life. Among other goals I had put before me in life, chief among them would be the *pursuit of the image* to make it say or mean something that I wished to communicate with others *(e.g. pp. 56-57)*. The power of communication via the graphic image is without bound; I saw that and wanted to be a practitioner of that.

I must credit my father for introducing me to the *pathway of woman*. This is a two-parter. As kids growing up, we all watched how our father revered our mother. Even after their relationship had long been history, Lenny never stopped his admiration and feelings for Therese. Although it was not healthy for Leonard to be so obsessive compulsive re: his ex; indeed, he caused himself much pain and suffering; what could also be taken from this aberrant adulation was the sheer magnitude of his love for *a woman*. To know that kind of love or to be close to that kind of love had a profound effect upon me.

The other manner in which I learned about *a woman*; how beautiful she could be and how untouchable as well, was when my father would take me to watch women dance *(in the 70's-80's)*. He always had the most respect admiring a woman dance as if she were posing for one of his canvases. As an artist-photographer I too had the most respect for each dancer, seeing at once the obvious beauty of female form but also the power that *dance* brought to the equation. This would have a big impact upon me later in life. *And one more very important "positive" owed to my father that he passed on to me is the love he showed for the common man in the street who had less than he <u>and</u> his "**color-blindness**" when it came to people. He introduced me to African American culture and I was very fortunate for that.* I remember his pride one day showing me his lifetime membership card with the **NAACP** – this was **LJD**.

Chapter 4: *The Devil In The House: Mental Illness Becomes Our Family Foe*
"I can not think of any need in childhood as strong as the need for a father's protection."

Sigmund Freud

During the early years of life together, I need to say that we had many unhealthy memories as well. Leonard was basically a very good man with a great sense of humor, extremely hard-working, (workaholic-yes), incredibly talented as an artist with a very big heart for his fellow man. I don't know when it started but something was happening to Dad. He was always very authoritarian and very intimidating and demanding, and you didn't want to incur the wrath of his temper because there were only so many beatings one could suffer. One occasion is branded into my brain. It was around 1958.

We lived in West Hartford on Selden Hill Drive, in a beautiful split level home. The third floor had one large room where three of my brothers and I had beds. One evening, the four of us decided to have a pillow fight, a harmless, let's have some fun, let's-be-boys pillow fight. We evidently made too much noise and were about to be taught a very valuable lesson – BEWARE of Dad! When he got to our room, he began, one by one, beating us in an apoplectic rage. My brother Richard was so genuinely fearful, he could not help spraying Dad with the contents of his bladder during *his* assault. After he had doled out what he felt he needed to upon my brothers, he came lastly to me, and I can still recall his words, *"And you get extra because you're the oldest and you should've known better!"* Thanks, Dad.

A couple more recalls from West Hartford and we'll move on. I remember camping out in the woods one day (we had a wooded area directly behind our home) and I decided to start a campfire. I had gotten into an argument with my brother Richard and I used *the "f" word*. When my father heard about the campfire and the use of this family taboo word, he didn't just hit me with his hands (Leonard had huge hands, was 6' and over 200 lbs and always in very good shape from his work ethic), he threw me crazily against the corners of the bare stairs going from the garage to the kitchen. I don't know how I escaped without any broken bones, but it was one of, if not the most painful of beatings I received from his majesty, the lion king. Just as his name Leonard has the word lion in it (el león), so too did the lion rage supreme in him. Indeed, he identified with these creatures, collecting their images in paintings and sculptures.   Obviously, these episodes of physical abuse did not occur without an accompanying emotional and psychological abuse component as well. *(I think I paid in full to use the "f" word freely now.)*

Our Dad was *different* from other Dads, very different as we were all about to find out. Dad would get sick and have to go to the hospital for a week or two or more at a time. That's when we started hearing the terms "nervous breakdown" and "schizophrenia" used around our home. It turned out the medical community had a hard time treating our father and were not sure what to label him for many years. He was like a guinea pig undergoing various trials of medications and none seemed to work very well. When they gave him Thorazine for what they thought were his symptoms of schizophrenia; instead of calming him down, his symptoms accelerated.   He endured the ravages of ECT, formerly known as electroshock and now as electroconvulsive therapy, and he complained to me how horribly he felt after these treatments. It took many years for the medical community to correctly diagnose Dad as a manic depressive psychotic personality disorder (bipolar) due to a chemical imbalance, controllable with a regimen of lithium carbonate, Li_2CO_3, a salt compound. [Glenn Close has a website with her sister Jessie, bipolar, whose son Calen is schizoaffective: www.bringchange2mind.org Here, they promote working together as families and individuals united to erase the stigma of mental illness.] -- *Hooray!*
Glenn Close Conscious Magazine #ITalk #StartTheConversation #StrongerThanStigma #BC2M
One event is forever emblazoned in my mind.   One day, when Dad was experiencing one of his terrible breakdown episodes, he took our brother Michael down into the basement. I was protective of my younger brother and followed them down. We had a furnace for heat. When the door was opened to that furnace, the fire was fierce and great and very scary if you were a little kid. I was perhaps ten but my brother was six years younger.   Leonard actually scared me as well but the psycho-emotional trauma that this little kid endured when that door was opened, and Michael was pushed into the opening of this inferno and held there as he hears his father yelling at the top of his lungs, "THIS IS THE FIRE AND THE DAMNATION THAT IS HELL AND THIS IS WHERE YOU WILL END UP IF YOU DON'T BEHAVE AND LISTEN TO YOUR PARENTS! ***DO YOU UNDERSTAND*****⁇**" Holy shit! I kept saying to myself. Holy f*kin shit!!! *(We all have our crosses to bear but I wager none are heavier than those of the mentally afflicted.)*
Boy, did I ever have a fundamental change of perspective about Dad and where my life was going. I knew for the sake of survival for myself and my family that we would have to be very careful about our every thought, word and deed around this unbridled volcano known as Dad. ***Indeed, a silent war of***

survival was about to be waged by all of us. It was the only way. Be strong, be patient, be understanding and be very careful not to awaken the monster within Leonard.

At about this same time our youngest brother Tommy was sleeping in a crib in the office of our father. His crib was very close to if not touching the desk in this office. One day, Tommy managed to reach the top drawer of this desk and find a small bottle of luminous paint (paint that glows in darkness). He somehow managed to ingest some of the contents of this bottle and in very short time was rushed to the emergency room with paint poisoning. We almost lost him. We received a call from the hospital that things did not look so well and suggested we pray for a miracle. Our Mom got us all together in the living room and we all prayed and prayed and prayed. Within the hour another call came in and we were told that things had taken a turn for the better. To this day Mom and the rest of us at the time believed we had just experienced a miracle. Today I believe that it was just not his *unlucky day*. Who knows why we are granted reprieves in this world; I know I have received my share of them. To acknowledge these moments of our lives as the *gifts of opportunity* to move on and do something more with ourselves might be a good way of looking at them; but I say, *'Do look that gift horse in the mouth and investigate as much as you can to leave nothing unturned'* - There may be hidden value to be found.

There were two very happy times that I experienced "on the Hill" *(91 Selden Hill Dr., West Hartford, CT)* where our home was situated. My first girlfriend *Hollis Fitch* lived across the street. I was the Catholic boy and she was the Protestant girl. It was infatuation at first sight. There was an offer for an ID bracelet on a Bazooka Bubble Gum wrapper. I was so happy to surprise her on her birthday with a bracelet that had her name on it. I've never forgotten her birthday on June 12th and on that day every year, wherever I am, no matter who I'm with, I have to shout out, *"Happy Birthday, Hollis!"* I've tried to locate her since just to see how her life has progressed but to no avail. *One begins to realize that some things pass your way just once in life and to be happy that you had that time.* But the feeling of "first love" cannot be adequately described. It is too special and good.

Our family dog, *Ta-day-yo, (the name I called him)* was very important to me. I bonded very closely with this mongrel mutt and he would come charging home when I would yell out my special call to him. I had just enough to hang on to for hope of a better day, a girlfriend and a dog. I was blessed in a sea of sickness. But these things did not last very long. One day our dog never returned home and soon after, the frequency of our father's hospitalizations having increased, we were forced to leave the suburb for the city, moving to another three story home at 715 Broadview Terrace, in Hartford, CT. Time to adapt.

It was 1960. I was just entering the seventh grade. Our father spent more and more time in treatment, at times committed to Norwich State Hospital for long stretches. Our family went from being relatively well off to filing for family assistance. But I did not harbor resentment towards Dad; rather, I felt sorry for him that he couldn't control his feelings and be that Leonard that most of us had grown to know and love as the great person he was before the "demons" took over his mind. I was the only one of his kids that made the 50-mile trip to visit him at Norwich State Hospital because no matter how much I had been abused, I had shared many good experiences with my father and had bonded very closely to him over the years. *Forgiveness is a powerful teacher both for the forgiver and the one being forgiven. *"FORGIVENESS is not something we do for OTHER PEOPLE. We do it for OURSELVES – to GET WELL and MOVE ON."* My formative years were relatively without incident until about the age of ten. This cannot be said of my youngest brothers who never really got to know their Dad when he was a healthy, functioning individual to be proud of. In this regard, emotional and psychological damage to them took a greater toll than it had with myself. For one of them, the ultimate price would be paid.

Our mother was now a single parent of seven kids struggling boldly to make ends meet. The State of CT paid for her training to be a hairdresser, she got licensed and weaned herself off of welfare. This was a remarkable success story. *She was born in Buckland, Canada, on the same day in the same year as Queen Elizabeth II of England, April 21, 1926.* She came to CT with her parents and seven siblings. She learned English, became a citizen and now was saving the lives of her own brood of seven souls. Times were very tough, sibling rivalry was always strong, and just surviving on a day to day basis became the focus of each one of us. Dad was not completely out of the picture. He no longer lived with us but when he was between confinements for treatment, he would visit Mom and us kids. His was an undying love for Therese. He was obsessed with trying to win her back and tried everything in his power to force the issue, not realizing that way too much damage had already occurred from his illness and it could never be. It was during these times that we all got to see the ravages of Dad's mental illness.

One begins to acquire an expert knowledge of the patient and his condition when subjected to it over a long period of time. I tried to understand every aspect of its manifestation in Dad so that I could learn for myself how best to administer to him for my own survival and his as well. I knew I would be charting my life in the direction of therapeutic intervention and was clear about my collegiate path to that goal. When he was in the depressive phase of his psychosis visiting us, described as *"Sheer Blackness"* by Glenn Close's sister Jessie who is bipolar, he would just sit there, legs crossed, constantly shaking up and down and absolutely mute. He would not speak. If you would ask him a question to engage him, the best you could hope for would be a nod for yes or no. It was really pathetic because if you knew the equilibrated, *normal* Dad of fantastic personality, this would not seem possible. Nor if you knew the manic phase of his illness could you ever believe this possible. The typical onset of a manic episode was very predictable; *(and I have often suspected that Dad sabotaged his own treatment, wanting to be in this state at times),* if he failed to take his medication, he would not be able to sleep at night. If he was up all night, that phase would be in full swing; he would be fully "*operational*"- these were the times when Lenny became very scary and dangerous to himself and others. He would go on a rampage, taking me with him wherever he went, controlling everything and everybody that or whom he came in contact with. If he walked into your home, he would rearrange everything to the way he felt it should be; if you protested, it didn't matter, he would do it anyway. This sometimes included spray painting messages on your walls such as *"God is Love"* - Many times the police had be called. They learned to come in "numbers" to arrest him because he was totally defiant of authority and was often very combative and resisted arrest. This usually resulted in another commitment proceeding. One traumatic memory of this manic side of Lenny was on a Thanksgiving Day. Our mother was a fantastic cook and baker. With what little she had to provide for her troops, she always made Sundays special and always with something homemade for dessert. You can imagine her efforts on T-Day. This particular Thanksgiving Day there was nothing to be thankful about; Dad was on the warpath. He was ranting and raving, putting us all in fear, and then began screaming out Scripture about the story of Isaac and Abraham. He was determined to re-enact the test of loyalty that God performed when He commanded Abraham to sacrifice his son Isaac. Abraham bound Isaac and was about to kill him when the angel of God stopped him. Dad was now going to test my loyalty. He was filled with himself, calling himself the Vicar of Christ, delusions of grandeur alive and well. What he proceeded to do horrified my mother and I. He gave me a large bottle of ink and told me that I needed to drink it all down. *(And I'm thinking, 'what angel of God is going to save me now?')* It was very hard to outwit the ol' man but in the state of mind that he was, needing to address every little thing and everybody, he could be distracted. Mom quickly diverted his attention to some other consideration out of the kitchen where I was standing with the bottle of ink in my hand. She doubled back, emptied the ink down the drain and told me to hold the empty bottle to my mouth as if I had just emptied its contents. Just not my unlucky day or *God* at work? I'll leave you to guess which way I was leaning. *Believing in a Higher Power or God or the Great Spirit *et al*, **or** believing in the

17

words of those such as Alan Watts, Arthur C. Clarke or Bertrand Russell, is something that each of us will have to personally decide for himself or herself; e.g., AC Clarke: *"One of the great tragedies of mankind is that morality has been hijacked by religion. Religion is the most malevolent and persistent of all mind viruses." Clarke insisted that Buddhism is not a religion, calling himself a 'crypto-Buddhist'.*

And there are these words, often attributed to H. L. Mencken: "Morality is doing what is right, regardless of what you are told. Religion is doing what you are told, regardless of what is right."

"Why A Belief in God Reflects A Lack of Faith" – Alan Watts: https://www.youtube.com/watch?v=Af815ksm4RU

Bertrand Russell: "I am as firmly convinced that religions do harm as I am that they are untrue."

❈ Buddhism is NOT a religion in the est tradition ~ it is *A Way of Life ÷ The Way of Kindness*

Dalai Lama: *"This is my simple religion. There is no need for temples; no need for complicated philosophy. Our own brain, our own heart is our temple; the philosophy is kindness."*

Learning To Survive In A Sea of Chaos

Defense mechanisms work; they sometimes are the only means of survival. *A person's ego needs to be protected and nourished and continually stimulated towards growth, a non-ending proposition. But this is a balancing act; too much ego or hubris (over pride) leads to tragic results* as so many Greek plays have shown. I utilized two approaches for my survival. They both may be forms of the same mechanism of escapism. The **first escape** I made was **into the world of knowledge** and books, my schooling and education. I loved to learn and knew that I would not get anywhere in this world if I didn't successfully pursue the ranks of the educated. I also wanted to be the best example I could as the oldest of five brothers to show that it could be done; there was a way out of the insanity that was our environment.

Albert Schweitzer: *"Example is not the main thing influencing others; it is the only thing."*

More than that, I felt I had a duty to do so; taking the 'easy way out' was not an option. I did well in school, graduated cum laude and was fortunate to receive a scholarship to attend St. Anselm College in Manchester, NH, a Roman Catholic college run by the Benedictine Order of monks.

The **second escape** I made was **into the world of motorcycling**. Everything I do in life I try to do with the utmost passion possible. This was never truer than with *my addiction to the motorcycle way of life*.

Finally, I could leave the world of powerlessness behind and assume control of my own life and destiny.

I would not be content to simply ride and enjoy the motorcycle experience. I was determined to develop motorcycling as an art form and to be totally at one with the machine in some sort of transcendental manner; I was the machine and it was me, literally. I was influenced by *Zen and the Art of Motorcycle Maintenance: An Inquiry into Values* by Robert M. Persig, a philosophical attempt to *"explore the metaphysics of quality."* I started riding in my senior year at Bulkeley High in Hartford, CT, but a *left curve* temporarily derailed me. In my physical for the job I was applying for with the City of Hartford's Park Department, my chest X ray showed an enlarged heart. Further testing showed that I had an *atrial septal defect*, a hole in the wall separating the upper two chambers which allowed for fresh, oxygenated blood to mix with used, de-oxygenated blood. This made for an inefficient pump as I was not able to supply the heart with sufficient oxygen. The heart being a muscle got bigger and bigger trying to compensate for the more demanding physical activities I was requiring of it. I was told if the hole was not patched or sewn shut, I probably would not live to the age of 40. So, on May 10, 1966, I went in for open heart surgery where they cut my sternum in half, opened my heart, sutured the hole and sewed me back up with stainless steel wire; a very traumatic experience I must say, especially the healing phase. There are what are known as muscle spasm attacks against one's own body. The body's reaction to having a lot of its tissue cut away is to have these really intense contractions of your chest muscle mass. Nothing they give you for pain prepares you for this. I was told that in some cases the contractions are severe enough to fracture one's own ribs. The other unforeseen feature of the surgery was waking up with half of my right chest muscle mass removed. I had just built up my body from three years of body-building, lifting weights religiously, and one day I wake up like a freak. Not a very pleasant experience, believe me. *(This same defect today is repaired routinely with non-invasive probe technology -- hooray! for medical advancement and the science of pain management -- born too early.)*

After healing from heart surgery, I began working for the Hartford Park Department and met Peter Potaski. Peter became my best friend in life and an intermediary to understand the teachings of Timothy Leary. I think the best way to describe Peter Potaski is to say he is truly a national treasure. A *"card-carrying"* lifetime member of the hippie movement, he is an erudite, scintillating mind and personality, great personal friend and invaluable asset to the field of psychological and psychiatric care. It was he and our incredible mechanic Jeffrey Moores who influenced me to look beyond chain-driven engines, to **BMW**, a shaft-driven transversely opposed powerplant with extensive racing pedigree from Munich, Germany, whose center of gravity allowed it to turn much more efficiently than the higher center of gravity of all other motorcycles in the world. BMW (**B-Mer**) = Bayerische Motoren Werke AG (Bavarian Motor Works) My first **B-Mer** was a '67' R-60, a 600 cc bike. Peter also had one and we took many trips together on those machines. A typical run would be to a Boston BMW bike shop or to visit some friends in Rhode Island. [In ABC's coverage of Steve Jobs' passing on 10/5/11, it was so cool to see Apple's *'insanely great'* visionary riding an R-60 as well, one from the good ol' days, just like our own.]

***Chapter 6**: College Years: Two Teachers Who Influenced Me Greatly*

One day in 1969, Peter came by and invited me to go along with him for a really big concert *(Woodstock)* that was going to take place on Max Yasgur's 600 acre dairy farm in upstate NY from August 15-18, less than a month after men had landed on the moon. I was always up for a concert and taking a bike trip but this time I had a real dilemma. I was a very serious student now attending Central CT State University and I was in the middle of researching and producing the most important paper I had ever attempted to write, *Lester Frank Ward: Pioneer Systematizer & Synthesizer of Sociological Thought*. I had been poring over Ward's *Pure Sociology (1903),* and other original resource material publications in the Trinity College library to understand and have a point of view about Ward's contributions to sociological thought. At the time of Peter's invite, nobody really knew how life-changing Woodstock would be; if I had only known, I probably would have forsaken my commitment to the above manuscript. As it turned out, this paper was to have a life-changing impact of its own upon me and for this reason I know I did not chose incorrectly to pass on Woodstock in order to produce it. Why had the writing of this paper so profoundly affected me? For as much as it had an effect on my mentor, **Dr. Paul A. Hochstim** from Vienna, Austria, who in turn had a major effect upon me. But first, *who was Lester Frank Ward? "Described as* **'the American Aristotle'** *Ward was an* **'apostle of human progress'** *who vigorously advocated for public education and the rights of women and minorities. The noted feminist, Charlotte Gilman described Ward as* **'one of the world's greatest men'** *and dedicated her book 'The Man Made World' to him."* (LFW: 6-18-1841 – 4-18-1913) Wikipedia

Scientifically trained as a botanist, Lester Frank Ward saw from his knowledge and understanding of the inter-connectedness of the causes and effects at play in the world of botany, a similitude with respect to the world of human relationships. From this human analogue perspective, he derived the concept known as *synergy*. He is the father of this concept that today is ubiquitously bandied about to the point of over-use of a concept gone viral. His description was:

*"**Synergy is the cooperative working-together of antithetical forces in nature producing the desired end or effect known as conation or creative effort.**"*

So, I turn my paper in, confident that I have given my best. After the papers are graded and handed out, Dr. Hochstim dismissed the class but asked me to stay, saying, after everybody had left, "I have some doubts that you are the author of this paper." I was angry and deeply hurt, having given so much of my time, energy and passion to this effort. I wear my emotions on my sleeve as they say and he saw how distraught I was protesting to the contrary. "I'll tell you what I'll do. You can come into my office and I'll give you an hour to write as much as you can about Lester Frank Ward on this legal pad." I agreed, he left his office and I began writing at the fastest rate of speed I could, my head was so full of this material. When he returned an hour later, I handed him the pad and he started reading the pages, one by one, not missing a word; and as he was two or three pages into it he began with some facial tics and slowly waxed emotional to the point of actual tears, and said this to me, "I'm sorry for doubting you. I am convinced you could write books." And without missing a beat, he goes to his file cabinet, opens the drawer and takes out and hands me a hard-bound copy of his dissertation, _Alfred Vierkandt: A Sociological Critique_ (1966), "I hope you accept this in apology." *Now that was a truly transforming experience for me.* It legitimized my worth as a writer and gave me that boost of acceptance of self that pushed me forward. It empowered me to want to do bigger and better things. I knew that if I put my total self into anything, only good things could come from it. Thanks, Paul, just what the doctor ordered. On the other side of the coin, I think Peter was thanking his doctor, Dr. Timothy Leary, back there at Woodstock for all the enlightenment he was receiving.

Chapter 7: *Pushing The Boundaries of Life to Understand One's Connection to Death*

I spent my first two years of college at St. Anselm's in Manchester, NH. It was about time in 1966 to finally be able to leave the toxic environment of my first 18 years. You grow up fast when you leave the cocoon of dependency and are forced to fend for yourself for everything. Other than the independence that this adjustment process afforded me, two events come to mind. I first learned to appreciate the benefits of *the most kind herb* that Nature was so gracious to provide our planet. Now I could speak about **The Great Hypocrisy** of our system of laws and justice to legalize alcohol, a deadly drug with many deleterious effects to self, family and society on the one hand and to deem as illicit, cannabis, a naturally occurring herb with relatively harmless effects. How arrogant and contemptuous man can be. The mentality is something like, "We'll just do whatever we want and control the people; we know what's best for the masses." But now the masses have risen up as decriminalization and legalization of cannabis have become the policy of several states in the U.S. today. In just four years since the defeat [11-2-10] of Proposition 19 in California (the Regulate, Control and Tax Cannabis Act of 2010) "support for legalizing marijuana has risen 11 points since 2010." (Pew Research Center for the People & the Press) The Marijuana Policy Project: *"Now that four U.S. states and the nation's capital have made marijuana legal for adults and the House has voted to end the crackdown on medical marijuana, there is more momentum than ever in Congress for ending marijuana prohibition."* We are slowly emerging from the **Dark Age of Prohibition** and the rampant imprisonment of untold thousands incarcerated in many cases for nothing more than the possession, cultivation or use of a naturally occurring medicinal herb- **cannabis**- one of the crowning achievements of the flora of Mother Earth.

http://www.theguardian.com/society/2016/mar/24/medical-experts-call-for-global-drug-decriminalisation?utm_source=esp&utm_medium=Email&utm_campaign=GU+Today+USA+-+Version+CB+header&utm_term=163894&subid=7398324&CMP=ema_565

*It is important to know what *is* harmful: from the CNN study [11-1-10] funded by the London-based Centre for Crime and Justice, "Study: Alcohol '*most harmful drug,*' followed by crack and heroin. Alcohol ranks 'most harmful' among a list of twenty drugs, beating out crack and heroin when assessed for its potential harm to the individual imbibing and harm to others, according to study results released by a British medical journal, _The Lancet_. A panel of experts from the independent Scientific Committee on Drugs weighed the physical, psychological, and social problems caused by the drugs and determined that alcohol was the most powerful overall. It was compared to 19 other drugs using 16 criteria: nine related to the adverse effects the drug has on an individual and seven on its harm against others. This makes it almost three times as harmful as cocaine or tobacco." Highly Recommended:
*CNN WEED 3 Documentary 2015   https://www.youtube.com/watch?v=QnVHxOPEbqc

The second event that had a lasting effect upon me has to do with a major paper I had written in 1967.

I was fascinated to know why, when this world has so much good to offer, when each day should be considered a gift, when there's so much good a person could put their life to, why would a person want to commit suicide? I was actually trying to reconcile these thoughts which I wholeheartedly believed in, with what I felt must be the unconscious thoughts of a death wish *I* must possess for not just riding motorcycles, but the way in which I rode them, always going faster and leaning closer to the ground than would have seemed cautionary or discretionary on my part.   So, to try to understand this phenomenon, I sent off to all the agencies of information I could find on the topic and amassed quite a few sources for my research into **the Big ?** **"Why does one want to commit suicide?"** I remember the 'bible' on the subject, the French sociologist Emile Durkheim's Suicide (1897), in which he talked about the major cause as being *a sense of normlessness*, what he called *'anomie'*. The more an individual was not part of some group ascribing to a set of shared norms or values, the more likely that individual would suffer the consequences of his or her own isolationism. *"Durkheim categorized four types of suicide based on the degrees of imbalance of two social forces: social integration and moral regulation:*

1. *egoistic suicides are the result of a weakening of the bonds that normally integrate individuals into the collectivity…An example of this would be unmarried people, particularly males, who, with less to bind and connect them to stable social norms and goals, committed suicide at higher rates than married people.*
2. *altruistic suicides occur in societies with high integration, where individuals are seen as less important than the society's needs as a whole. (the opposite of egoistic suicides) An example would be the soldier in military service.*
3. *anomic suicides are the product of moral deregulation…People do not know where they fit in within their societies. Durkheim explains that this is a state of moral disorder where man's desires are limitless and, thus, his disappointments infinite. Economic boom or disaster contribute to anomie.*
4. *fatalistic suicides occur in overly oppressive societies causing people to prefer to die than to carry on living within their society." (Wikipedia)*

National Suicide Prevention Lifeline   1-800-273-TALK (8255)   www.suicidepreventionlifeline.org

I include the above definitions of suicide for the benefit of all readers seeking answers to the Big Why?— but especially for my family after the loss of one of us to suicide, to be revealed at the proper chronological stage of events. *But why have I referred to my writing of this research paper as an event at St. Anselm's?* Because I learned a valuable lesson. You do not put in the hands of another something such as original resource material so that a person can plagiarize or outright steal it out from under you. I made this mistake. An upper classman came to me, pleaded that he just wanted to get some ideas to write his own paper and I was credulous enough to go along and trusted this individual. That was the last I saw of over 30 pages and two months of research into the subject of suicide. *I was too naïve and too trusting*; I now am more cynical and a lot more careful towards my fellow man. There are a lot of bad people out there and many times they are cloaked in sheep's clothing – *Be Wary…Don't Be Fooled!*
[Summary of above: Beware of "Confidence Men" (& "Con Women" as well, as you will see in Ch. 15)]

Another event that was to have a profound effect on my life and qualify as a *near miss* as well was a trip I took with one of my best friends in life, Chuck Horvath, to Seaside Heights, NJ, in the summer of 1969. Chuck was an expert surfer and we traveled to this stretch of coastline for the renowned wave sets favorable to his sport. It seemed like a perfect day, the waves were beautiful and the surfing was great. But nobody had checked the weather forecast for this day. It was like a scene out of a movie. The skies darkened, the waves picked up and the temperature plummeted. When the lightning and thunder began, all the people on the beach picked up and ran for cover; all the people except Chucky, going back in to ride the big waves and me as I continued to throw myself into the giant waves on shore.

It got to a point where we were obviously flirting with death but we agreed that we each were having such an overwhelming experience of nature's primal forces that we could not bring ourselves to say, *"We're out of here!"*- it was worth everything to experience it. It's not that we had a death wish- we had a *LIVE* ('liv') wish! We wanted to live to the fullest degree, to experience *in total* these seductive forces. What happened was that Chucky almost didn't survive. He caught a rogue wave that had taken him under for a long period of time. I kept looking for him for the longest time thinking I had lost him when I finally caught sight of him with his board coming in from the distance a couple of breakers away. He was in a bad way. I had to physically hold him up and walk him out of the surf. His lungs had taken in so much water he had lost his voice. He tried to speak but could not for a very long time. We were both very thankful that his life was not sacrificed to the primal forces that had seduced us.

For the next several days, now back in CT, I began having flashbacks of this event, playing it over and over in my mind until one night the experience came flooding back to me in an episode of automatic writing. The following words were written in October, 1969, and have not left my consciousness since that time. I did not have to think of these words- they came to me in a rush. It's now more than 40 years later and it's as if this event just occurred yesterday--

The Way

Misty rainin' 'pon my face

As I indulge the Fringe.

Rushing, roaring, splashing 'tself

'Gainst Rock and shore

Till I can walk no more...

And yet more and more and more...

Nature speaks to all who listen.

Wants to know you, be your friend.

You will want, too, if but...

You chance to find the way.

The way to know the Storm is to be its prey.

Let it stalk, make its play –

Show you're not afraid of its splendor and its might.

Offer no resistance and there'll be no fight.

Then indulge and feel and reel.

Tell all your thoughts aloud.

For She will listen and resound.

Only glad for your soul that you have found **the way** --

Now need none ask, "Canst this be so?"

But: "Can not it always be?"

Sheer rapture 'pon beauty.

Ecstatic delight.

Mind-bending revelry, orgy of life --

So much from so little of you:

This life-locked synapse.

Mutation complete: neither a victim,

Being same to the Whole --

Forces together, daring the lot --

MAN'S MIND

MEETS

SOUL'S

MIGHT!!

22

I had lost contact with my good friend Chuck Horvath for several years. Turns out he had made two trips to Japan following his dream there (after trips to Thailand and Hong Kong). Finally, after exhaustive efforts on both our parts we reconnected in August of 2011. I asked my friend to share with the world his perspective on surfing, why it has been such a big part of his life and such an addiction, as the motorcycle had become such an addiction in my life, and Chucky sent me this magnificent description: *(Reprinted exactly as provided to me by Charles M. Horvath – cmhsurfinghi@yahoo.com)*

"I AM FREE and ALIVE when I am SURFING!!!!!!! Surfing means so much to me. It is my salvation. All else may fail. People will let you down. The ocean is always there. Dropping down a wave, especially a big wave is a rush so blissful and intoxicating; it makes me feel ALIVE. From tiny nerve endings on the feet to the very top of my head! I have free fallen on 20 foot waves. Imagine jumping off a two or three story building, not jumping, but sensitively freefalling, floating on the green-blue wall of rushing water and somehow make it to the bottom of that 15 to 20 foot face. Nerves in the toes on the board connect with ocean and you 'make the drop'!! WOW!! What a rush! All in an instance! Only seconds have elapsed, but you are ALIVE!!! Total consciousness!!!!!!!!! On small waves, you can dance along the water. Walk and run on water. Makes me think of one other who walked on water. You might have heard of him. Name was Jesus. I think we got something here! Then we have the aqua blue sheet cover the body, 'in the tube'. Total euphoria! I love dropping down a wave and touching the moving wall of water and I merge with ocean and become one with her. I feel the power and beauty! This is what surfing in its purest form means to me!"

"The Japanese word for memory, OMOIDE, is a powerful concept.
The good memories are powerful-healing, strengthening."

"Aloha! Yes, yes, there is good and bad in all. I expressed good and positive feelings about surfing. Now, the negative. Getting held under on a big wave is like DYING!!!!!!! Tons of water hitting you, DARKNESS, trying to breathe. Running out of breath. Lungs about to burst!!! Then a quiet! Silence! It's all over! I'll relax and slip into the deep sleep! Then a ray of light! I grab my cord and pull to the surface! I'M ALIVE!!!!!!!!! Surfing is not all fun and euphoria. The crowds can be brutal. Men and women at their worst fighting for possession of the wave. Mankind has always lusted after beautiful things. The golden waves are desired by many, and sometimes that desire can be manifested in a very ugly way. It happens. It is not good, but it is what is. I search for the good and the perfect wave. Chuck"

The Watercourse Way ☯ Compassion•Moderation•Humility

It's as if, in order to be the most *alive*, paradoxically, there is a connection to one's death. Riding the motorcycle is another such example as the one provided above; I never felt more free or alive than all those times aboard that iron horse. TOTALLY FREE & ALIVE – this is the exhilaration of motorcycling as the world passes you by. And yet many times I seemed to be playing with death in the way that I rode. An interesting correlative viewpoint on this subject is a statement made by Jim Arender from the 1965 "underground cult classic documentary of the psychedelic 1960's," *Mondo Hollywood*. Arender was a multi-time world champion skydiver and had these pearls of wisdom for us:

*"A parachute jump allows as much freedom as you can possibly have. Whether or not you survive is dependent upon you. You alone make the decision whether you will live or you will die. **I think that living fully is intensified by experiencing the various parallels of nearly dying.**"*

In December of 1971, our father and his wife Christine, who had gotten married about a year before, brought forth our latest brother Mark, named after our brother who never did make it home from the hospital. When signs of maternal abuse upon his person presented at about age one (cigarette burned into his arm for incessant crying), I was determined *not again*; another child in the custody and care of our father and his wife Christine would not bode well for the continued physical and emotional abuse that was guaranteed to occur. I now was a Social Worker with the City of Hartford (as of September, 1972) and had a legal duty beyond my personal conviction to have Mark removed from his injurious environment. My mother and I gave testimony to the authorities why we felt there were sufficient grounds for this action and soon Mark was placed with a very loving family, the Myhr's. He remained in the Hartford area for a few years with access to his parents and then relocated with his adoptive family to California, where today he is a successful adult pursuing his career in engineering. *Kudos to Mark!*

In the summer of 1971, I married for the first time to Constance Rita Ann Albert. She was my sister Lucille's best friend, a couple of years younger than me, her family living only a couple of blocks from our family residence. Her background like my own was French Canadian. We were both virgins. I guess you could say I was a late bloomer at 23. I was not prepared to marry at this time and it was not my intention to do so. I wanted us to live together first. Her parents would not consent to our living together unless we were married; so, essentially, I married in order that we could live together. This did not bode well for the success of this relationship. Furthermore, we agreed to wait *at least two years* before trying to have a child. Based on the birth date of our son Lee Matthew on March 15, 1972 *(the Ides of March)*, Connie became pregnant approximately two *weeks* after our marriage date. It was a great experience having Lee, however, and I have no regrets about his addition to my life. Watching your child being born is an overwhelming experience that transcends any other. The miracle of life coming forth from the woman you love is something to behold and something that reaches to the very core of your being; it is truly a life-changing event. *It was one of the three best moments of my life.*

A couple of months after Lee's birth, I graduated from Central CT State University with a BA in Sociology. A couple of months after that, on July 10, 1972, I had a date with a cosmic phenomenon. My dedication to photography was second to nothing, including the motorcycle in my life. *(Actually, it was more like an ongoing war between the two and eventually I would have to choose one over the other.)* The total solar eclipse that I was about to experience meant a great deal to me. Throughout all time on this planet, these total solar eclipses have meant a lot of different things to a lot of different cultures. (An example is Mel Gibson's movie *Apocalypto* – *a movie I highly recommend*.) I had sent away to Kodak and to the Hayden Planetarium in New York for as much information as I could find on how to properly photograph this once in a lifetime event (for some) of our immediate cosmos. My friend Andy Gumkowski and brother Michael DesRoches didn't want to miss this event either; so we all traveled from Hartford to Nova Scotia and then took a ferry to Prince Edward Island, bound for Summerside, where the band of totality would guarantee the best view possible, clear skies permitting.

Latitude: 46.3507°N, Longitude: 63.7811°W Duration: 1min, 52.1s, Magnitude 1.009 (from the *NASA Eclipse Web Site*, www.eclipse.gsfc.nasa.gov). *"I like to compare different types of eclipses on a scale of 1-10 as visual spectacles;"* says NASA's leading eclipse expert Fred Espenak of the Goddard Space Flight Center, *"if a partial eclipse is a five, an annular eclipse is a nine and a total eclipse is a million. It is completely off the charts compared to any other astronomical event."* [MSNBC 5-19-2012]

When we arrived there, in the countryside of Summerside, PEI, we began to worry. The skies were overcast and it didn't look too promising: www.rasc.ca/publications/nationalnewsletter/nn-1972-10.pdf Solar Eclipse July 10 from Prince Edward Island, *"All Prince Edward Island was under high-running cirro stratus cloud in the afternoons of July 8th, 9th and 10th. Rain developed on the 9th, but the 10th was dry and sunny, if hazy. A minute before second contact a fracto cumulus cloud obscured the sun completely, but cleared about three seconds before totality began, so that the inner corona was easily seen."*

As the time approached 2:00 PM, the beginning of the moon encroaching upon the sun's disc, I yelled out, "Clear skies, please! Clear skies!" And *as if like magic* my calls were answered ⊛ the winds picked up and the clouds raced away from the sun, giving us a clear, unobstructed view of the drama that was beginning to unfold. This is what Don Juan meant by ***stopping the world*** and being fully in the moment. I can't explain to you how breathtakingly beautiful those two minutes of totality were ☀ It's as if somebody shut off all the light in the sky so that all you could see was this intensely beautiful ring of fire. *We were transfixed, in awe and in some mysterious way-- changed from within, forever.* It all became so clear how insignificant we humans were in relation to *the big picture*. Three celestial bodies in perfect alignment and three human specks witness to it; no other humans around, with all the animals freaking out, "Where did our day go?" (The egrets were screeching, the cows in the distance were bellowing.) *So nice to have been given these moments-one of the three best experiences of my life.*

This same eclipse has been popularized in song by Carly Simon. "In 1973 Carly Simon scored the biggest success of her career with the classic global smash, *You're So Vain*, which includes the lyric, *'Then you flew your Learjet up to Nova Scotia to see the total eclipse of the sun,'* presumably a reference to this (July 10, 1972) eclipse."- Wikipedia *(Band of totality of this 1972 total solar eclipse included the following Canadian Provinces: Nova Scotia, Prince Edward Island, New Brunswick, and Quebec.)*

There is a phenomenon referred to as "solar eclipse addiction". Once you have experienced one total solar eclipse, you crave to partake of another and another. I can attest to the addictive properties of this ritual and for a look at the well-documented passion of another, visit 'pioneer synthesist and composer Wendy Carlos', self-proclaimed 'coronaphile': www.wendycarlos.com/eclipse.html

Barbara Carrera, as bag lady and street urchin in the movie, *Love Stinks*, *"But that's all life is....just a bunch of moments...but once in a while you steal a good one."*

This is how I described at the time in 1972 this otherworldly experience:

The presence of clouds which have totally obscured the progress of the moon's encroachment upon the sun's disk suddenly as if magically disperse quickly from the vicinity of the stage as the final sliver of the sun's crescent melts into a breathtaking cosmic aura of totality.

For two minutes during the constant snaps of the shutter and repositioning of the camera's tilt, I submit to a natural wonder of the universe, transfixed, as if under hypnosis by this awesome and ecstatic interlude.

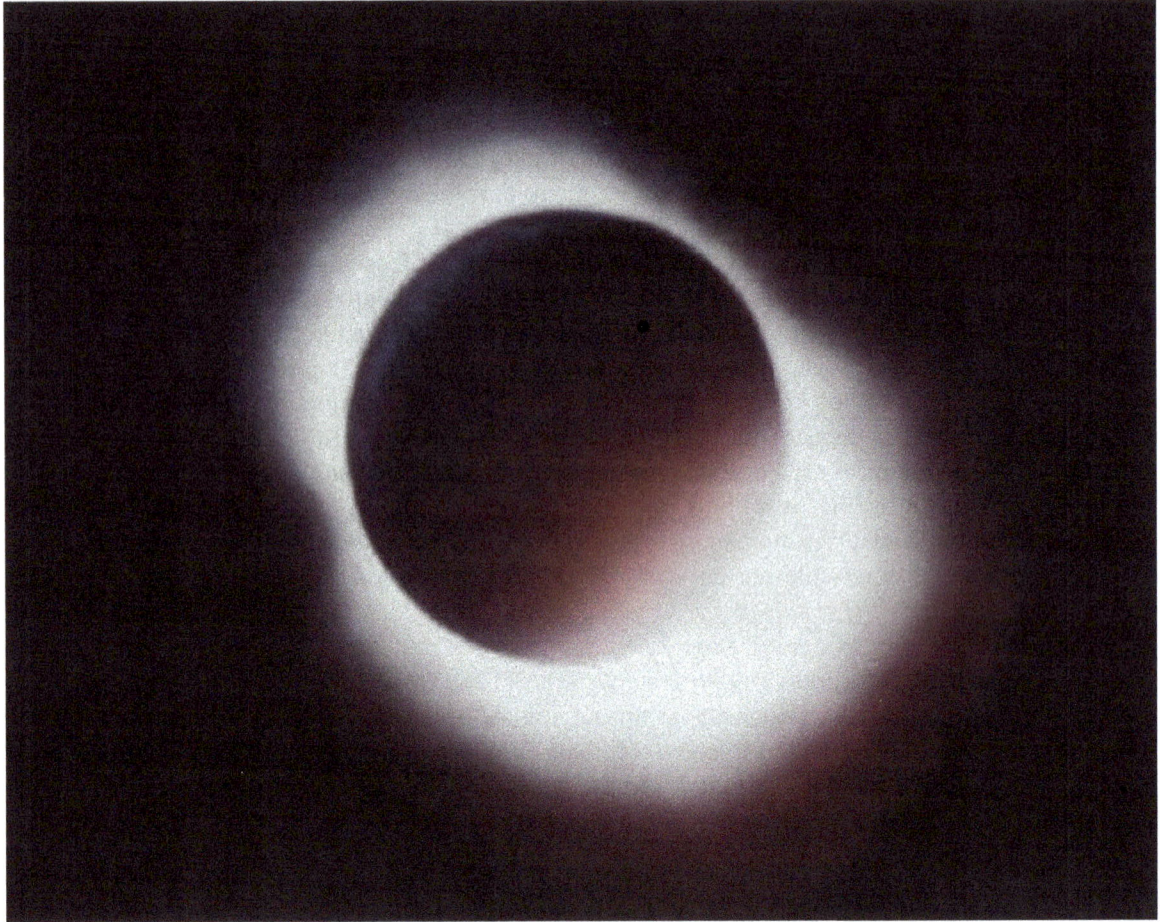

Cosmic Energy ☀ *Total Solar Eclipse*   *Summerside - P.E.I.*   *July 10th • 1972*

Chapter 9: *Social Worker with City of Hartford, CT & A Case Study of Suicide*

A couple of months later, I was hired as a Social Worker with the City of Hartford's Department of Social Services, working out of the Hollows Center on Park Street. My supervisor John Cosker recognized my experience administering to Leonard's manic depressive disorder and for that reason my caseload had a disproportionately higher number of individuals with mental health issues. I was kind of the 'resident expert' if you will. Carl Jung said, *"Knowing your own darkness is the best method for dealing with the darknesses of other people."* The other "Social Workers" in this field office had been hired for this job with degrees in English and History and anything but social services' training. I could never understand that. As time went on, I felt that their interest was strictly to hold down a job, NOT to sincerely be an advocate for social or personal improvement in the lives of their clientele. I remember the English major referring to his charges as "douche bags" and "dirt balls." I was appalled. A little more of my naïveté was replaced with the true reality of the way things were. I was disillusioned for thinking that we were all there sincerely trying to make a difference in these peoples' lives. There were other workers there who were trying to make a difference as well, but they were in the minority.

One of the cases that affected me deeply was the case of a 23 year old woman 'Ms. K'. She had been recently discharged from Hartford Hospital's Adult Psychiatric Clinic, and was assigned to my caseload for emergency assistance services. She appeared to be a little agitated but had a very amiable personality. I counseled her re: adaptive strategies she might consider for her aftercare adjustment back to "normal" living. I made an appointment to see her the following week and she went on her way. A few days later I received a letter from her at my office telling me that she had re-entered the hospital. In addition, she told me that she had strong feelings for me and wanted me to visit her at the hospital. I immediately shared her letter with my supervisor to get his idea on how to proceed with a situation like this. His words, as close to my recollection as possible, were, *"Dennis, I think you should not react right away. You have over a hundred cases that need your major attention. Maybe in a week or so you can make an official hospital visit to see her and try to set her straight."* A few days later John Cosker came into my office with a news clipping from The Hartford Courant. It was the obituary of 'Ms. K'. She had been discharged the day before, went straight to her apartment, opened up her gas oven, and ended her turmoil and suffering. I was shocked, taken aback and began to second guess every decision I had made when she was alive and not so well. I began to *internalize guilt* for not having done something more or better for this soul. And then I remembered the paper I had written on suicide back at St. Anselm. And I recalled one of the findings of the study which I found to be most valuable in dealing with this series of events. A study was done to determine the rates of suicide among professionals. The group of professionals with the highest rate of suicide was *psychiatrists*. I'll never forget that finding, or the reason given to explain it. The study went on to state that the reason suicide was so high for psychiatrists was because so many of them had *internalized guilt* for having failed their patients who also committed suicide. I realized I was having a natural and predictive reaction to this suicide by my client and I knew I needed to stop blaming myself, to believe I had done all I could do and, in the final view of things, probably nothing I could have done any differently would have had, ultimately speaking, any different outcome. I was happy I had written that paper. It was stolen but I still owned it.

Chapter 10: *Existentialism, the R-90S & Khalil Gibran– Three Forces of Power Ready My Soul*

As a youth I had become disillusioned with *religion* and I felt I was headed towards the priesthood. *It was my "mental slavery."* But when the priests no longer had answers to my existential meanderings of philosophical thought, I simply lost faith. And when the writings of *Jean-Paul Sartre* started making more sense to my life's existence, I was hooked on the Reality train. I now found myself proselytizing for what it was to be *totally real,* alluding to the concepts of existentialism and to the works of *Carlos Castañeda*, a Peruvian anthropologist who studied the Yaquis of Sonora, México via shaman Don Juan Matus. The following excerpt is from the 2003 seven-time Best Documentary film, *Flight From Death: The Quest For Immortality*, 'hailed by many as a life-transformational film.' Sartre is quoted as saying:

"Everything has been figured out except how to live. So perhaps the better question is not, 'What are we to do with death?' but, 'What are we to do with life?' Life exists in individual moments and it's up to us to make sure that those moments are vital, inter-connected and vast; that our process of living, of contributing to the collective experience of life, is embracing, nurturing and meaningful to create a masterpiece out of life, a life we would willingly repeat and to live it again and again for all of eternity. This is what we can strive for."

http://www.theguardian.com/books/2016/mar/04/ten-reasons-to-be-an-existentialist

I had studied the works of Sartre and many other philosophers when at St. Anselm College in such course offerings as: *Philosophy of Nature, Metaphysics, Logic, and Ethics. (1966-1968)*

For a time I began disseminating my views about *reality* to anyone who would listen. My friend Peter Potaski surprised me one day with a box of business cards he had made up which said: "Dennis DeRoche, Reality Merchant." Largely, the propositions I was promulgating were those from Carlos Castañeda's three books, *The Teachings of Don Juan: A Yaqui Way of Knowledge, A Separate Reality* and *Journey to Ixtlan.* There were some useful teachings, I felt, to gain from the Toltec tradition of the indigenous Yaqui belief system *for all of humanity* and I just wanted as many as possible to benefit from them. Probably the teaching from shaman Don Juan Matus, the "Man of Knowledge," that freed me the most was the concept to accept one's death as an ally that you carry with you on your left shoulder so that henceforward every moment can be lived to the fullest. He preached about being the *impeccable warrior*, one who is ready to face his death in any given moment and thereby able to live every moment as if it were his last, a teaching I pretty much took literally, adapting it to the motorcycle experience. By accepting this teaching fully, I was totally *freed* to ride.

(Another to learn from of great value in the Toltec tradition is Don Miguel Ruiz, author of *The Four Agreements** and *The Mastery of Love*.) *1. Be impeccable with your words; 2. Take nothing personal; 3. Don't make assumptions; 4. Do the best that you can*

Correspondingly, a very wise sage for humanity's enlightenment offered this prescription:

"The secret of health for both mind and body is not to mourn for the past, worry about the future, or anticipate troubles, but to live in the present moment wisely and earnestly." Buddha

At the Hollows Center I became known as "Wolfman,"my co-workers addressing me as "Wolf"or "Lobo." By 1973, I had purchased a new BMW R-75, a 750cc machine, and was coming to work in full dress leathers with long hair and a full beard. The dress code was very relaxed and I was being totally real about the image I was presenting. I was perhaps doing my job in a better way, with more confidence in self because I was accepted for who I was, thanks to John F. Cosker, Jr., NASW. [1/17/36 – 5/12/09]

I kept the R-75 less than one year because BMW was getting ready to unveil their newest addition to their line of superbikes, the R-90S café racer, a 900cc offering. I was a total BMW addict by this time and had to own this thoroughbred as soon as it was available to the public, which turned out to be March of 1974. This was the dream bike that I had hoped and longed for. It was a beautiful machine. The standard paint job defied description; it was smoked silver-black with gold highlights. It was a work of art and science by those unrelenting German and Italian engineers. It had a 5-speed gearbox with racing carburetion from Del Orto of Italy. It had a real throaty, highbred racer sound when fired up; it was something special. So what does someone like me do who is so obsessed with the BMW experience, now that he has his dream bike? Well, take that trip of a lifetime of course. I began planning my dream bike-trip adventure. I had been saving vacation time for two years and now was entitled to take an entire month off at one time. *The demands from within me were about to be met –*

There is one person who deserves a lot of credit for transforming my factory ready R-90S into a highly tuned hybrid racer and his name is Jeffrey Moores, the best BMW mechanic I have ever encountered and the best rider I have ever known. We would ride at 2 AM when most of the rest of the world was asleep so that the roads were much more *ours* than could otherwise be. JM was a transplant from California doing business out of a barn in Wethersfield, CT, dba *Moores Cycle Supply*. I remember him going through a box of high quality bits to perforate my discs so that my brakes would perform to maximum efficiency with greatest heat dissipation. German steel is for real; it's very high quality tough stuff. (Perforated disc brakes were not standard issue for the first model R-90S.) Nod to the best, Jeffrey Moores, an uncompromising talent whether aboard his two-wheeled rocket or setting up your own. Much respect to this maestro of motorcycles. I was fortunate to have known this special brother.

Time For Respite   *Cedar Hill*   *March • 1974*

Chillin' in the Cedar Hill Cemetery in Hartford, CT - one of our favorite riding places with all of its winding roads, *far from the madding crowds* and filled with solitude and peacefulness, my brother Tom with his Suzuki and me with R-90S. *(Canon FT placed 'on the rocks' in self-timer mode to capture two brothers 'of the Rocks')* We had other special places that we and our brother Michael would take trips to, but probably our favorite was *Middlefield Lookout* at the top of a mountain bordering Beseck Lake, in Middlefield, CT. Our grandfather Wilbrod DesRoches (born in 1900, died in 2000 – *was an amazing human being* – seen smoking his White Owl cigars to the very end) had built 7 homes on a horseshoe-shaped piece of property right at the lake's edge, 6 of which he rented out; and we were always fascinated as kids visiting our grandparents, taking boat rides and climbing that mountain to get a bird's eye view of the valley below – *where eagles fly.*

I wanted to plan the perfect trip and not forget anything in the preparation of it. I had already perfected the sound system requirements from the R-75. I had gone to the local army-navy surplus store, purchased two Navy flight helmets, gutted the earpieces and installed *Sennheiser* headsets in their place. Thanks to my brother Richard DesRoches, who was something of a genius with electronics, I was able to plug the two stereo helmets into any source unit provided. I chose an auto-reverse *Pioneer* cassette player which I mounted on top of the gas tank. I fashioned a carrying case from the old leather boots Peter had given me for a wedding present three years earlier. I was almost set to go. I wanted to camouflage the wires running from the helmets to the junction box and therefore decided to sew on some green, gold and brown velour to that end. The seat on this bike hinged open from the left side where a tool pouch was contained and plenty of room was left over for personal items as well. After

29

inlaying this compartment with velour as well, it was ready to receive a handful of pre-recorded 90 minute DNR cassette tapes. Next to the BMW, my Beautiful Majestic Woman, as I called it *(from an anthropomorphic and anthropopathic view of this gorgeous beast),* I was addicted to music. I thank my Fate that I grew up listening to *(I say)* some of the best music that has ever been recorded in all of time: *Pink Floyd, The Moody Blues, 'Emerson, Lake & Palmer,' Santana, The Beatles, Elton John, 'Crosby, Stills, Nash & Young,' Miles Davis, Iron Butterfly, The Eagles, Dan Fogelberg, Jethro Tull, The Rolling Stones, It's A Beautiful Day, Cat Stevens, Jimi Hendrix, The Doors, Janis Joplin, Bob Dylan, Judy Collins, Bob Seger, Led Zeppelin, The Grateful Dead, The Allman Brothers, and The Band-* and others more whom I'm sure I'll regret not mentioning at this time. They were my co-pilots even when I did have a passenger on board.

After three years of marriage, the relationship between my wife and I had drifted irretrievably apart, and soon we would be divorced. Peter introduced me to a woman named Peggy in Rhode Island who was suffering the loss of her entire family from a fatal car crash that killed her husband and two children and for which she was found responsible, a case of vehicular homicide from alcoholic intoxication. She was having a hard time adjusting to reality and seemed to be living in her own dream world. I was going through my own marriage withdrawal woes and she offered me *The Prophet* (1923) by Khalil Gibran to read. 'Gibran was an inspirational poet and artist from Lebanon.'
"The Prophet became extremely popular in the 1960's counterculture. Gibran is considered to be the third most widely read poet in history, behind Shakespeare and Lao-Tzu." This book affected me deeply. It was more like a bible about all aspects of living spoken about with true wisdom. I have since given it to a number of individuals both in English and in Spanish because it has the power within its pages to profoundly affect one's perspective about life. It is not a book you just read and put aside; it is a masterpiece to be looked at again and again and to be utilized as a book of inspiration to live one's life for those who would allow themselves to do so. Thank you, Peggy from Rhode Island.

Chapter 11: The "#1 Chapter" In My Life (August 1-31, 1974) —
Bringing Thoughts, Hopes & Dreams Into Reality: Trans Canada-USA-Mexico Tour
I had just experienced *The Grateful Dead* the night before taking off for my trip and was totally stoked and energized for my marathon adventure. I would not know what I captured on film for weeks *(p. 57).* The time had finally come. My bike trip was scheduled for the entire month of August, 1974. Three different people had professed a desire to make the trip with me but one by one, as August 1st approached, the only one who was going to be going on this trip would be me (which is probably the way it should have been – after all, this was *my dream*). Of course I would take the second helmet; you always prepare for the unexpected. My loosely planned itinerary was to go north from Hartford, CT, to Niagara Falls, continue on up into Canada, travel all the way across Canada to Kamloops, head south across the border to Lake Chelan, WA, where my friend Chuck Horvath was picking apples, continue down the coast to Sonoma County to visit Bobby Corcoran (another transplanted friend from Broadview Terrace), then head for Mexico, come back up through AZ to the Grand Canyon, traverse the rest of the USA to Richmond, VA, where my brother Paul was living, and head for home. I actually stuck to the plan pretty closely with a few digressions; after all, *"diversion is the soul of touring."* I wanted to start the trip with a symbolic gesture. I decided that the first day of riding I would not stop until I had traveled 715 miles, since that was the # of our family address on Broadview Terrace. I held to it but with some justifiable regret. *Mile # 715* put me in a terrible downpour of blinding rain somewhere in Canada. The closest semblance of shelter was a park of some kind, and low and behold, a family had pitched their tent and they were in for the night. This was my first opportunity to experience the people of another nation. They saw the condition I was in, drenched to the bone, cold and shivering and they immediately offered their station wagon to sleep in that night. How great was that. The moment I started having

second thoughts about the decision I had made, some good people stepped up and put all that to rest. I was very encouraged from the first day out by this wonderful show of Canadian hospitality.

When Coefficients Become Deities

Niagara Falls was very impressive. I viewed it from the American side and was trying to imagine being one of those daredevils in any one of those contraptions that had been used in times gone by going over those falls for the ride of a lifetime and in some cases the ride of their death. The immense power and tremendous fury of so much water passing right in front of you *(as close as they will allow you to get)* is daunting. The experience of taking it all in for an hour or so is akin to re-charging one's batteries and it gave me a newly acquired respect for the forces of Mother Nature. And as a biker, much more than a car driver, one needs to have a very healthy respect for the Laws of Nature, forever mindful of the *coefficient of friction*, that variable which allows one to remain upright on a two-wheeled balancing act known as motorcycling. For real, homeys, for real!! All of a sudden it occurs to me that the words *Metzler* and *Continental* are not just the names of tires on my bike, but *'deities'* to be revered *for* life.

Even when it's dry, there can be a patch of sand or ice in front of you. And then there's black ice and rain and all the other things Nature can throw at you; and all that may pale in comparison to one other ingredient in the mix as well, other human beings! Eliminating that last ingredient is the bane of the existence of the freedom rider.

I figured if I was going to make this trip and arrive back in Harford, CT, by the end of August, I would need to travel approximately 300-500 miles per day (X 31 days). For every couple of days I rode 500 or more miles, I was entitled to take a day off and chill. After Niagara Falls, I continued towards Toronto and then to Thunder Bay, Ontario. Once back on the Trans-Canada Highway somewhere in Ontario, I saw way up on the horizon another biker. Now my style of riding, especially for highways like this, is to cruise around 80-95 mph. If I see another biker in my rear view gaining on me, I increase my speed to not permit a pass. I didn't relish being passed by anyone; I liked, wanted and when I was able, I insisted on clear road ahead of me. The sense of freedom and adventure for me diminished when I let others in front of me; because, almost inevitably after a pass, they would slow down, forcing me to do the same.

So, I eliminated that scenario altogether by staying in front of all traffic if possible. Of course, you must allow the vehicle behind you to gain upon you until you could determine if it was law enforcement, before initiating these vanguard maneuvers, because you didn't want to complicate matters with a speeding violation. *'Who, me, officer? I was just being totally real!'* Yeah, right, I'm sure that would fly.

The Race Is On To Be Out Front

Anyways, I see this biker way ahead of me and I start closing the gap between us. The R-90S was an awesome machine. A slight twist of the throttle and in milliseconds you could accelerate from 80 to over a 100 mph with no sweat. I closed the gap significantly up to a point and then I noticed that this rider began doing just as I had described. He turned it on, not wanting to be passed, and the race was on! I believed there was no bike I couldn't catch but I had to hand it to this rider- he did a respectable job holding me back as much as he could. Just as I had gotten into passing position, he slowed down and took a quick exit. I decided I would stop also and meet this individual. No wonder he was doing so well in those turns, and now it was no surprise to me- he was riding an *R-75!* The R-75 was the best handling motorcycle BMW ever built. It was considerably lighter than the 494-lb R-90S and for that reason could dump into a turn with much more agility. Having ridden both, however, I was not giving up much in handling, and for all the extra power and speed of the "S"- I wouldn't have it any other way. This biker and I had a lot to share about our rides and he ended up being a kind of tour guide for the remainder of my trip across Canada. I don't remember his real name but I called him *"Canada."* Ironically, he was returning from a trans-Canadian tour *he* was doing, wanting to visit every province in his country. One of the reasons I had decided to go across Canada is because both my mother's and father's families came from Québec, the French-speaking province north of Vermont and New York, and I felt there was a strong connection with this country that I needed to more fully explore. *The maple leaf on the Canadian flag had special significance to me as my great grandparents were producers of maple syrup in Canada and my most prized photo is of g-dad Wilbrod at 7 with his dad Philipe in front of their sugar shack in 1907. I had a chance to meet Philipe when he was 88 and played a couple games of checkers with him. **He whopped me!***

As Close As You Can Get Between Keeping It & Losing It

I have two lasting memories from my trip across Canada. One of them was almost my death. We were riding high in the mountains of Alberta, the only two vehicles for miles way up in the wilderness reaches of this province. The highway ran real close to the cliff-side mountains we were traversing. With no warning whatsoever, I had a blowout of my rear tire, which threw me into a vicious wobble from side to side. It was very reminiscent of the wobble episodes I had with the R-60's infamous Earles fork design. I wrestled my steering fiercely to regain control and came oh so close to going over the side of that mountain! Makes you appreciate life so much more! I call this experience a *left curve*. You always have to be ready for the unexpected, even more so on a motorcycle. Remember Murphy's Law, "Anything that can go wrong, will go wrong." I was to have one more of these *left curves* come my way before my return home. These *"unknowns"* can be pitched by Mother Nature, mechanical breakdown or human interaction. I prefer either of the first two coming my way over the latter. (Remember how *Easy Rider* ends?) When you undertake an ambitious trip like this trans-Canada-trans-USA tour, you need to go prepared. I would not have taken this trip without a spare tube, three tire irons and hand pump. And, just as <u>Zen</u> <u>and</u> <u>the</u> <u>Art</u> <u>of</u> <u>Motorcycle</u> <u>Maintenance</u> would have it, I knelt at the edge of that mountain and fixed that rear tire. Felt so great to get back on board and push on through those mountains.

Banff National Park – Crown Jewel of Canada

The other lasting memory I have is of Banff National Park in Alberta. This biker I had been traveling with was very familiar with the beauty of his native country. He told me the most beautiful part of his country was this Banff National Park area, 2500 square miles of the most gorgeous stretch of the Rocky Mountains with many ice fields and pine forests. He knew just where to go and led the way through areas I never would have experienced. The awesome beauty of these mountain passes was spell-binding. When you've never seen anything like this in your life and it's all of a sudden put in front of you, you really do appreciate it and it really does enrich the soul. These are the kinds of experiences that become part of you, that transform you. Our trip together was about to end. "*Canada*" lived in Prince George, British Columbia. He continued north from Kamloops and I continued south. I had experienced the wonderful hospitality of the Canadian people my whole trip throughout Canada, proud to say that this is the country from where my parents' heritage had come.

Lake Chelan & Chuck Horvath

I now had my sights set for Lake Chelan, WA. This is an apple growing region and my good friend Chuck had decided to move to this area for the summer working the orchards. He knew I was coming and when I arrived there was a big party waiting for me. Chuck was living in a communal arrangement and all of the folks here were really righteous. It was refreshing to be among friends and people close to the earth. Chucky had come to Washington from Hawaii where he had been living. He was the *Big Kahuna*, the die-hard surfer who wanted to experience the waves of as many places around the world that he could and he did. As mentioned earlier, he has lived many years in Hawaii and visited Hong Kong, Thailand and has been to Japan twice. But this addiction of his was not without its residual effects. One of his ears had gotten infected from his surfing in Hawaii, and now he needed medical attention. So I took him to Seattle, a couple hundred miles to the west, and he caught a flight back home to Connecticut where his family insurance would pick up the tab for his medical treatment. Chuck Horvath,

The Endless Summer Kid – one of the finest human beings I have ever known ✳ Aloha Nui Loa

Oregon Coast Highway & Pamela Madison – the Supreme Being of my Marathon Adventure

Riding through Stevens Pass in Washington State was very reminiscent of my trek through the Rocky Mountains of Alberta -- grandiose, majestic panoramas, big rock country with rivers through the mountains, everything of natural beauty and none of it touched by man. More than 36 years have passed since I took this trip and Stevens Pass is still up close and personal for me. The beauty of west coast USA is unsurpassed. As impressive and awesome was Washington State, so too was Oregon. The coastline highway I followed was very curvy with many switchbacks, providing a very enjoyable sight-seeing tour, often times with full views of the Pacific to my right, waves endlessly crashing the rocks and shores below. In the distance up ahead of me, I espied two people on the side of the road, a man and a woman. As I approached, the woman stuck her thumb out; so I stopped. They had agreed that if a biker stopped and she was so inclined, she would go with that person. She didn't take very long to decide. Within a minute she was aboard with knapsack in tow. I'll never forget her name, *Pamela Madison*. She was about 22 years of age, very attractive and at least an inch taller than my 5'9". She was very intelligent, a most engaging personality and she was to be the most important person I would meet on this mega trip. We had long discussions about music and biking and what we were doing with our lives and she was totally stoked to be listening to the wide-ranging musical selections I had on tap in perfect hi-fidelity via those *"open-air" Sennheisers*. We rode for several hours and decided to detour to her stomping grounds in Medford. We went to a bar where she had worked and then to a friend's home close by where we aimed to get cleaned up. While Pamela was showering, I was in the living room talking with her friend. After about five minutes, Pamela's voice could be heard, "Oh, Dennis…" I kept talking with her friend. About 15 seconds more and once again, "Oh, Dennis…" This time her friend says to me, "Dennis, I don't think you should keep her waiting." To which I immediately got up, walked over to the bathroom and realized I was in for a very nice surprise. Off came the leather pants and shirt and in I went to get clean and share the experience with her. As you know, we men think with two heads, and often times our brainless head can get us into trouble before we know what hit us or before we know what we hit. Well, this little guy was no more such a little guy; he was *'thinking'* just fine and as he would have it, Pamela and I became one with each other enjoying the fruits of Mother Nature. *Thank you, Pamela Madison, for being so totally real, so totally free, and for risking total aliveness within yourself.* The next day we decided to visit her Dad who lived deep in some woods by himself, fashioning knives for a living. I'll never forget the moment Pamela introduced me to her Dad. "Dad, this is Dennis, can we use your waterbed tonight?" Talk about someone who didn't mince words. The terrestrial body of water we were about to enjoy for the evening was a king-sized version; there were no complaints.

The Day of Reckoning

The next day we had a long talk. She invited me to Ken Kesey's annual bash coming up soon that was held every year in Eugene, OR. [Ken Kesey, author of: *One Flew Over the Cuckoo's Nest* (1962)]. She said that she and her Dad had been going to it for the past several years. I told her, as much as I would love to go with them, I had an itinerary that I needed to honor; that I was still employed as a social worker with Hartford, CT. Then we started talking about motorcycles. Pamela said she had ridden with a lot of bikers, and some of them pretty good, and what she experienced with me was something she really enjoyed, but she felt like I was *'playing with death in every turn'*. She did not feel comfortable leaning so low into the turns and thought that maybe the best ending to our relationship would be if I could get her down to a California beach, we could kiss and say "good-bye, it was nice," and wish each other a good life. To paraphrase her, *"Dennis, while I see that you are an expert rider, I also feel that the motorcycle experience has been all-consuming in your life and therefore you cannot control how much control it has over you. In order for you to take back control of your life, you probably need to start thinking about if this is something you can realistically sustain."* Her words hit with the full force of REALITY. She was being totally real with me, not mincing words, and she appealed to my intellect.

Just like when she appealed to my *id* in the shower and was very effective then; so too had she reached my *superego* (to borrow from Freud) and made a real difference to my philosophical perspective of life. This was not an ordinary woman. *Thank my Destiny or Good Fortune, I had finally met someone to help me make sense of it all and it happened to be a total stranger hitchhiking on the Oregon coast.* I am indebted to Pamela Madison. It's truly amazing and wonderful the people you meet in life. The next day, per our understanding, I took Pamela to a northern California beach and we said our good-byes. I had the feeling that if nothing else really great happened on this trip, it wouldn't matter; I had a clear purpose and direction vis-à-vis the motorcycle trip I was on - going forward. And that was an important turning point for moving on with some of the other aspects of my life that up until then were being pushed back or forsaken, such as: *"How to maintain a healthy relationship with a woman when I'm already married to an iron maiden,"* and *"How to further develop my career in photography when so much of my energy and assets are tied up in two wheels."* *Oftentimes life gives you what you need; you just have to be *awake* enough to notice it and do something about it.* I was awakened and I was going to do something about it. *(Horace Wells, a Hartford, CT dentist, who is credited as the discoverer of modern anesthesia, has these words engraved on his tomb: "I sleep to awaken; I awaken to glory." Wells noticed the anesthetic effects of nitrous oxide and did something about it.)* His grave in the Cedar Hill Cemetery where we rode our bikes was the one that impressed me the most.

For more on 'waking up', see YouTube video by Alan Watts, "The Way of Waking Up."
https://www.youtube.com/watch?v=fcPWU59Luoc&list=PL936809BAE67BF725
https://www.youtube.com/watch?v=tCbHg243-AE   https://www.youtube.com/watch?v=9miTS53auUk

The Redwoods & Bobby Corcoran

Time to visit Bobby Corcoran. He grew up on the same street as Chucky and Connie and my good friend Mitch Pawlowski whose mom always made me happy with kielbasa sandwiches and pierogi. Mitch was fond of saying, *"If it feels good, do it!"* It's a philosophy very similar to, *"Go with your heart,"* a philosophy highly touted by the very successful Steve Jobs of Apple fame as the way to live one's life.

Bobby came from a family of plumbers and he was Irish through and through. He was a musician back in CT, the lead guitarist of a group called *Liquid Lite*. Now transplanted in California, he found himself an ideal home in the redwoods of Rio Nido close by the Russian River in Sonoma County, just north of Santa Rosa. Talk about an idyllic paradise, he was living in a log cabin surrounded by redwoods with a sign artistically rendered over his door, Gentle Funk. There was a loft inside and a hammock down below.

It was really something special. We visited for several hours, checked out Guerneville which was close by, offered thanks to the sativa gods and then I reluctantly got back aboard my teutonic steed one more time. All I could think to say to Bobby Corcoran was, "Congratulations for having found nirvana!"

Tijuana & Ensenada

I continued my journey along the California coast until I reached the border. I wanted to experience both neighbors to the north and south of our country and so Mexico was to be my next stop. After crossing the border into Tijuana, I was quite shocked and taken aback as to the conditions of living in this country. Whereas in Canada much is as it is in the US of A, there was nothing in this part of the world that reminds you of anything you might have known or experienced heretofore, a veritable shantytown of pervasive poverty before me. When I got to the commercial district, I parked my ride and began checking out the different storefronts. Something else I had not experienced before was the very "in your face" style of aggressive marketing that a lot of these vendors utilized. They would try any method they could short of jumping you in order to separate you from your *green*. The most memorable of all was when, unbeknownst to me, I had walked along the sidewalk in front of a brothel. A woman darted out up to me, grabbed me by the sleeve and asked, *"You like to sucky, fucky?"* Wow! I was shocked. I decided to saddle up and kick on down the road to the next major coast city, Ensenada.

I went down by the ocean, passed a day at a beautiful beach practically by my lonesome -- and then I decided it was time to head back. I picked up a bottle of mescal+*gusano* and re-entered the Lower 48.

Grand Canyon & Blessings From The Sky

Next stop, Grand Canyon. I had heard so much about this *"must see"* natural wonder that I would be remiss not to include it. It was all that I had ever hoped to experience. So many others before me have attempted to put into words what cannot be fairly stated and so many more have tried to put into photos what cannot be depicted-- this is the magnitude of the wonder known as *Grand Canyon*. You absolutely have to experience this place in person. There is only one parallel I could draw from my experience that had something in common with this vastness of time and space- the 1972 total solar eclipse in Prince Edward Island. In both cases *'man'* is reduced to the smallest, most insignificant speck of dust, that it's a wonder he has accomplished so much as he has. We've managed to land two men on the moon with the Apollo 11 spaceflight on July 20, 1969, *and that was an awesome feat!* -- but next to all that has been accomplished in this place over millions of years-- well, *you* be the judge.

It's interesting that the only days of precipitation I experienced on this entire 31-day excursion were the very first day, the very last day and the day I was witness to this natural wonder. The first and last days it rained; my day visiting the Canyon I was greeted with an ice storm of hail all around me. I saw it as

kind blessings from the sky. **What a way to cap a day!** And put a cool exclamation mark on this trip*!!*

Trying to recount a trip I had taken 36 years ago is a little difficult. It would have been great if I had kept a diary or tried to condense into words, years before now, all that I had encountered. What I am sharing are the events that have been seared into the fiber of my being, that have stood the test of time in my memory and that I hope will inspire someone else to go out there in the wilderness and seek himself or herself as well. What I have learned is that the individual who submerges himself into an all-encompassing experience such as this will undergo a metamorphosis of sorts; you can count on a "new you"—a new way at looking at life or a new way of being "you"--

Cadillac Ranch   ['*Cadillac Ranch*' released as a song in 1980 on Bruce Springsteen's The River.]

Crossing through Texas I passed through Amarillo. On the outskirts of this city is what I call a *must see* all-American attraction. It was established in June of 1974 and consists of 10 old Cadillacs from the years of the "fins", from 1949-1963, that are buried in the ground nose first, one in front of the other, the same distance apart, and they are buried up to about half their body length. You are encouraged to put your own graffiti on them if you so chose. But for me, the most interesting aspect of this outdoor sculpture is the fact that the artists, known as the *Ant Farm*, had these cars installed at an angle corresponding to the Great Pyramid of Giza in Egypt. Why, I don't know, but it makes you wonder. Long live the great American spirit! [Coordinates: 35°11'14N, 101°59'13.4W – current home of this sculpture]

Life And Death Decisions – *(Analogy: Nations* RESPECTING *Each Other's Rights = Survival & PEACE)*

The next recall that comes to mind is that other *left curve* I referred to back when I had a blowout in the mountains of Alberta, Canada. I was getting closer to the eastern side of the country now, riding through the West Virginia mountains. It was a very sinuous stretch of mountain roads, very curvy. As a rider you're constantly leaning left or right to negotiate curvy roadways. The problem sometimes arises when the curves are quick and short that you have very little time to allow for debris on the road surface if you are already committed to a lean in order to negotiate that curve. Such was the situation I was faced with. As I had indicated earlier, *the coefficient of friction may be viewed as the relationship between life and death, that principle of physics that allows the motorcycle to remain in an upright position. When you lose traction or friction, there is nothing for your tires to hold on to.*

I was leaning way over to the right, committed to my line in a blind curve *(meaning you can't apply your brakes at this time or try to change your line within that lane)* when up pops a large patch of sand that a trucker more than likely had shed. I was going to go down for sure if I didn't use the oncoming lane as an escape route. But this was a blind turn and I didn't have the luxury to know if there was a vehicle coming towards me in that lane. These are the times for split second decisions, micro-millisecond decisions that you really don't have time to think about. These are gut decisions that you execute without thinking. So I went for it. I used the entire oncoming lane of that blind curve, just hoping it would not be my unlucky day and I would survive to see another sunrise, another human smile and be able to recount all of these great adventures I was having. Such is Fate. You win some and you lose some. Sometimes you just have to go for it and risk it all; sometimes you have no choice. *As long as one sincerely pays homage to RESPECT at all times -- *for* all people and *for* all the forces of Nature, and one has prepared himself/herself to be that *"impeccable warrior"* as Don Juan puts it, there's nothing more that one can do that is in one's control.   And there's something to be said for: "Character is Fate"

*There is a *collective unconscious* operating out there and all of our actions are connected to others.
V-Star to Change the World since 2010 has been harnessing the power of TM for world peace from one million children assembled annually in Thailand: https://www.youtube.com/watch?v=4VV8wDyxhwM Dr. John Hagelin: "We all have the opportunity now to permanently change our world for the better. Why not give peace a chance?" www.tm.org/blog/video/world-peace-from-the-quantum-level-david-lynch-and-john-hagelin/

World Peace Progress: www.PermanentPeace.org   More on Peace in the World: pp. 80-81

Richmond, VA & Paul DesRoches

Happy to have cheated my demise, I continued on into Virginia and after having been on the road for 28 days or so, I finally reached a familial oasis, my brother Paul's home in Richmond, VA. Paul had two sons, David and Paul, from his wife Carla.   I was happy to have influenced my brothers about the virtues of the BMW experience. My brothers Tommy, Michael and Paul all had B-Mers and it was one more way for us to connect with something in common. So Paul had a keen appreciation for the trip I had just taken.   There are those who would say that a strong rivalry existed between Paul and I. We both had gone through college and were considered "intellectuals" and I guess some of our tête-à-têtes were memorable. Actually, we were both very strong-minded about our positions on issues; yet and still we usually got along fairly well at the same time. Throughout life we have managed a healthy respect for each other; he in Virginia, and myself in whatever state I happened to be living in at the time. (I have lived in Hawaii, California, Arizona and Florida) We could have been a lot closer, I suppose, but time and distance away from each other's worlds took its eventual toll on our relationship.   Paul is a multi-talented individual; an expert at decorative woodworking, *(I remember he hand-crafted a dulcimer that came out pretty damn good!)*, a *Photoshop* maestro, and a musician of stringed instruments. A truly talented person. He is now happily married to his wonderful wife Karen living the good life in VA.

On September 30, 2010, yesterday, as I am inserting these words, I met Paul's son David, my long lost nephew. Living my life from afar all his years growing up, we never got to know each other. Well, I'm pleased to say that after a flurry of e-mails in just one evening, we now know quite a bit about each other and look forward to a rich relationship going forward. David is a very talented photojournalist and media consultant who has spent part of his life in Africa and can be solicited at: www.daveroch.com

Last Stop: New Haven, CT & Richard DesRoches

After a day or so at Paul's, it was time to head for my home state of Connecticut. I had one more stop to make before home base. My brother Richard and his wife Sally lived in New Haven.   We were closest in age and pretty close to each other when we were young, but as time passed we grew further apart. The motorcycle played a big part in Richard's life as well. He preferred dirt bikes and one day he and I were riding through Penwood Park in Avon, CT, he on his *X-6 Hustler* and me on my *R-60*. I think he wanted to show off how fast he could make it through the trails on his *Suzuki* while I was just out for an enjoyable ride through the park. (A 600 cc touring bike does not race a 250 cc dirt bike) Anyways, he went ahead of me and soon was out of sight. But the telltale, high frequency sounds of his two stroke engine could no longer be heard. I started looking very carefully from side to side, trying to see if he'd gone off the road somewhere and then I saw out of the corner of my eye down about 20 yards in the woods to my right he and the bike laying down close to each other. He had hit a tree close to the trail with such force, part of the hardware from his handlebar clutch assembly was firmly left embedded in the tree. But he was a lot worse for wear. He had evidently slapped the tree so hard with his thigh that it opened up like a split watermelon. We had to think fast. And the first consideration was stopping blood loss. I wrapped his army jacket around his thigh and had him transported to Hartford Hospital's ER. Here's where the story gets interesting. The attending ER nurse, Sally, came to his rescue, nursed him back to health, and after some preliminary courtship, the two of them got married. This happened over 40 years ago and they are still together today, proud of their two children Kathy and Eddie. Yeah for motorcycles! They can bring you love! *And awaken the power and freedom within your soul.*

The Marathon Is Over: For The Road & For My Life

It was time to rendezvous to the start/finish line, 109 Franklin Avenue in Hartford, CT. I had kept a close tracking of my mileage for the trip and I had traveled exactly 10,333 miles (16,533 km) in that month of August, 1974. I had experienced quite a lot in one month's time and somehow had become a *new me*. I don't think you can take a trip like this and not become somehow transformed by it. I had decided, in no small part due to the brilliant observations of Pamela Madison, that the motorcycle experience going forward might turn out to be a crippling proposition, that I needed to gain control back in my life for those endeavors that I had effectively forsaken; namely, the further pursuit of my photographic career and the furthering of my education in the form of an MSW degree in order to become a more effective player in my chosen field of social work. I had to view the continuation of the motorcycle way of life and these other endeavors as mutually exclusive events. I could not entertain the two side by side. I had taken the motorcycle experience to its logical conclusion, allowing it to totally consume all of my energies to the detriment of my involvement with the other considerations of my life including and probably most important of all, the ability to have a healthy, wholesome loving relationship with a woman. I was the one essentially at fault for the divorce with Connie- the motorcycle had gotten to play too big a part in my life usurping from me all of my resources. Carl Jung: *"Every form of addiction is bad, no matter whether the narcotic be alcohol or morphine or idealism."*

Being totally real here, I was a bigamist, married (on the one hand) to my iron maiden parked outside, ready to make love at any moment to its power and speed, and (on the other hand) to an actual flesh and blood woman who cared about and loved me for real. I knew what I had to do to regain control of my life and, *truly speaking, there was no relationship that meant more to me than one with a loving, significant other to share the joys and mysteries of life together. I wanted that more than anything else and it became my #1 goal in life, one that I would relentlessly pursue and then maintain, once I had acquired it, hopefully, for the rest of my life.* No other goal is more important than that in my view. Your heart comes first, your soul follows. But when you are at war with your soul; your mind wants to tell you what are your priorities but your heart has a passion for an experience much greater, then the issue is not so easily resolved. In words of Khalil Gibran: *"Your soul is oftentimes a battlefield, upon which your reason and your judgment wage war against your passion and your appetite…Your reason and your passion are the rudder and the sails of your seafaring soul. Therefore let your soul exalt your reason to the height of passion."*

I had made up my mind that I would pursue a Master's Degree in Social Work so that I could make more of a difference in peoples' lives by intervening at an administrative level rather than to be confined to the ranks of *line worker*. After having completed four years as a caseworker with the Hollows Center, I felt I needed to do something to change the operation of *business as usual* in the provision of social services to the eligible population. I was very unhappy (having been on welfare as a child) to witness the way these "social workers" were treating their clientele. What I saw was a system ostensibly set up for the needs of lone individuals and families but actually was being manipulated and perpetuated for the job security of these caseworkers. I submitted a very detailed resignation letter to Nancy Fleming, Director of Casework Services with the Hartford Department of Social Services, summarizing my reservations above, calling my view of things a "Big Hypocrisy."

Before my employment had ended with the City of Hartford and before we leave this all-important venue of my professional life's experiences, there is a chapter that needs to be told re: my love life. Two of the Social Service Aides at the Hollows Center were from Puerto Rico, *Carmen Rodriguez* and Jose Vasquez. I was very attracted to Carmen Rodriguez. She was a very beautiful woman from Ponce but married and so our relationship was strictly one of friendship. My friend Jose, realizing how much I was smitten by the calm, self-assured ways of this Latin woman, introduced me to a friend of his, *Gloria Guadalupe*, also from Puerto Rico. ♡ A former singer from the island and also very beautiful, we had a relationship that lasted about six months or so. She spoke no English so that communication was at times difficult as I had just only recently decided that I would learn Spanish as a second language. I loved the Latin culture. It seemed to me from my observations and involvement with this community that their families were more close-knit; *family* was not only important as it is for every other culture, *family was everything*. I began to feel very envious, wanting to have this same closeness of commitment to each other in my life. Having come from a fractured family home environment, I was oh, so hungry for that which I had just discovered to be the most satisfying relationship I had ever experienced. *I felt that I might not be satisfied in life unless I could find that special lady of Latin persuasion.** But I took a long, hard road to get there. I made a few mistakes along the way and paid a very high price at times before I was to have and hold the woman of my heart that I had been seeking for so many years. Never give up. **(I need to state unequivocally that my years together with Jennifer Rebholz I was very satisfied.)*

Chapter 12: *"Life Is What Happens To Us While We Are Making Other Plans" Allen Saunders*
My plan was to terminate employment, head south to Miami and put myself in position to apply for and matriculate to the University of Puerto Rico. Between 'terminating employment' and 'heading south,' a lot more happened that I wasn't counting on- because one cannot control everything in the face of Fate.

   En Español: *"La vida es lo que nos pasa mientras estamos haciendo otros planes."*
(This quote, incorrectly attributed to John Lennon, has been verified by three sources as a quote of Allen Saunders-it first appeared in a 1957 Reader's Digest edition of 'Quotable Quotes') Quoteinvestigator.com

Carlos Hernández Chávez 🗿 *Artist, Musician & Humanitarian Activist*

Another colleague of mine who worked out of a different field office and who became a close personal friend was Carlos Hernández Chávez, born in the heart of México in the city of León, in the state of Guanajuato, México, about 3½ hours northwest of Mexico City. I found Carlos to be a very multi-talented individual. Beyond his employment as Social Worker for the City of Hartford, he is well known throughout the Harford area for his artistic genius. Carlos has an extensive portfolio of paintings and other media as well, but is perhaps most famous for his large murals that always have an important educational and political message. (He can be seen and heard on YouTube at: art.culture.life/Carlos Hernández Chávez: http://www.youtube.com/watch?v=ycGEHwi2gGk) CHC: "The culture of a people is really the signature of who they are…I have this philosophy about life that the more you give, the more you receive, whether it's directly or indirectly, to the circle of people that you appreciate and that you love and that you like and that you work with." As a social activist, Carlos is involved with Concerned Citizens For Humanity, promoting human welfare and social reform. "What we try to do is empower people to improve their lives and to improve their health, etc." In addition to his vast range of visual artistry, Carlos is a superb guitarist as well, as you will hear. carlos.hernandezchavez@gmail.com

Carlos calls me *el lobo* and I call him *el coyote*. He once painted my face in the image of *Quetzalcoatl*, the feathered-serpent being of Aztec mythology, who "represented life, motion, laughter, health, sexuality, and the arts and crafts of civilization...." (Myths Encyclopedia: Myths and Legends of the World) The following is from the French ethnologist Laurette Sejourné: *"What makes Feathered Serpent a king is his determination to alter the course of his existence, to initiate a journey to which he is forced only by inner necessity. He is sovereign because he obeys his own law instead of that of others; he is the source and origin of movement."* I would say: *'What makes one king of his own destiny is his determination to alter the course of his existence, to initiate a journey forced upon by inner necessity.'*

And lastly, from Dwayne Edward Rourke, *"From humanity's earliest beginnings, the work of those who have embodied the Feathered Serpent spirit, has been to help heal and redeem a fragmented humanity, through a reawakening of sacred view, and the re-establishment of sacred order."*

Thanks to the perspicacity of Chávez, he was able to see these operating tenets which indeed had been defining my life's path. As artist-photographer, Carlos' work can be seen on the front cover of this book's first edition, face painted and photographed by him in 1974 just before I embarked on my North American bike tour. People often reacted with shock and disbelief at this photo but really, for me, it represents the duality of the conscious and the subconscious constantly at play controlling our lives, as well as the left and right brain functions operating synergistically in harmony, the sum effect of their efforts resulting in who we are as *human being* in a world impinged upon by the complementary forces of *yin-yang* in balance. And lastly, I was the *warrior* that Yaqui Indian Don Juan Matus speaks about, readying myself for the battle (*the trip* I was about to embark upon), ready to face my death in any given moment *and at the same time able to experience and appreciate each and every moment of life to the fullest degree possible.* There really is a lot we can learn from our Native Brothers.

Laurie Doster - Supernova

Carlos knew my love of photography and thought I might appreciate seeing and photographing a play he was in, *Man of La Mancha*, in which a mad knight Don Quixote was famous for jousting at windmills that he believed were evil giants.   The actress and singer who played the dual role of Aldonza the whore and her counterpart persona Dulcinea the pure vestal virgin was Laurie Doster. I was overwhelmed with her performance, her passion as an actress and her voice as a singer when she belted out, *The Impossible Dream*. I met her back stage and she invited me to the cast party she was having at her home in Killingworth, CT, about 50 miles from Hartford. It was the dead of winter with a fierce storm and very high winds when the Friday of her party came. I guess you could say I was a freak of nature because I rode my motorcycle exclusively throughout the year. It was masochistic to say the least. I felt that a regimen of Spartan training would toughen me up and keep me in good stead. This can better be described as *"mortifying the body in an effort to subdue the ego"* as Joseph Goldstein writes in "The Buddha's Sacred Journey." I would also describe this as *beating the ego down to reach humility*.

I really suffered for this decision. Connecticut gets cold in the winter and when you add the wind-chill factor, it could become humanly impossible to ride a motorcycle as fast as 50 mph. This was the worst experience in my life riding the two-wheeled beast. Never before had I experienced winds so fierce, that I was nearly blown off the highway. I had to lean deeply into the winds and could barely maintain upright at 40 mph. It was terrible. The temperature was below freezing and I had never been colder in my life! I thought I had prepared sufficiently with my leather jacket inside a full length raccoon coat with ski goggles and gloves. But Mom Nature just laughed at me and had me begging for mercy. I had to stop on at least two separate occasions to warm back to life my nearly frost-bitten *huevos,* if you dig.

The Iceman Cometh! By the time I reached Laurie Doster's home in *Killingworth (a symbolic name of a town to say the least for this death-defying journey towards it- but Laurie was worth the risk),* I was the last one to show up for the party. When the door was opened to my arrival, the people were shocked that I had biked my way. I had a mustache complete with snow *and icicles* hanging from it! It didn't

look very *normal*. It wasn't. This experience more than any other is what gave me the resolve to select only lower level latitudes with lots of warmth and sun as places of residence for the rest of my life. *(Hawaii, California, Arizona and Florida)* After everyone had left the party, I had time alone with Laurie. She was a very interesting and talented lady. She had a pet dragon hanging from a ceiling corner she called "Oh-be-die-ya," and she had a collection of *death masks* from around the world mounted on all her walls. She kept a copy of CG Jung's *Dreams and Philosophy under her pillow* and her hobby was studying psychic phenomena. The next day she uncovered another talent of hers. She took me to her local church, unlocked the main doors with her own personal key and took me up to the base of the belfry tower where a magnificent old organ sat. Then she told me, "Play something…just play whatever you feel." So I started messing around with the keys and it actually sounded halfway decent. She goes, "Good, good, not bad at all." It's all about *improv*, you know. *Improv* is the name of the game." Then she sat down and wowed me with some *really* good keys. We left the church and she told me, "I want to take you to one of my hangouts. But you've gotta promise me, you won't ask me to play anything. They always want me to play something when I go in there." She took me to the Madison Steak House. Sure enough, the staff pleaded for something on their house piano. I tried to remain quiet but I think I managed to say something like, "I'm not gonna plead with you, but it sure seems like you'd make a lot of people happy around here." And she responded, "Oh, OK, maybe just one song." *What she did next is part of my soul for life. There are some life experiences that become part of who you are and stay with you forever. This was one of those. With all the passion of a seasoned professional, she proceeded to belt out, Roberta Flack's* Killing Me Softly with His Song. *Wow! What a performance!* I felt so privileged for the moments I had been able to share with her. She had plans to go to New York and make the Big Time. I had plans to travel south and continue my education. About a year later I received a call from Carlos H. Chávez, "Remember Laurie? She had a car accident on her way home about a week ago and she was killed." *Shock. Hurt. Disbelief. Only 19 years old! What A Special Lady She Was!!*
(I began to have thoughts that her death might not be accidental from a number of cues I was receiving- but I didn't want to go there.) But we cannot forget the power of one's Character as determining one's Fate -- Laurie drove her Datsun B210 recklessly wild on her country roads and I told her so – it was like she had a death wish.

Chapter 13: *THE GREAT INJUSTICE OF MY LIFE: Knocked Down By Anti-Blackism In Connecticut: ONE WAY to a DEAD END   * (see p. 120 to learn why 'Racism' not used in this titling)*
A giant roadblock was about to alter my life forever. I had gone to a nightclub in downtown Hartford, Connecticut, and met and befriended an attractive black woman, Joyce, with whom I danced the night away. When the two of us left together on my motorcycle (June 29th 1976), we were headed for another establishment. I made the mistake of going the wrong way up a One Way street and before I knew it, I was being pulled over and cited. What followed is very painful for me to recapitulate.
I refer to it as **Tragic Tuesday 62976**, THE GREAT INJUSTICE OF MY LIFE. Case: H14H-CR76-198480
(("Please be advised that this case has been physically destroyed in accordance with Section 7-13 of the Connecticut Practice Book. Date of Disposition: 7/19/76, State of CT Records Center, Superior Court"))
Phase 1 of the "Great Injustice" I was co-operating with the officer, *Jimmy Doyle*, giving him my license and registration. This seemed to be a normal traffic stop to me so far. However, things changed very quickly. The officer called on his radio for assistance. When the second officer arrived, the tone changed completely. In a very aggressive and forceful tone, Doyle turned and ordered me, "Get into the car!" Keep in mind there was no dialogue between us; I had not given this *representative of the law* any reason to arrest me. There were no drugs, there was no gaff from me, there was nothing. And then it became obvious; the motive had to be 'anti-blackism' (white officers). If you do not do exactly what a police officer tells you to do, it's called, "resisting arrest." So, when Doyle abruptly ordered me into his car, I didn't have the right to question him. I know that now. What I said to his demand was, *'Why do I need to get into the car? I didn't do anything.'* And that's when the beating began. The two officers

started throwing blows with their *billy clubs* all about my head. I yelled at them, *'Will you stop hitting me!'* as I raised up my arms to block the incoming blows to my head and body. It escalated and they would not stop, so I ran down the hill away from them. I'm thinking *'Oh, shit! They might shoot me in the back!!'* I ran down the hill where there was an intersection and police cars pulled up from two directions as several cops with guns drawn chased me down. I sustained the beating of my life, my head was bloodied and filled with contusions. What they did next I'll never forget. There were four or five *'officers of the law'* participating in this brutality. *They each grabbed a limb of my body and stretched me out in four directions and then pushed me towards the pavement stopping ever so close from finishing the job, their way of saying, "We can snuff you out just as easy as this!"* The whole time they're beating the crap out of me, I'm yelling, *'I'm a social worker with the City of Hartford, somebody check it out! I didn't do anything!'* As if there is only **ONE WAY** to be and we cannot cross ethnic lines to be with someone of a different color of skin -- this **is _NO WAY_**! That was *Phase 1 of the "Great Injustice"* --

[I describe this event in YouTube video *by Gregory Polone: "Never Let Injustice Go Unchallenged"*]

Phase 2 of the "Great Injustice" - Our family's attorney was Eugene Cooney. The charge was dropped to misdemeanor assault on two police officers and resisting arrest. Keep in mind, I never struck back at any time; the only thing I ever did was block their blows with my arms raised up; and for that I'm charged with *assault*. So I have my meeting with Mr. Cooney, a family friend and neighbor. In my mind we have a very strong case to counter sue for false arrest, police brutality, and damages. I was very naïve. What Cooney told me next, what he advised me to do, destroyed a piece of who I was forever. He advised me: "to not do" *He said it didn't matter that I was innocent and didn't do these things; that I had a very good chance to do prison time; that I should plead "guilty" because you can't win against the police. "They're not going to find 5 or 6 officers guilty …this is unwinnable."* So, I can't stand up in a court of law and profess my innocence to something I have been accused of; and, contrarily, I must say "guilty" when asked "How do you plead?" And then Cooney added, *"I don't want you to say anything, not one word."* I couldn't even have the satisfaction of having the court document my side of the story. I was just supposed to take it like the victim at the whipping post, accept it, let them get away with it, and somehow continue my life as a social advocate fighting for the rights of others to stand up for what's right and just. *A piece of me died forever.* **I did not stand up and fight for what was right.** I didn't want to do "time" so I played along and lied to the court that I was guilty. *How warped is all that!*

Remember the words of Selassie I: *"Throughout history it has been the inaction of those who would have acted, the indifference of those who should have known better, the silence of the voice of justice when it mattered most, that has made it possible for evil to triumph." I am haunted by these words.*

I went along with my attorney's recommendation **but** I was not guilty of total inaction in this case. What I did do was probably responsible for why this case was expunged less than one month later-- *something I did not learn about until many years later when a background check was done on me.* On my day in court, I came with a three page type-written brief of all the events that transpired on June 29, 1976. I waited until the case was heard and headed to the Clerk of the Court to pay my fine. I pleaded with the court employee in this office to please attach this actual version of the events that transpired in my case because I was not allowed to speak at my own trial per insistence of my attorney. I was very emotional, explained that I was a social worker with the City of Hartford, CT, and that this was going to be the only way that the real story will ever be known by anybody and the only way that I could contribute to justice being served in this case. I was fearful that this would not be permitted per the rules of procedure but the court employee took the pages I had given and attached them to my file. I felt a very big sigh of relief that I had been able to accomplish something in this case and hoped that it would make a difference. I firmly believe today that this case was destroyed because somebody in a position of authority such as the judge in this case had a chance to read the truth and effect a nullification. Never sit by and do nothing. *There is always something one can do to make a difference.* Doing nothing is not acceptable. And doing the little you can do might be all that is necessary to turn the tide to you.

Stand Up For What Is Right - Never Let Injustice Go Unchallenged Leonardo da Vinci - *"Nothing strengthens authority so much as silence."* So now I speak out. *("better late than never")*
*[*I was not totally real when I did not stand up for what was right; because of this I have deprived myself of the benefits of total freedom and aliveness throughout my life, forever dogged by this false conviction, even though this case was documented as 'destroyed'. It comes up on background checks and requires extra hoops for me to resolve all the issues. Who can say how many times I may have been passed over for this malignment.]*

If what happened to me in 1976 by the HPD played out today in any number of American cities, you can bet that I most probably would be killed by a trigger-happy cop. The pathology of the police out of control in the US is pandemic. Today the police in America are killing more than a 1000 people a year- at a rate 70 times its Western neighbors. "Since 1990, police officers in the United Kingdom have killed exactly 58 people. In the last two weeks of December, 2015, American cops killed 60 citizens- it took the English cops 25 years to do what American cops did in just the last two weeks of December." **We are now sending our police chiefs to Scotland to be trained on how *not to kill* its citizens. The above is why I refer to the police in the United States as *Coward Nation*.   *http://thefreethoughtproject.com/cops-kill-often-scotland-learn-kill/*
*** *For a 24/7 real time accounting of USA police killings*: *http://www.theguardian.com/us-news/ng-interactive/2015/jun/01/the-counted-police-killings-us-database*

Chapter 14: *Time To Re-Boot, To Re-Invent Myself: Communal Living Rules*

It was at this time in my life, trying to make a clean break from the events of my past, that I removed my middle name, Leonard, and the two "s's" from my last name as my father before me had done; I would henceforth be my own person and begin the rest of my life anew. I took up residency in Bloomfield, CT, in a beautiful home shared by my friend Peter Potaski *(Eldorado Rollfast)* and his girlfriend Toby Snyder (whose home it was), her two kids, a couple of other friends of ours, Gary Franchi *(Ace Nolo)* and Joy Dickey- and Gary's Flying Frisbee Dog *Tank, The Dude.*   Although my time there was limited to only several months or so, some of my best memories were from this communal living arrangement that I shared with these great people. When the chemistry is righteous among the ones you are living with, it is truly something special. It was a vegetarian household and both Toby and Joy were exquisite chefs. Each person had his or her own duties to perform as part of the family; kind of like Ward's synergy, the co-operative working-together of all the individuals to produce the desired end of creative effort. My humble task was "pots and pans" - who didn't mind scrubbing those vessels when 'dem viddles were so good! I remember taking my son Lee with me to visit these folks because I wanted him to meet these people and to experience how I was living my life, now that his mother and I were divorced. I spent as much time with him as I could, often times taking him for nature walks through the woods. It was going to be tough; I was going to be heading south to find my way in the world and Lee would be growing up without his father at his side *yet always remain very close in his father's heart*. Every person that lives is destined to make his or her own way in the world. Sometimes the choices we make anger, offend, and alienate the ones we love most. These are not intended outcomes; these might be referred to as *collateral damage*; they are unintended outcomes that necessarily attend the decisions that we make. Hopefully, with the passage of sufficient time and understanding, the process of healing can be made complete. I have no greater wish than this. dd   (see p.129, Wayne W. Dyer)

"Goodbye, Yellow Brick Road" – Agiocochook, Home of the Great Spirit (House of the Wind - dd)
The time to hang up my leathers had come. All those fantastic excursions I had taken with so many great people to the top of Mount Greylock in Massachusetts and to my favorite place in all of the continental United States, to the top of Mount Washington in New Hampshire, truly a sacred place, [known as *Agiocochook* to pre-Europeans, an Abenaki Indian name (from the Wabanaki Confederacy) meaning *Home of the Great Spirit*, and also *home to the highest winds recorded by man* on this earth (231 mph, 372 km/h, on April 12, 1934)], co-pilots including Chuck Horvath, Robert Bourque, Steve Cooney, Tom DesRoches and Connie Albert. And I must not forget Pamela Madison. Thanks for the memories, all! I trust you have a few of your own. Life is for the living. And we must all move on. I'm thinking of *'The Wheel,'* that tremendous song from the *Grateful Dead*, where Jerry Garcia sings about life as a big wheel that continues to go round and round- nobody can stop the wheel. But

we *can* modify the cog to our wheel; i.e., go faster or slower or change it up if we like, anything but the same old speed. ('*The Wheel*,' from the 1972 self-titled album *"Garcia"* with Hunter and Kreutzmann)

Yin-Yang As Cuirass: The Journey Continues With Taoist Teachings As My Spirit Guide

It was not easy bringing myself to the actual point of selling my *"S"*. But once I could not realistically see its presence in my future plans, it became possible. With the $ received from its sale, I purchased a 1966 VW van. It was light blue, needed some work, but had a lot of potential. I'd always wanted a van that I could live in, call my home and be proud of. Like everything else I touched, it had to be an artistic expression of me. That meant, first and foremost, to replace the VW insignia on the front with a black and white *Yin Yang* in its place ☯ The definition that I was fond of for this Taoist symbol: *"all the positive and negative energy of the universe in harmony."* I thought there could not be a better message to communicate to others -- *a kind shield* -- respecting the rights of all *via* The Three Treasures of Taoism ~ Compassion, Moderation, and Humility. Since I had developed a certain style of riding over the years, I knew it wasn't going away overnight. I felt I would probably drive this van in many ways similarly to how I had been accustomed aboard my two-wheeled dream machine. So, for that reason, I cut out some reflective tape for the left rear quarter, *"Espíritu de BMW,"* *"Spirit of BMW."* I decided that I should have curtains running across the rear window, controlled from the driver's position with pull cords to open and close, thereby preserving the privacy of my inner sanctum from prying eyes, bright headlights, and any other distractions from outside the rear of my domain. Of course I would use the same green, gold and brown velour I had used for covering the stereo wires from my helmets. That allowed me to have a connection or continuity into the next chapter of my life.

[By the way, an aside of interest: I didn't feel right selling my stereo system with Sennheiser-installed helmets; I preferred that another R-90S rider I had come across in my travels have them; it was a way of perpetuating something special in the right hands-- it just felt like it was the right thing to do.]

(It's not always about $ in this world; sometimes the feeling you get from not taking it is better than it, itself; not becoming any richer financially- yet improving the human condition, becoming richer inside.)

Another requirement I had was to have a four inch foam mattress at least 74" long, and above it a hammock. The hammock idea came from my Rio Nido log cabin experience. It was a fun alternative for rest, sleep and making love. When I had been living in my apartment on Franklin Avenue, I painted my living room walls and ceiling flat black, and installed a 4-foot black light on each side of the room. If you visited my art space, I encouraged you to pick up a brush and Dayglow paints that were stocked by the door and "do your thing" artistically anywhere you liked, ceiling or walls. Most memorable was the cattail astrological clock painted by the twins Lynne and Linda Cicero. I reproduced this black light art-space in miniature in that microbus. My brother Michael's artistic brilliance really shined inside that bus! When it was night and the mini 12V black light was on, his creativity was quite something to behold. I rounded out my new home with a Sony stereo system. Ready to roll. I felt like the State of CT did not deserve to have me living there any longer-- I would always feel like a prisoner after my false arrest and the corruption of a clean record. I needed to start my life anew without the baggage of the past upon my shoulders. I was off to Miami, the Magic City, as it is known. It was the summer of '77.

The Power of FRISBEE ☮ *For Ritualistic Indulgences Suffused By Ecstatic Euphoria*

For several months I lived in the streets of Miami. The neighborhood was accustomed to my presence. I was always trying to start a catch session with my Frisbee and for that my street name became *Fris.* People were shooting up heroin and escaping any other way they could in the streets around me. I was trying to do social work at a grassroots level, to challenge the *mental slaveries*, the false belief systems that allowed for so many dependencies. I used the Frisbee as a tool to bring people together, to put them back in touch with something pleasurable, something that was euphoric in and of itself. For me, FRISBEE was an acronym that represented the *Power of Freedom* in action. Those seven words above pretty much describe the ritual of throwing this disc around and the great feeling you get doing it. I felt a further connection to this pastime knowing that the history of this sport is directly tied to CT. It was the freedom of spirit of several Yale University students in New Haven, CT, flying *Frisbie Pie* plates to one another which began the phenomenon known as *frisbieing* from which Wham-O, Inc. adopted the name of *Frisbee*, not to conflict with the *Frisbie Pie's* name in use. After having been engineered into a wonderfully aerodynamic flying disc, it has spread throughout the world as a recognized sport of competition. *But I prefer to enjoy the non-competitive aspects of this great ritual, refusing to regulate and codify that which remains most enjoyable in its purest form, simply the reflection of each person's self, their aura and essential being.* Who you are will come out in how you throw and catch this magic disc. I for one say, 'Forget the rules and let's play!' It is interesting how far people will go with this Frisbee. Ed E. Headrick of Wham-O, Inc., who is known as the "Father of Disc Sports," obtained the Frisbee patent for his professional model on 12-26-67 (applied for on 11-1-65) which now included *raised rings* for improved stability, allowing the disc to fly much more accurately. According to Wikipedia, *"Upon his death Headrick was cremated and, in accordance with his final requests, his ashes were molded into memorial Frisbees and given to family and close friends."*

I totally understand. And if I could arrange it, I would do the same - ⊗ ☉ ☮ ☯ ☺

I used my vehicle by day to travel to job assignments that I received from Manpower in downtown Miami. At night I would just sleep in my van on the side of the road after cleaning up in the common bathroom of an old rooming house nearby. I lived like this for several weeks until one day I was warned by the MPD that living out of my van on the street was illegal; so I rented a room at the Miamian Hotel and parked it legally in their parking lot. Soon thereafter, I was faced with a blown engine and couldn't go anywhere. Because it now appeared to be abandoned, it was much more susceptible to crime. I was robbed. Most valuable to me was the crocheted afghan that my grandma Marie LaFlamme DesRoches had given me just before she passed away and the beautiful painting that my friend Carlos had given me that was priceless. The feeling of being violated when you're victimized is one of the worst and there wasn't a damn thing I could do about it. I agonized over having to tell Carlos the terrible news.

Chapter 15: *Moment of Biggest Regret In My Life*
Oftentimes, after a hard day of labor, I would go with my working partner from Billings, Montana, to a Cuban restaurant to eat a decent, close to home-cooked meal of black beans and rice, with chicken and sweet plantains and finish off with a *pastel de guava* and a Cuban coffee. One day while enjoying this end of my day with 'Big Red' Bill Henderson *(a Vietnam vet suffering from PTSD who always carried his razor sharp flying stars with him and who would go into "take cover mode" from any jet passing overhead),* a couple walked in and sat down at a table near to the food bar where we were eating. I couldn't help overhearing the conversation they were having at some point when it became clear that the woman was planning some sort of motorcycle tour of Europe. And then I had to hear these words, as she went on to her male companion, "The only question remains, should I get a Harley or should I get a BMW?" Now how am I supposed to stay on my stool and let that question go unchallenged given my life's history? Absolutely no way was I *not* going to get involved. (AND THAT BECAME THE MOMENT OF BIGGEST REGRET IN MY LIFE) So, what do I do? Well, of course, I had to march right over to their table and immediately interrupt, "Excuse, me, folks, I couldn't help overhearing your conversation, and there is only one answer to your question—it has to be a BMW! There's no comparing the two if you want the best ride in the world to tour Europe." And I went on and on about the virtues of BMW and why she would regret any other decision and I finally shut up and returned back to my friend. As they were leaving, this woman gave me her number and said, "I'd like to talk more with you about this motorcycle you're so crazy about. Give me a call, OK?" I wish I had thrown that paper away. I wish now I had lost that damn number. But I knew too much about *this* subject; hell, I was the self-appointed world ambassador of BMW, how was I supposed to resist the pulpit now? I could not and I would not. *ERROR!*

Lies, Entrapment & "You Can Get Anything You Want In This Cuban Restaurant"

Was there ever a time in your life that you wish you could take back? This was the one by far for me. Her name was Joanne. I started seeing her and a relationship ensued. I was still too trusting and too naïve for my own good and I was going to pay a very big price for that. This might be referred to as a case study in pathological confabulation. The first big lie that she perpetrated with lots of emotion and *real tears (she was a very skillful actress)* was that she was dying of osteosarcoma, bone disease.

She told me she might have a year or so to live and all she wanted to do before she "passed this plane" as she put it, was to have the experience of bringing forth a child into this world. She said she was looking for the "right man" (*or the right patsy* I should add) who she could be proud of to carry out her last wish. I know some of you are reading this thinking, "How could anybody fall for a line like that?" Right? You haven't met this person. She turned out to be a criminal con artist supreme and had powers of persuasion that I have not seen nearly equaled by anyone. If one knew how persuasive Lenny was, our Dad, Leo the Lip, and the saying "You can't con a con-artist," one would be shocked that she conned Lenny as well; he also was one of her victims. She knew how to play to people's emotions and to their pocketbooks. So I'm hearing all this and we've already begun a relationship together and I'm thinking this would be a really great thing I could do for her, kind of like an act of social work that had not yet been imagined. *"It's cool to be kind"* as they say *'but in the right measure'- *don't allow yourself be taken advantage of like I was.* I began to have my doubts when I could never speak with any medical personnel about her condition. I should have insisted on speaking to her doctors who did not exist and I did not. The ruse continued. Taking too much on faith is naïve. Prospective mates need to be vetted.

Lesson: 'Standing Up For What's Right' Sometimes Can Be Painful – But It Must Be Done

At about this time (while she was a waitress at *Sambo's* on Biscayne Blvd & 36th St.), I continued working out of Manpower in Miami. One day after work, I entered The Red Pig Pub, a bar I knew. The lady bartender inside was an acquaintance of mine and was heavily involved with a patron she was trying to remove from the premises. She had stepped from behind the bar and was demanding that he leave and it was beginning to get physical. I felt I needed to come to her aid; I approached the man and told him, *'You'd better leave now. If she wants you to leave, you need to go.'* He punched me square in the face. We fought for a minute or so and I threw him very hard to the ground. When he didn't jump up to continue, I turned my back for a few seconds and that's all it took for him to jump up and jam me with a knife he must have had concealed on his person. Welcome to the streets of Miami! I was in shock as I watched him dancing around in front of me, looking to attack me once again. A Puerto Rican friend of mine *Flaco* jumped in between us and saved my life, exiting this murderous felon. *Reprieve!* The knife had entered my liver and I was rushed to Jackson Memorial Hospital in Miami. The police who came to my bedside didn't make things easier when they said to me, *"We don't mean to scare you, but there's a chance you might not make it to tomorrow. If you could give us a description of this person, it would help us to get this guy."* Fortunately, the internal bleeding stopped and I took a turn for the better. I didn't have much desire to remain any longer in Miami. I had been handed one of life's vicissitudes. It was time to think once again about my plans to pursue a graduate school education.

Destination Phoenix: Time To Roll

Joanne and I decided to do a "drive-away" where you transport someone's vehicle across country in exchange for use of their vehicle to move yourself there. She had connections in Phoenix to put us up for a week or so and I could apply to graduate school from that area. My plan to attend the University of Puerto Rico was not to be. My VW bus that I was hoping to ship to Puerto Rico had a blown engine and I couldn't afford to fix it. I needed to consider a university stateside. The only university among the ones I considered that would accept late application in the summer for attendance in the Fall was Arizona State. I applied, was accepted and entered classes the Fall semester of 1978. No sooner had I completed the first semester and things had fallen apart. She had gone somewhere for a few days and when she returned, she noticed some marks on my legs. She started accusing me of being with another woman saying the marks were *"proof positive of bed sheet burns,"* if you can believe that! It went from an irrational response to a totally blown-out psychotic episode which sent me packing. I had had enough. I left the graduate program, got all my things together and returned to Hartford to regroup.

Headed For Hawaii To Begin A New Life

I decided I would go visit Chuck in Hawaii. He was employed by Royal Hawaiian Airlines and at least I could continue my life with a good friend in a strange place. When I left Hartford for the 77 hour bus ride to the west coast, I told my father, "Whatever you do, don't tell her my plans that I'm going to Hawaii." I trusted my father and gave him Chuck's address in Maui so he would know where I was. When I arrived in Maui, I wasted no time getting work. I landed a job with Horizon Foods delivering health foods all around the island of Maui. I may have had the job for two weeks and one day I came home to the room I was renting, ransacked of all its contents. *Leonard, who had a questionably close relationship with Joanne, had betrayed me and given her my address.* She had taken my route map out of the room as well and knew where I would be at what part of the day. I arrived in Lahaina and she was already waiting for me at the store I was delivering to, taking product out of the van and throwing it in the street, screaming some kind of crazy shit at the top of her lungs. I'd get to Kaanapali and the same scenario would repeat. This was obviously a very sick individual. I barely kept my job. About a week later I received a package addressed to Horizon Foods. I opened the package and to my horror and the horror of my boss was the shirt I had purchased for my son Lee with a pile of human feces on it and note attached, "This is what I think of you and your son." She was very jealous of my time talking about or money being spent upon my son. The Spanish refer to *celos enfermisos*, the jealousy sickness. But clearly in her case it went a lot further than that. This was pathological behavior being exhibited by a psychotic individual. She held me at ransom. She had all of my photographs and personal belongings hidden away somewhere. I didn't want to risk losing everything I owned; so, like a fool I kept playing her game. *Que error!* **What a mistake! I never felt any lower than this in my life with anybody!**

Back To The Mainland: My Life In Pieces

We flew to Seattle, she purchased a '73 Super Beetle, and we set out for Alaska. I had some tremendous opportunities for photography and took advantage of them during this trip to Mt. Denali and Fairbanks and back to Anchorage and Haines Harbor, Alaska. I had some great photos of the indigenous people of Whitehorse in the Yukon and many other places, and all these photographs were later taken from me and destroyed by her. I was a total fool and wrong to be with her and I'm making myself sick writing about it in this moment. I had allowed myself to share time on this earth with this loathsome human being who manifested nothing more than the psychosis of narcissism to the nth degree! *I was so accustomed to living with Dad's mental illness, that it didn't faze me to take it on in someone else. If I had just been a little more careful or minded my own business,* **HELLO!**

After this trip we resided in Oceanside, CA - right at the ocean's edge - for about three months. Then we returned to Arizona so I could complete the second semester of my first year *in the Spring of 1980*. On February 16, 1980, Joshua was born. No sooner had I completed this semester three months later and all hell broke loose again. We had no car. I rode my 10-speed (*Le Vent Noir*, *the Black Wind*, an Austro-Daimler machine) to classes; and on weekends I rode seven miles to a security guard shift I had, putting in 24 hours a week. One day after a night class, I returned home and realized that my wallet was not where I usually kept it. I was starting to get very upset because I distinctly remember where I had put it. She "helped me" looking for it but to no avail. I went the next day to Valley National Bank where my account was to alert them. When possible, we always went to the same teller who knew us on a more personal basis. When I explained to her that my wallet apparently got lost, she looked at me with an incredulous look, and to my utter shock and ire, she says to me, *"Dennis, she came in here yesterday with your wallet, took all the pictures out and ripped them all up."* The last straw had finally come. I raced home with the truth about what she had done destroying my most personal possession, then lying about it pretending to help me find it. I told her our relationship was over and I would seek custody of Joshua in order to save his life from the psychotic monster that she was. The next day was a Saturday. I went to my job for the usual 12 hour shift. *When I returned "home" -- there was an empty trailer space. She had found someone to hook up our trailer and she was long gone from the scene with Joshua and all my personal possessions in tow.* Joshua was my whole life and I was hurting deeply and I needed to heal. I called the Tempe PD, filed a child kidnapping report and got involved with Child Search. I was a guest on a television program, "Parental Kidnapping," hosted by Fox TV personality Michael Dixon in Phoenix, AZ, to bring light to this growing phenomenon. But I wouldn't see him again till he was 13.

Chapter 16: Transformation: VIP Jennifer Rebholz, Life Saver & Game Changer
I had a couple of friends from graduate school who put me up for a couple of weeks until I could re-group and get my feet back on the ground. Then I answered an ad for construction personnel and got a job full time as a laborer in construction. I worked for Sky West Development Company as assistant to the superintendent until the 19 buildings of 16-unit apartments were completed - 304 apartments.
During this time, I ran into a woman who had known Joanne and I when we were together. I asked her to go to a concert with me to see the jazz guitarist *Al Di Meola*. She accepted and we enjoyed a fantastic evening of great guitar virtuosity by one of the world's greats. Little did I know that this woman, *Jennifer Rebholz*, was a guitarist in her own right. When I took her to her apartment, she surprised me and started playing her 12-string *Alvarez* quite beautifully. *We made wild and passionate love and all of a sudden things didn't look so bad.* Jennifer was a junior at ASU studying for her Elementary Education degree. I somehow had been trapped in a very toxic relationship for two years and now was finding peace and tranquility in a very healthy and promising relationship. I was with such a wayward and ill person and now found myself with such a good and healthy person. I supported Jennifer's dream to *go public* someday, to sing and play her guitar. She had a vast repertoire of covers and plenty of good original compositions, needing now only to surmount some confidence issues. I surprised her with her dream guitar, a six string *Ovation*, and now she was really on a roll. *Jennifer was one of the most important people in my life, a very giving, loving, wholesome human being. I learned how to love and be healthy and to appreciate a woman for all the things that a woman can be. I will always be indebted to that special lady from Indianapolis who gave to my life so much that I was craving and needed.*

Chapter 17: The Rockford Years: (June, 1981 – June, 1993)   Learning To Wear Many Hats
One day Jennifer showed me an ad for *electronics assembler* with Rockford Corp., home of the world famous *Rockford Fosgate* car stereo amplifiers and speakers, among other products. Paul Grissom interviewed me and I was hired. The next day, another prospective employee came in to be interviewed, Darrell Chapman. He also was hired but as a technician as he had experience in electronics from the Navy. We were to become very good friends over the next 12 years. Darrell went on to become Vice President of Production and married Kathy Berg, our very amicable Human Resources Manager. Rockford Corporation, a venture capital group, had just purchased *Fosgate Electronics* of Phoenix, AZ, and decided to relocate to its adjacent city, Tempe, AZ. The big expansion was on. There were no tech benches and we were increasing our staff rapidly. I was pretty good working with wood, so I volunteered to build as many benches as required. They started calling me *D-Wood* and the name stuck. Todd Didlo came with the old company and was responsible for painting and screening the entire product line. What started out as a fledgling operation of a small handful of assemblers and technicians, a purchasing agent, Jeanne Pepper, a superb marketer in Kevin Campbell, and a brilliant engineer in

John France, turned into the premier car amplifier and speaker company in America with close to 200 employees. Cindy Babers deserves a special note of mention for all she did for everyone. Yeah, Cindy!

I had the unique opportunity at this company to wear many hats. I held positions of Fosgate Production Manager, Quality Control Manager, and Acoustat Production Manager. But more than anything else, I had the opportunity to begin my own business providing video and photographic services as needed.

I started *Studio D Video & Photo*, providing product photography and company training videos for marketing. Lastly, I established *Rock & Soul Power* with my friend Dwain Soultaire. (*Roche* is French for Rock; *viz*, the names of two of our favorite music genres, *Rock* and *Soul*, worked out just fine).

I now had half the people calling me *D-Rock* and the other half calling me *D-Wood*. It was kind of funny. This was a transformer winding operation providing the Rockford line of car amplifiers and processors with the necessary power supplies required. Unfortunately for us, because we had run such a profitable enterprise with almost 0% error rate, the business was taken out from under us by the then presiding president. He actually came to us and said, "You guys are making more money than my marketing people with this winding business, so I've decided to give the business to a friend of mine." He was a bishop in the Mormon Church and had a side business finding employment for his church members.

It's absolutely amazing how greedy people are at the top of the food chain. But he got his and was fired as president when the corporation was deemed "not profitable enough." What goes around comes around. At least this time anyway. To balance the 'bitter taste in my mouth' about this leader of ours, there was something that he needs to get credit for. He was responsible for bringing the charismatic Stephen R. Covey to Rockford to teach a workshop on self-improvement, *The Seven Habits of Highly Effective People.* This book provides some very helpful habits and I will summarize them here:

Habit #1. *Be Proactive*: Focus on the Things You Can Actually Do Something About.

Habit #2. *Begin with the End in Mind*: Begin Everything You Do With a Clear Picture of your Ultimate Goal.

Habit #3. *Put things First*: Manage Your Life According to Your Needs and Priorities.

Habit #4. *Think Win-Win*: <u>Integrity</u> – Stick With Your Feelings, Values, and Commitments.
<u>Maturity</u> – Be Considerate of the Feelings of Others.

<u>Abundance Mentality</u> – Believe There is Plenty For Everyone – (As opposed to a Scarcity Mentality).

Habit #5. *Seek First to Understand*, Then to Be Understood (Learn how to Communicate Clearly and *LISTEN* to Others).

Habit #6. *Synergize*: Two Heads Are Better Than One (*cooperative working-together*- *Lester F. Ward*).

Habit #7. *Sharpen the Saw*: Allow Yourself to Grow by Maintaining A Balanced Program in the Four Areas of Your Life: physical, social/emotional, mental, and spiritual.

Habit #8. *From Effectiveness to Greatness*: <u>Find</u> <u>Your</u> <u>Voice</u> and <u>Inspire</u> <u>Others</u> to <u>Find</u> <u>Theirs</u>.
(An 8th is added to unify all the others.) [I'm hoping this book is an example of this -- hoping to inspire others to find <u>their</u> voice.]

I have a lot of fond memories from my 12-year hitch with the "Rockpile," as Soultaire liked to call it.

I was very humbled by the honor bestowed upon me, *Employee of the Year*, at the 1988 annual Christmas party at Tempe Mission Palms by our CEO John Bartol because it was voted upon by my peers. Once again, I would like to thank everyone for their faith in me and their support of me. As with any successful enterprise, it is the cooperative *working-together* of many team players in the knowledge that *the whole is greater than the sum of its parts* that makes it all possible. *(Paul A. Hochstim)*

Jennifer and I got married in 1985 and bought a modest home in Mesa, AZ, where we hosted most of the company parties. I think I can say that we contributed to the culture of Rockford lore with the likes of Carlos Castrejón, George Rocheleau, Darrell Chapman, Kathy Berg, Kevin Campbell, Roger & Debbie Miller, Mischele & Don Riggins, Todd Didlo, and Lynette & Dwain Soultaire among others as well. The Rockford family circle with Jennifer was really the only non-dysfunctional family I knew in life. (My *family of orientation* left a lot to be desired as did, due to seeking my own development and fulfillment in life, my *family of procreation.*) We took ski trips together renting cabins up on the Apache reservation, and bonded further perhaps than any average-normal company might be seen doing. I remember Patti Cromwell as the camp director. As Rockford's official Purchaser/Inventory Control Manager, she was well-suited at taking charge of all the logistics of these types of events. And then there was Camelback Mountain, a very popular climbing destination on any given day of the year. If you were in Olympic shape, you might be able to do the climb in less than 20 minutes (I can only remember Scott Clifford); if you were a mere mortal like the rest of us, you probably would need more like 25-50 minutes. I think my best time (at age 40) was 26. You could easily have a heart attack going up this mountain, your heart pounded so fast and hard, and your gasping for oxygen was off the charts! Long live the Camel!

In 1993, after the passing of our CEO Bartol, there was a scramble for power and a not so *Subtle Gallows* was about to wreak havoc as a head hunter was hired (space does not need to be wasted on *his name*) and the wholesale decimation of the ranks of those who had made it all possible for there to be a Rockford Corporation in the first place was underway. In the name of "progress" the company was *reorganized* and all the key or major players who were responsible for creating the company to its then present form of excellence were chopped at the block, excised out, terminated from existence – are you getting the picture? Corporate America had shown its ugly head and a rude awakening was had by all.

Chapter 18: A Lazarus Moment: Joshua Returns To Life

At about this same point in time (1993), there came a knock to my door one day. It was Joshua. After having been kidnapped by his mother at three months of age, he now shows up at my door like a revenant at the age of 13. I will save the drama of our personal reunion; suffice to say, it was not easy. Joshua's mother evidently had accumulated sufficient guilt by this time and decided to permit a relationship between us. She was totally unapologetic about her actions 13 years before this time.

Unfortunately for Joshua, the years reared solely by his mother had allowed him to become a criminal like his mother. She had successfully taught him how to lie, cheat and steal. But before we got to know that, here's what happened. One day, not far removed from the reunion, Joanne went into a rage about something or other and attacked me with a knife she had on her key chain, cutting me in front of our son. I called the police and filed a report and began legal proceedings against her for child kidnapping and for aggravated assault. To make a long story short, I won the legal process and was awarded full legal custody of Joshua. She was only allowed supervised visitation in a controlled environment. My wife Jennifer and I had an opportunity to make a real difference in this young teenager's life. When Joshua's personal files were sent to me from the various educational institutions, we realized we had a very disturbed kid on our hands. He had a long history of aggression and violence towards girls, had been involved in criminal activity including breaking and entering, drug use and sale, stealing, etc. I took his knock at my door as a sign, as an opportunity to try to save a damaged human being and to try and make a difference in his young life before it was too late. Jennifer was so excited to be given the opportunity to have a son and make a positive difference in his life. In her own words to me, *"Bringing Josh into my life was a natural progression of my love for you. I rejoiced in bringing Josh into our lives because he is a part of you and YOU were my family. In my heart he was OUR family."*

She was so good to him and tried so hard be the ideal mother. But it was not to be. We started to get calls on an all too regular basis from his school officials. He was continuing the behavior that he had been written up for, from the other schools he had attended. Nothing we tried seemed to work. He did not care to change or modify his behavior as he continued to glorify the *gangsta* image.

We had placed Joshua in the expert care of a very highly recommended Certified Professional Counselor, Adele Mayer, early on at the first indication that we had a troubled child on our hands. She corroborated our worst fears, *"Out of the thousands of children that I have treated over the years, Joshua is one of the sickest."* That was scary. We continued trying to help him turn the corner in his life before it was too late but nothing we tried would sway him from the path he had chosen. By the time he had turned 16, he was expelled from school. We were not able to make a difference in three years. I decided that the State of Arizona was the only option left for him; maybe their expertise or professional staff could intervene in ways that we could not. So Joshua was placed in State custody. He continued his juvenile years on the same path that he had been on. He glorified the prison life and now he would get his wish. He successfully graduated to a life in prison. All I know is that if I had been in his life during those 13 years, he would have turned out entirely different. The damage had been done throughout his formative years and he had little chance of survival. *And his mother roams free!* The older that I get, the less and less justice I see in the world. And I'm living through it now as I'm writing these words. **We cannot live somebody else's life for *them*.** If we allow ourselves to be used and abused *ad infinitum*, we will ultimately pay the highest price and give ourselves up to the unending process. Each person must find his/her own way in life and not depend forever on others to live their lives for them. If clear choices continue to be made rejecting the laws of society or the moral character-building of parents seeking the best for their progeny, there really is no other option but to move on in life knowing that you have given your all and your best and not feel guilty for the hard and inevitable decisions that must be made. Sacrifice as much as you can but to sacrifice your person totally as if you don't count, no. *You do count.* And you're not worth anything to anybody if you're not worth something to yourself.

Chapter 19: *Jennifer & I Seek Our Own Paths*

After 14 years living together, 10 of them married, Jennifer and I went our separate ways. She was very crucial to my emotional development and stability. The changing dynamics of personal relationships are a fact of life. There is a birth and growth phase and a maturation process but all this needs continued nurturing and constant attention for the relationship to remain viable. Too often, the dynamics of estrangement can be set into play at which time the sunset can often be seen on the horizon. I believe we were a positive influence on each other's lives and the lives of those around us. After our divorce, I remained in the home for a while longer. I had converted our garage into a video editing studio and it had served me well for eight years (1988-1996). It now needed to be torn to pieces to make way for the next buyer/occupant. This was very difficult for me - *like destroying "who I am."*

Creative Productions from Studio D Video & Photo
Following the Light *"The beauty in the art of image-making is in the light, how much, what kind, and from whence it doth shed."* -- *unknown*

The very definition of photography is the relationship between light and film (or in these days between light and the electronic sensor). In my craft of photography, *paying homage to the light* is *essential #1*. *Essential #2* is *paying homage to kairos*, a Greek word that has as one of its definitions *the right moment of time* - I came upon this word in a letter that CG Jung had been writing to Herman Hesse and was apologizing for the lengthy delay in responding to his friend but went on to say that it's at such times as these, *la kairos, the right moment of time*, when the act of writing can be performed correctly. I immediately adapted this word to perfectly describe what photography is all about; i.e., capturing *kairos moments in time, the right moments in time* –
Michael Caine, in the movie *The Destructors*, had these lines:
"Do you know the difference between an amateur and professional photographer? The amateur thinks for a moment first and then takes the picture; the professional photographer takes the moment and thinks about it afterward."
And what about your vision, how you see the world through your lens? From Carl Jung himself:
"Your vision will become clear only when you can look into your own heart; who looks outside, dreams; who looks inside, awakes." ♡ That pretty much sums up what it's all about. *Happy imaging!*

For many years I marveled at the creative possibilities of video production. Practically anything you could imagine to be shown in motion with sound could be achieved. This is the level of image processing I wanted to be at. I was determined to provide video production services as part of my business. I had no experience in video production or editing, *(beyond the Super 8 movies I had made many years earlier manually spliced together)*, but I knew I could be taught how to do it. I just needed to find someone who was experienced and wouldn't mind sharing their expertise with me. I asked around where video equipment was being sold and was referred to Mike Fish in Mesa, AZ, whom I met and was gracious enough and agreeable to the task of teaching me the basics of video editing with a controller and three VCR's. I needed only then to add a special effects generator for the transitions of scenes and learn the technology of audio and computer interfacing to make it all happen. I happened to be at the CES show in Las Vegas when the *Video Toaster* was unveiled to the public which essentially put in the hands of the individual the equivalent of $100,000 worth of gear for the purchase price of $1,500. This was a very high tech video processing board built around the architecture of the Amiga computer which revolutionized the industry as it was known up until that time. Overnight, fledgling video editors like myself could now compete with the big boys with all their expensive electronics and equipment. So I needed to marry my Amiga computer with a Video Toaster and learn how to use it. I took a course with Michael Montandon, "How to Use the Amiga for Video Production" and met Dick Fifield, an old Air Force vet from the Viet Nam War married to a Vietnamese woman. Dick was a master of the Amiga computer and would come to my new video studio in Mesa, AZ, and teach me everything I needed to know. I was finally prepared to offer video production services to the public. I needed to purchase a professional ENG camcorder, wireless microphone system for interviewees and all the related gear that would be required to provide mobile services professionally. I wanted a high-tech look that would be comfortable for clientele in my converted garage, so with the help of master craftsman Rick Dunn (Dunn-Did-It-Enterprises, Unlimited), we designed a "space ship console" with large center section and two wings, the center housing the three VCR decks with editing controller and special effects generator and monitors, the left wing housing the Amiga/Video Toaster and printer and the right wing housing all audio equipment (audio mixer, equalizer, tape decks, turntable and receiver).

Finally, the studio was sound-proofed with acoustic tiles throughout and invitations were sent out to celebrate its grand opening (thanks to Jennifer Rebholz). *It was time to rock and roll.* My biggest client was Rockford Corporation. It took some doing but eventually I got accustomed to the technology and comfortable in my skin providing the services required. I had produced a lot of memorable videos in my home studio. I was the editor of a widely distributed B-house selection, *'Traces of Death,'* that became a cult classic for the horror crowd. I was not happy working with the subject matter provided to me for this major editing assignment, but I wanted a full-length feature credit and I refused to do pornos. Other than the *How To* training videos I produced for Rockford and the IASCA (International Auto Sound Challenge Association) car competition documentaries, I was most partial to the production I put together for my mother's 70th birthday party in 1996, *"The Life & Times of Terri & The Revolving Worlds Around Her: A Celebration of 70 Years of Accomplishment."* I got my four brothers and two sisters to each send me a collection of photographs of their lives with their families and an audio recording with a personal message to Mom. I put all seven of these packages together with separate music behind each one and she viewed it with all her family around her on her special day. I put every ounce of heart and mind and soul into this production and there is nothing I could ever do that might ever surpass it. It was an experience of catharsis, renewal, and love. Two other video productions that I enjoyed putting together were *Jamaica*, a personal documentary of my stay on the island from June 15-July 1, 2000, and *Take You Down*, a music video of the Phoenix, AZ, five member, all-female hard rock band, *Whiskey Blu* (Sept 1992). This video can be seen on YouTube -- **Whiskey Blu**: "Take You Down" MTV Video --

In addition to being the official photographer for *Whiskey Blu, The Kind,* and the *Country Casuals (with Wayne Ryznar, Ralph Holda and Kevin Gubilee, and now with Al Fichtel in WRAVIN),* my portfolio contains the following portraits: *Pink Floyd; Dr. John; Don Henley; Neil Young; Maynard Ferguson; Billy Cobham; Leon Russell; Stevie Nicks; Tom Petty; Stevie Ray Vaughan; Airto Moreira; Walt Richardson & The Morning Star Band; Jenna Rae; Peter Storn Project; Hans Olson; Wally Traugott of **Capitol Records**; Carlos Hernández Chávez; Timothy Leary; Oscar Peterson; Ella Fitzgerald; The Grateful Dead; Wayne Gretzky; Daniel Abebe of **Rasta Tings**; Ras Pidow; Gregory Isaacs; Rita Marley; and Luciano.*

One of my favorite portraits is of Airto Moreira who I call the guru master of percussion. After attending one of his concerts at *Chuy's* in Tempe, AZ, I came away stunned and amazed how one percussionist had mastered just about every sound making instrument that existed and played each of them so well ('85'). I had a chance to meet him back stage and found him to be a terrific person. I told him I would love to have a signed enlargement from one of my shots that evening and if he didn't mind, I would send him two 11X14 prints, one for himself and one he could return to me at my address. He had no problem with that idea and I was able to do the same with Wayne Gretzky and Timothy Leary. I never met Wayne Gretzky; I sent a proposal along with photos to his management to accomplish the same goal (2-12-84). Timothy Leary's portrait is one of my favorites as well. I guess I could call him the guru master of mind manipulation- as he certainly received a lot of notoriety for his contributions in this sphere of activity. Rockford's engineer George Rocheleau invited me to hear Leary's lecture, *"How to Operate Your Brain,"* in November of 1992, in Phoenix, AZ. We've often heard that a person's eyes are the windows to their soul. Dr. Leary had taken a pose and was almost catatonic in thought focused on one point and his eye was so crystal clear in the lens that I did not hesitate to take the moment. He was very cordial with me and I was amazed at the access he permitted, agreeing to give me his home address with no problem whatsoever in order that I could send him two enlargements that I might have a signed portrait of him. I never heard of anyone trying to obtain signed pieces this way but it seemed to work for me.

The two most creative portraits I have ever produced *(and probably the two most important images as well for what they represent)* are each examples of *painting* *with* *light*. They are each about two seconds in exposure time but differ radically in every other respect. One of them is the B&W cover portrait of the band *The Kind* which is described on *p. 55*. The other is a color transparency taken at night of the *Grateful Dead* on July 31st of 1974. Quite a number of fans at their outside concert at Dillon Stadium in Hartford, CT had purchased those multi-colored plastic glow sticks and every so often someone would set off a red rocket flare which was like a signal to answer by throwing your glow stick in the air. I figured that if I could take a two second shot and push process the film 2½ times, (ESP-1), I might get lucky on the exposure, wide open at f/3.8 with my *Vivitar* 85-205mm zoom lens. I was using a monopod and could therefore stabilize the light paths of color, (as opposed to a mass of indiscernible vibrations of color). I pre-focused on the last battery of missiles, waited for the next rocket to ignite and followed as best as I could, rock steady and slow, the path of the rocket as it sailed in one big arc in the sky. The patterns of light produced by the glow sticks looked like so many human vertebrae with extended ribbons of color *bowing* as if in homage to the giant red path of the rocket flare, symbolizing as it were, the *Grateful Dead* or **The Source** itself. I call it: *Paying Homage to The Source* *(p. 57)*

Over the years I have had the opportunity to photograph numerous portfolios. Two of them define my best work. The beautiful dancer Lyssa Clark of Gypsy Magic from Apache Junction, AZ, performed her snake dance routine while her mother accompanied her on drum. We scheduled an outdoor night shoot at their home and the images, via specially placed lighting in the trees above her, lent an ethereal, otherworldly quality. This was perhaps my favorite photo session of all. Also one of my favorites were the portraits of Alexandra Anastassopoulos, a woman of Greek and German descent and quite frankly one of the most beautiful and most intelligent of women I have ever known. Her natural ability in front of the lens also contributed greatly to a very memorable and successful shoot. She was opposed to being photographed for several years until one day when I received a phone call from her that she had changed her mind and that we should schedule a session. These shoots are from the period of 1998-99.

Timothy Leary *"Eyes Fully Open to Knowing and Seeing"* *Nov 28th 1992*   *10-22-20 → 5-31-96*

An American psychologist who "encouraged the use of the drug LSD for its therapeutic, emotional and spiritual benefits, and coined the words, **Turn on, tune in, drop out**." *(Wikipedia)* I met him at a Mensa meeting held in Phoenix, Arizona, on November 28th, 1992, his topic for discussion, *'How to Operate Your Brain.'* "For more than three decades Timothy Leary has been designing methods which empower individuals to *think for themselves* and *question authority*." (<u>Greater</u> <u>Phoenix</u> <u>Mensa</u>)

From David Colker, *Los Angeles Times,* and reprinted in *The Hartford Courant* on 8/28/95:

Leary: "When I found out I was terminally ill, I was thrilled...*How you die is the most important thing you ever do. It's the exit, the final scene of the glorious epic of your life. It's the third act, and you know, everything builds up to the third act.   I use the term, 'voluntary dying'. It's a nice way of saying, 'killing yourself'...When you think about it, there's nothing to lose."*

53

In addition to Timothy Leary's advocacy of LSD "for its therapeutic, emotional and spiritual benefits," there is increasing evidence from medical studies that hallucinogens are being found to greatly affect with positive outcomes the injured mental states of many. My brother Paul DesRoches emailed to me, on 1-7-2012, the following words of encouragement from this realm of medical progress in the field of mental health from a Los Angeles Times article entitled, *"Testing Hallucinogens for Therapeutic Use: Unlocking the Secrets of Altered Consciousness,"* by Melissa Healy:

"Janeen Delany describes herself as an 'old hippie' who's smoked plenty of marijuana. But she never really dabbled in hallucinogens – until two years ago, at the age of 59. A diagnosis of incurable leukemia had knocked the optimism out of the retired plant nurserywoman living in Phoenix. So she signed up for a clinical trial to test whether psilocybin – the active ingredient in 'magic mushrooms' – could help with depression or anxiety following a grim diagnosis. Delany swallowed a blue capsule of psilocybin at Johns Hopkins University in Baltimore. She donned a blindfold, a blood pressure cuff and a headset playing classical music. Then, with two researchers at her side, she embarked on a six-hour journey into altered consciousness that she calls *'the single most life-changing experience I've ever had.'*

In the 1960's and '70s, a rebellious generation embraced hallucinogens and a wide array of street drugs to 'turn on, tune in and drop out.' Almost half a century later, magic mushrooms, LSD, Ecstasy and ketamine are being studied for legitimate therapeutic uses. Scientists believe these agents have the potential to help patients with post-traumatic stress disorder, drug or alcohol addiction, unremitting pain or depression and the existential anxiety of terminal illness. 'Scientifically, these compounds are way too important not to study,' said Johns Hopkins psychopharmacologist Roland Griffiths, who conducted the psilocybin trial. In their next incarnation, these drugs may help the psychologically wounded tune into their darkest feelings and memories and turn therapy sessions into opportunities to learn and heal.

'We're trying to break the social mind-set saying these drugs are strictly drugs of abuse,' said Rick Doblin, a public policy expert who founded the Multidisciplinary Association for Psychedelic Studies in 1986 to encourage research on therapeutic uses for medical marijuana and hallucinogens. *'It's not the drug but how the drug is used that matters.'*

Last January, a team led by UCLA psychiatrist Charles Grob reported in Archives of General Psychiatry that psilocybin improved the mood of patients with 'existential anxiety' related to advanced stage cancer. The benefits lasted at least three months.

Delany said her 'trip' awakened a deep and reassuring sense of 'knowing.' She came to see the universe and everything in it as interconnected. She sensed there was nothing more she needed to know and therefore nothing she needed to fear about dying.

'When you take the veil of fear away from your life, you can see and experience in such a present way,' she said. 'I don't have to know what the future is. Every day is the day of days.' "

Just as psilocybin has proven to be a very effective tool for the terminally ill, so too has MDMA, Ecstasy, proven to be most effective with sufferers of PTSD. "One pharmacologist called it 'penicillin for the soul.' Ecstasy has a reputation for dissolving anxiety and fear, suppressing social inhibition and enhancing one's willingness to trust others. PTSD sufferers avoid reminders of their pain or shut down at the prospect of facing it. A dose of Ecstasy appears to help these patients revisit their traumas and reflect on them without fear. *'It can connect people more with their emotions without them feeling they'll be overwhelmed by them,'* said psychiatrist Michael Mithoefer of Charleston, S.C., a clinical investigator for the Multidisciplinary Association for Psychedelic Studies." For more: https://erowid.org *Most recently, there are the well-documented therapeutic benefits of the plant vine **ayahuasca (brewed with DMT)**, a plant that has been utilized by shamans for centuries in the Peruvian Amazon.

The 2014 documentary '*Ayahuasca Nature's Greatest Gift*' "explores ayahuasca's benefit as a tool for growth and the potential medical uses for the field of psychotherapy as a powerful medicine for healing for the treatment of depression, anxiety, sleep disorders, phobias, PTSD, drug and alcohol addiction."

https://ayahuascahealings.com/ayahuasca-retreats-usa/ ≋   ≋   ≋   ≋   ≋   ≋

Band Manager of *The Kind*

My other involvement with the music scene was as manager of the three piece band *The Kind*.

The Kind's self-described sound "electro pop new wave" was akin to the sounds of *Dépêche Mode, Erasure, and New Order.* Members included front man Jim Cochell- keyboards, vocals and songwriting; Floyd Williams- keyboards, vocals and songwriting; and Rick Flaherty- lead vocals.

In deference to *paying homage to the light* as one of the essentials of photography, I wanted to create something memorable and different for the band's album cover. The next page is an example of *painting with light.* I gave each musician a mini maglite and asked them to spell out KIND. I asked them to find a meditative space within themselves and trace each letter backwards with outside members responsible for one letter and the inside man responsible for the IN, *three unique talents uniting the light of their beings into one bright sun, fixing their signature with photons in space.* I call it: *Paying Homage to Kindness (cover photo)* [Double "K" in photo ⇔ *Kindness is the Key*]

Have you been *kind* to someone lately? Let's everyday show our kindness to others, OK? We all thank you. One of my heroes in life: *"My religion is simple, my religion is kindness"*-- Dalai Lama *Technical*: Second curtain flash synch with Canon EOS 620, about 2 sec./T-Max, 1989. [Jim Cochell currently with *TransAtlanticCrush.* * Video: 'SHINE' on YouTube; also: 'Try' at reverbnation.com]

We *tried* to put on a concert at Cactus Park in Scottsdale, AZ, and I even had a permit, but when neighbors started calling the police during their sound check warming up, it had to be cancelled. So, what's a manager to do? Change the venue. It had been advertised and lots of people were showing up, so I changed the venue to my home in Mesa. I had a fantastic music system in my home. As manager of the Acoustat Division of Rockford Corp., I was able to procure a set of Acoustat 4400's for a price far below cost- for a pair of the most beautiful sounding speakers in the world! Listing at $4000 a pair, they were electrostatic type speakers that used vibrating wires, not cones and magnets like conventional speakers. They were 7' 11" high, about 3-4" thick and about two feet wide. You had to hear them to believe them! They were powered by a Hafler Pro Audio Transnova amplifier, the signature, top of the line amplifier offered by the Hafler Division of professional audio gear. The two were made for each other. The Acoustats required lots of power to run most efficiently and the Hafler put out 500 watts a side of the cleanest and most stable power in the industry. It was a match made in heaven. At high levels of amplification, this system could be heard at least a block away in all directions with absolutely no distortion! Eventually, the police were called by some neighbor and I had to shut it all down, lucky to not get arrested for all the minors that were there that night. When it came time to sell my home, this music system was the hardest to let go. I knew I would never be this fortunate again, to own such a system as this. I set up the system in the home of Gladys Caquimbo until I was in a position to find a buyer I needed. I ended up trading this dream system to my mechanic Jerry Secor of Apache Junction in exchange for a red, 1988 Toyota Celica in 2003.

Re: The following two pages -- The page opposite *Paying Homage to Kindness* is another example of *painting with light*, a time exposure of about two seconds of a rocket flare and glow sticks sent into the night sky at a *Grateful Dead* Concert on July 31st 1974 *(the music of Kindness and Love)* at Dillon Stadium in Hartford, CT, titled: *Paying Homage to The Source* -- I needed to juxtapose these two images not just because they both record multiple moments of light in time but because one speaks to the other – For me, The Source is Kindness, Kindness and Love *is* The Source --
It is the deepest message that seems like the simplest message. But it is profound truth as well.

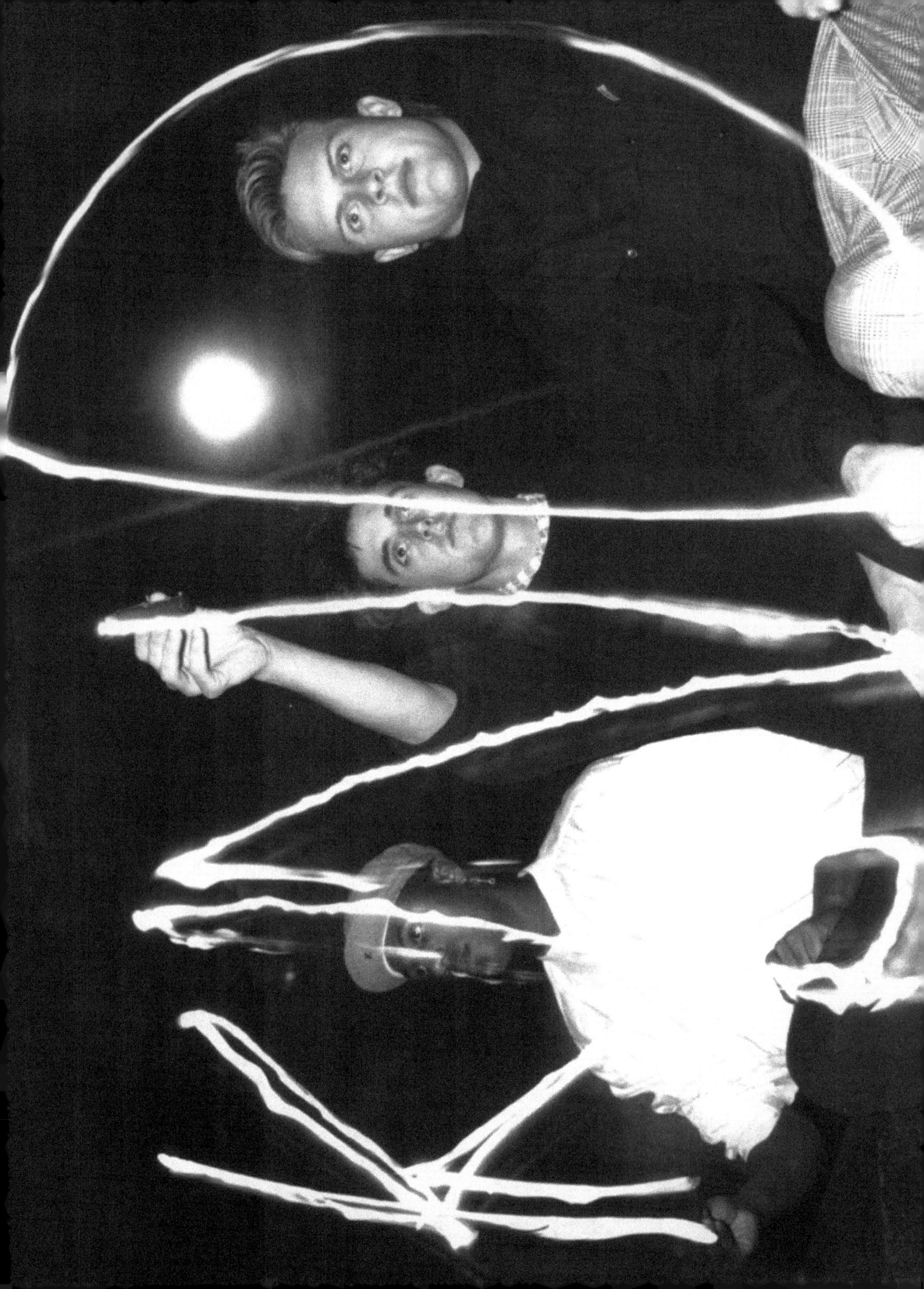

"Paying Homage to Kindness" ***The Kind***
Floyd Williams, Jim Cochell, Rick Flaherty -- Gold Canyon Desert, AZ - 1989

"Paying Homage to The Source" ***The Grateful Dead*** *in Concert - July 31, 1974*
Dillon Stadium, Hartford, CT

Cab Driving Days

After Rockford, in the year 1995, I took a job as a cab driver with Neil's Cabs in Apache Junction. I didn't have this job more than three months but in that short period of time I came in contact with a multitude of different people. Of all those people, two clients became friends for life. One day, one of the other drivers, Bill Cross, called me and asked me if I could pick up his girlfriend Christel Reuther since he was tied up and would not be able to do so. Christel has become one of my best friends in life. I got to know her two daughters as well, Roxy and Alexandra. One of the great things about these three women is their cultural heritage. Christel is a native of Germany. She married Alex, a native of Greece. The two girls lived in Greece for a number of years and learned to speak, fluently: Greek, German, and English. If you are a friend of theirs and only know English, you need to be prepared because they actually go off into their Greek and German worlds, leaving you in the dust as you try to survive in their midst. Over the years in their home I was very fortunate to partake in many authentic Greek and German dishes. Authentic Greek salad is to die for with fresh feta flown in from Greece! Now you have a reason to throw back an ouzo or two. And if it wasn't for Christel I wouldn't know about the world's best beers, the very finest of them all being the black lager *Köstritzer Schwarzbier, especially if drawn from the keg!*

Spencer Land: President of ***High Country Archery*** *(from the files: "It's a small world, isn't it?")*

The other person to whom I am indebted from my short history as a cab driver is Spencer Land. I got the call to pick up this guy at a hotel to take him to Falcon Field, a small local airport. We started talking about flying because my friend Terry Wright is a commercial jet pilot. I inform Spencer that I had just started cabbing; that actually I'm a photographer who needs to supplement his income. I showed him my fold-out business card that I had put a lot of time and money into designing and he was favorably impressed with the card, saying to me, *"You know, I have a company in Tennessee and we're going to be hiring a photographer for our upcoming annual catalog."* 'Oh, really, what kind of company is that?' And he answers me, *"High Country Archery"* '**No way!** My wife and I's closest friends are archery hunters (Don & Mischele Riggins) and they're always bending our ears about HCA. Wait till I tell them I picked up the president of their favorite bow company.' *"You know, you should consider submitting a proposal to photograph our product line."* 'Absolutely, I'll do it.' So, with that, I dropped him off by his plane as he got ready to pilot back to Tennessee. How many times do you say to yourself, *small world, isn't it?* Thus began a professional relationship that was to net me four different assignments, the last one almost taking my life.

I was very serious about writing a very polished proposal and deliberately low-balled my professional fee so I would have a better chance of being selected. I proposed that I would charge the company $500 a day to shoot its product line. I also expected to be paid for my flight back and forth from Phoenix, AZ, and for room and board in Tennessee. When my offer was accepted, I was a very happy camper! I had a lot of experience doing product photography at Rockford and now I could look forward to a new adventure in a new environment. When I arrived, Spencer met me at the airport and took me to a motel. As I was about to check in, he turns to me and says, "Forget about this, why don't you come stay with me and my family, how'd that be?" I couldn't believe it. I get to stay with the *pres* at *his* digs! When we arrived at his big, beautiful home, he introduced me to his lovely wife Joye and their two kids. The hospitality was amazing. I was treated like one of the family. It took five days to shoot the entire product line. In addition to those shots which were taken with my Mamiya 6X7cm camera, I photographed one of his "stand out" employees who had worked previously as a model. She posed with Spencer's cowboy hat, leaning on one of the bows. One of those shots was made into a poster and distributed at the archers' annual ATA Convention (Archery Trade Association) in 1996.

One night, towards the end of my stay with my gracious hosts, Spencer starts in, "*Dennis, I can see from your proposal that you can write. Would you be willing to write the High Country story?*" I couldn't believe it; he was actually considering that I write the rags to riches history of his journey in the archery business. I said something like, '*Wow, that would be an honor. But if I were to do this, I would need to do research, meet the key people involved and conduct interviews so I could get all the background information necessary.*' "*Not a problem, it all started in Idaho. I have some business there in a few weeks. I could go pick you up in Phoenix, we could fly to Idaho and I'll rent two cars. I'll give you names and addresses and the rest will be up to you.*" '*Great! Sounds like a real good plan. Let's do it.*'

*Writing The **HCA** Story*   (*Director James Cameron: "Failure is an option but fear is not."*)

I went with Spencer to Idaho. *What a way to travel, in your own personal flying machine!* The views from the air thousands of feet up flying over Arizona, Utah, Nevada and Idaho were breathtaking. What a fantastic way to see our beautiful country! We arrived in Idaho, went our separate ways and took care of business. I had a very memorable visit with the Geidles, an old couple who owned lots of land and who had given Spencer his first "seed" money to begin development of his new bow concept that was to revolutionize the world of archery. They had nothing but the best to say about Spencer and Joye, considering them "their kids". They helped Spencer a second time in his career and were most instrumental in his success for keeping things financially afloat. Two or three more contacts and I felt I had a pretty good picture as to how I would proceed with this all-American success story.

After we had finished our business, we climbed aboard and *set sail* once again for the wild blue yonder. After about an hour in the air, we were in trouble! The de-icers were not working. We had lost all electrical power! Spencer got very quiet. This is a very cool, calm and collected guy. Not much fazed him; but, as I found out later, he was more than worried; *fear had begun to set in*. The transponder couldn't function without electricity, so the only means of communication was his cell phone. We were getting heavier and heavier with ice on the wings and descending more rapidly than you'd like when there's only mountainous terrain for miles around. Spencer began looking for a place to land but there was none. His plane didn't have GPS but he did have a hand held personal unit with him. He also had a map of the area and a list of airports for the different states we were flying through. He kept searching for an airport that would be our best shot to make it to before running out of time. And just when you think, 'we're doomed' (it felt like shit), he decides we can make it to this podunk, non-descript patch of a landing strip. He immediately calls the airfield and says, "We need to emergency land **now**--make way!" No permission here, we're going for it! What a damn good pilot! He maintained his cool all the way.

After we had landed somewhat forcefully, Spencer turned to me and said, "I didn't say much because I didn't want to scare you but that was a lot more serious than it looked. We were in a bad situation." So nice to have returned to terra firma without having been put there against our will. So we waited for a 20 seater twin prop to take us the rest of the way to Phoenix, AZ. We finally board this bird and we're off once again. *What are the chances that two consecutive flights would experience life-threatening mechanical or electrical problems?* No sooner had we climbed to altitude and one of the engines gave out. There was a lot of sputtering going on and it seemed like Fate had not dealt us its last hand for this day. We were forced to make an emergency landing in Page, AZ, close to the northern border. Now there would be a scramble for the only three cars that could be rented. Spencer spear-headed that campaign. I consider myself an expert car driver, so when I say this guy was just as good on four wheels as he was on two wings, it's for real! I couldn't understand why he felt so comfortable at 90-100mph all

the way to Phoenix and I said so and he pulled out a card he had with him that said something like Provisional Police. OK, fine; I feel better now. OK, Fate, you had enough?! It felt so good to be alive and well again and in my own custody (as it will once again when I'm free of this GPS monitor attached to me). [I like to tell myself that this whole day spent getting back to Phoenix in one piece was Fate's way of saying to me, *"That's what you get for terrorizing all those poor souls on the back of your motorcycles for all those years!"* It was now my turn to be the passenger *out of control*.] *"What goes around ..."*
I couldn't wait to get home and start putting this story together. It took me about two weeks to write the text. I would call it: *The HCA Legacy: Right On Target! Portrait of An American Success*
So my studio would have to wait before a date with the wrecking ball. Because, I needed to isolate and print out some stills from the video I was given, honoring Spencer's coach who was like a father to him. And the word processor of my Amiga 2000HD would be needed to write it all down. I made two copies. It was probably my best piece of writing since critiquing Lester Frank Ward. I sent off the manuscript. I didn't need to enclose a bill. I knew Spencer would see the effort and compensate me accordingly. A couple of weeks later I received a check in the mail for $2000. So, he paid me $2500 for the photo shoot, $2K for *The HCA Legacy*, and an additional $500 for photographing his brother's wedding in Mesa, AZ. *Not bad for a cab ride!* I was on a roll with this benefactor of mine and I was excited to see what next he might have in store for me. And that's when it got dangerous and I got careless and agreed to do something for him that I had no business giving serious consideration to...

Learn To Say 'No!' When You Should & Try Not To Be So Naïve (*'Don't Bite Off More Than U Can Chew'*)
The last job he asked me to do for him I should have refused and I'm lucky to be alive at this time writing about it. He asked me to do some detective work for him. He told me about his cousin who tried to **run him over** after Spencer denied him a job in his company. This was a shady character involved with a drug operation and always up to no good. Spencer told me **he always carried a gun**, so be careful. He wanted me to follow him and take footage of him; to record the places he would go and anything he might be up to. But he also asked me to, at some point, let his cousin see me with the camera trained on him. I should have declined. I'm not a detective, I didn't have a gun and I'm going to piss off someone who's already once tried to *kill my boss!* Dennis, say *No!* Dennis doesn't say *No*; I don't know what I was thinking; I get it- I *wasn't* thinking. So the day comes. I set off following this Cadillac with my Neon rental and already the parameters are changed; he's got a buddy with him. We're talking two big boys, black shades, in their late model Cadillac. I followed them for a few miles. Maybe they felt my presence or not but they started making risky pass maneuvers to get through the traffic on this long winding country road. Not one to shy away from those kinds of maneuvers, I stayed with them. After a while, they probably realized that this Neon was just too much a part of their scenery. So I let them see the camera trained on them. And right away they're pissed. They want to see who the hell I was and what the hell I was doing. So I saw them quickly turn around to come my way and I in turn did the same and now they're behind me giving chase! What was I thinking, how else can this scenario unfold? Now I can drive a damn car and take it to the limit but you know those Neons just were not cut out to keep up with, out-run, or have anything else to do with those big ol' Cads. I was beginning to wonder what I had ever done to Spencer to have been put in such a situation as this. Surely he must have given thought to the possibility of these events taking place. After racing down this country road as fast as the Neon could go for some time, the caddy was closing the gap. When they positioned their car in the oncoming lane to force me over or get alongside, I went into the oncoming lane to block them. We went back and forth like this for awhile- and then I had a thought. I put my right signal flasher on and began to slow down. I had created a little distance between us. The driver got out and approached my side of the car. I waited till he had almost come up to me and then I floored it. I was able to buy a few precious seconds but I know this will be a short-lived moment. Within about 40-60 seconds the Caddy's threatening again

to overtake me. All seemed lost and I kept saying to myself, *'What the hell were you thinking; this is f*kin' crazy!'* How helpless is the feeling when one loses control of a situation.

And just when my fate seemed to be sealed, I heard the most beautiful sound I ever heard. Did you ever think you would call a police siren the most beautiful sound in the world? Thank Whoever, Whatever. When the State Trooper got to my window, I spoke fast, *'I'm so glad you stopped. Those guys are trying to run me off the road. I'm a detective from Phoenix. I was hired by the cousin of the guy who's driving who tried to kill my friend, Spencer Land, the President of High Country Archery.'* "You got a detective's license?" *'No, I don't sir. I was just hired to follow these guys and document their movements; they're supposedly involved in a drug operation.'* "Alright, you wait here; I'm gonna talk to them." He comes back to me, "Look, you're not from around here; you don't know who you're dealing with and things could have turned out a whole lot differently if I hadn't come along. Here's what's gonna happen: you're gonna go in this direction and they're gonna go in the opposite direction. You better go back to Phoenix where you came from and leave your friend's problems to him." *'Thank you, sir. I appreciate it.'*

It's not like in the movies, folks! So, enjoy your endless shoot-em-up good guys-bad guys crap; just remember, it's only entertainment. You get a couple of bad asses like this who mean to do you harm and you better start recalling how nice it was to be alive and free- for real. Sorry, Spence, no more jobs!

It was time for my life to take a completely different path - it was time for Peace & Harmony -

Chapter 20:   *Time For A Paradigm Shift*   * * * *A Peace Machine Is Born* * * *

It was time to move on with my life. Our house had to be sold. The studio that had served me so well for all those video productions would become no more than a memory. Where would I go from here? One thing for sure; I didn't want to repeat this scenario of buying a home and having to vacate it and destroy my very means of survival, my studio. It was time to seriously consider an alternative living arrangement. And then the *light* came on in my head. I would purchase a small motor home and would try to develop a mobile photography business whereby my studio would be your domain. I would change my name from *Studio D Video & Photo* to *Studio D Mobile Photography*. At about this time in my life (1996), I was very involved with reggae music and dance. It occurred to me that I could convert this RV into a symbol of Peace dedicated to the message of Bob Marley. I was a frequenter of *Likle Montego Jamaican Café*, the best reggae dance club in the valley, owned by Marcus Wright. The authentic Jamaican cuisine was really something special. My friend Errol Henry from Spanish Town in St. Catherine was lucky enough to have his mother in their kitchen. She would prepare the best jerk chicken, rice and peas with sweet plantains that you could ever have! *And those XXX MACKESON Stouts!*

It became clear to me the more that I pondered over it, that I would paint my RV as a tribute to Bob Marley, Jamaica and Reggae music. I purchased a 1975 Dodge Camper RV for $2500. I decided to paint the entire right side of the RV as the Jamaican flag. A giant saltire from upper left corner to lower right and from lower left corner to upper right painted in GOLD: (represents the natural wealth and beauty of sunlight); the upper and lower quadrants in GREEN: (represents hope and agricultural resources); and the left and right quadrants in **BLACK**: (represents the strength and creativity of the people). It has been said that the Jamaican flag is the only flag in the world that does not have a color of the American flag in it. On the left side of the motor home, I reproduced a very accurate to scale rendering of the island of Jamaica, filling the entire side with it. In the middle of the island complete with mountains, rivers, and parishes was their motto: *OUT OF MANY, ONE PEOPLE*. The back of the RV was painted the Rasta colors, equal parts GREEN, GOLD, RED. My license plate was *JA LAND*. I had an African American airbrush artist paint a portrait of Bob Marley on each of the cab doors. I wanted the spirit of Native America as part of the artistic rendering and so artwork from Hopiland was reproduced on the engine cover. The air conditioner on top was equal parts red, gold, and green. The back window was covered with an air-brushed sheet of aluminum by Dale Daniel of *Rocky Mountain Airbrush*. It was painted from the original artwork that I had commissioned from Clinton Taylor (renowned artist and sculptor of Southwest Native American themes) in August, 2001. I told him I wanted an original concept of *Great Spirit* shrouded in Rasta colors, breathing life into the heavens - it was a triumvirate project--

dedicated to SPIRIT ~

Two different reggae music groups were interested in having the vehicle for their bands but it was my home and I was not interested. Not one square inch was not covered in something different than when it had arrived in my possession. I wanted to create a spiritual space, an inner sanctum of higher consciousness, a place of comfort and peace. This became my home for the next six years; it was a work in process the whole time and became known as the Bob Marley RV. I referred to my home as the *Peace Machine* or among close friends as *Peggy Sue,* named after Buddy Holly's big hit song in 1957.

I had written a mission statement for its *raison d'être*:

The Peace Machine

"This vehicle has a mission and its mission is PEACE - dedicated to communicating or teaching the values of universal freedom, brotherly love and human understanding--values which acquired lead to PEACE among men, women and children. It is my opinion that Bob Marley **(Feb 6, 1945 – May 11, 1981) --** *more than any other person*, has had the greatest influence with his lyrics and music the world over to bring about **Unity and Understanding and the Brotherhood of Man, One Love -** This vehicle is a mobile testament to Bob Marley's life's work and his contribution to humanity and hopefully will serve as both a reminder and bearer of the messages he communicated to all of us. That is why the *flag of Jamaica* covers the entire right side of this camper motor home and the *island of Jamaica* covers fully the left side with the most important message of all: OUT OF MANY, ONE PEOPLE and why also the Rasta colors Green, Gold and Red which symbolize *Earth, Sun* and *Blood* cover the entire backside of the vehicle. The portraits of Robert Nesta Marley on the cab doors are rendered to capture so much of what the man was all about - the *spirit of freedom* - emancipating the mental slaveries of people's minds. So many people are held powerless by whatever system keeps them down—they are the downtrodden—those whose individual rights have been taken away or diminished to the point of destroying the human spirit. [Unbeknownst to me then, I was writing about myself now as well.] And then there is the portrait of *Great Spirit* replacing the back window; and finally, above *the point of power* on the engine cover is artwork *dedicated to* the Hopi way of life, to *peaceful co-existence* with all living beings—elements of Native American belief systems incorporated to serve as guides for this vehicle—wherever it is supposed to be and for whomever it needs to be in their presence."

ONE LOVE

The Peace Machine – Holding the Bob Marley Freedom Flag with me: (L-R) Tarenah Edwards, Marina Wilson and Iesha Edwards, all daughters of the photographer, Kristie Edwards. (July, 2001) Portrait in window is of Goyathlay (Geronimo), Chiricahua Apache and Native American leader, who with his band of resistance fighters was "one of the last major forces of Independent Native American warriors who refused to acknowledge the United States occupation of the American West." A Freedom Fighter like Bob Marley, although his fight was for the right to keep the lands of his people free from foreign domination and control. "On his death bed he confessed to his nephew that he regretted his decision to surrender. He was not allowed to return to the land of his birth."

[Quoted statements credited to Wikipedia]

I have had the opportunity in my life to meet a fair number of so-called 'famous people' and at times it was for no other reason than because *The Peace Machine* brought us together. A woman came up to me when I was parked in a Mesa, AZ mall and introduced herself as Dennis Brown's wife. That was truly amazing (Dennis Brown aka *The Crown Prince of Reggae*). Another time when I was in Phoenix, AZ parked at a Reggaefest venue, my friend from Ethiopia Daniel Abebe of *Rasta Tings* asked me to help him with his booth and that's when the promoter and Rita Marley stopped by. I had the opportunity to photograph Rita with Daniel (who had grown up with Ziggy Marley and knew Rita very well) and then I had my photo taken with Bob Marley's wife as well. That is the closest I came to Bob Marley himself. I have always regretted not only not meeting the man but never having been to one of his concerts as well. But at least I could for six years share with the world his messages of Unity and One Love via the mobile tribute of the Peace Machine in his name.

Hopi (Hopituh Shi-nu-mu) The Peaceful People

My favorite words from Bob Marley's songs:

Get Up, Stand Up, Stand Up For Your Right
Get Up, Stand Up, Don't Give Up The Fight
Get Up, Stand Up, Life Is Your Right
Don't Give Up The Fight

"Emancipate yourself from mental slavery.
None but ourselves can free our minds."
-- Marcus Garvey

Just can't live that negative way…
Make way for the positive day.
Life is one big road with lots of signs;
so when you're riding through the ruts,
don't complicate your mind. Flee from hate,
mischief and jealousy. Don't bury your thoughts.
Put your vision to reality. Wake up and Live!

"Until the philosophy which hold one race superior
and another inferior is finally and permanently
discredited and abandoned…WAR!" -- Selassie I

Robert Nesta Marley

"Me only have one ambition, ya know. I only have one thing I really like to see happen.
I like to see mankind live together—Black, White, Chinese, everyone—that's all."

Chapter 21: *The 'Peggy Sue' Years -- Living Life Totally Real, Totally Free & Totally Alive*
I was excited about a reggae concert that was coming up and I knew I had to be there. *Peggy Sue* would be baptized in a sea of Rasta-conscious humanity. The debut of the Peace Machine was at hand.
When the actual day finally had arrived and I managed to find just the right place close by to the entrance/exit of the large event to park, the magic began to unfold. People were already reacting to this mobile island tribute to Marley, Jamaica, and Reggae. Several different groups of reggae music were to perform that day. The crowds were growing and the mood to shake one's booty was increasing to unstoppable. [I give thought to Alan Watts' last book, Tao: The Watercourse Way (*Go with the Flow*)]

Dance As All-Powerful Medicine & Celebration of Self **(Spanish translation: p. 67)**
If you know about reggae music, you know how infectious it is upon your soul, how contagious it is to dance to. Once you make the original decision to allow yourself the freedom to let loose and move your body, you have begun the pleasure journey that will take you to many beautiful places. As human beings, we are made to dance. When I studied Cultural Anthropology at college, we explored myth and myth-making of the various peoples of mankind throughout history. In no culture was it found where "dance" did not play a central role in the defining of a people's existence whether to celebrate life or death or anything in between. In Africa there is a saying, "If you can talk, you can sing; if you can walk, you can dance." Dancing to Reggae music is unique in that there is no prescribed way to do it. (→ p. 67)

It was important to boldly show the motto of Jamaica, *-- OUT OF MANY, ONE PEOPLE --*
because I can think of no more powerful or meaningful message that should be shared with the world than this one, also to be known as: "The Four Colors of Man: WE ARE ONE HUMAN RACE"
It's a shame that many die-hard Utopians like myself, while we can never stop trying to push the Peace agenda for all the world's citizens till we die, secretly harbor the dark feelings of the pessimistic realist at the same time. Oh, how we all wish it could get done and there be a future for our childrens' childrens' children and forevermore. But then reality begins to set in. But we can't stop trying to make a difference; there's still some time left on this beautiful planet of ours and the torch of positivity must continually be passed with the hope of a better future for all of us.

But I believe the window of opportunity comes with an expiration date --which may not be too far away!

It is important that the true story of genocide and ethnocide that was the history of Jamaica and the Caribbean be known. The Arawak/Taíno people of what was once known as the island of Xaymaca, the Island of Wood and Water, were systematically hunted down and destroyed, sharing the common legacy of all Caribbean peoples at the hands of Columbus and the other conquistadors.

The history books need to be rewritten and Columbus Day needs to be replaced with Indigenous Day!

We need to help restore the culture and Indigenous heritage of the Taíno people and foster their rightful identity. They never died out. www.TainoDaca.com The people of the Dominican Republic and Haiti and Puerto Rico and Cuba and Jamaica will thank you. And the same applies to all Native

Indigenous cultures wherever they may be threatened. *~ cultural identities must be preserved ~*

The Great Spirit or Wakan Tanka of Native American Cosmology

The more I learned about Native American belief systems, first from my readings of Carlos Castañeda's Yaqui Indians of Sonora, México, and subsequently from my many years living in Arizona, the more I appreciated what our Indigenous Brothers and Sisters had to say about our world and their reality-view of it. I had always been very close to nature but now I was beginning to acquire a much deeper connection to all living things, beginning to see and know that all physical beings may have a metaphysical component to them, a connection beyond the physical realm. The animistic view *(that might be compared to Bergson's élan vital, the life force in all living things)* that a **Great Spirit** flows through and connects all living things to each other; and, if you are so inclined to believe, to the world beyond, presented itself to me.

I wanted **Great Spirit** to be the *spirit guide* on the journey I was taking. On the front of the Peace Machine the energy of the Peaceful People, the Hopi, was symbolically placed in art form above the engine power source to represent the Power of Peace; and the energy of **Wakan Tanka, The Great Mystery**, was placed on the backside of the motorhome acting as a kind of rudder influencing the paths I would be taking in the many trips that came to define my Peace Mission journey in tribute to Bob Marley, Jamaica and Reggae Music, the most powerful and contagious *spirit dance* music the world has ever known.

It's not like you're at a Latin club and Salsa or Merengue or Bachata is playing and there is more of an urgency to dance a particular way. That's what makes Reggae so much fun. Nobody really cares how you dance. Bob Marley is famous for his *spirit dance*. He allowed himself to get into a trance-like state of mind, and the spirit of his soul took over when he danced. We can all dance in a similar way. Let the music come into your soul and dance how you feel in that moment. I believe through the process of *spirit dance* -- *healing* is most possible both for the dancer and those around him or her; that it is an effective vehicle to contagiously affect people with good, positive feelings and it may be looked at as an effective way to actualize the goal we all refer to in reggae circles as *ONE LOVE ♥ ONE HEART* I've been saying for years the way I dance is to use my body as an instrument and interpret the music I hear. As a percussionist, I'm always reinforcing my knowledge of the music and this in turn positively affects the self-expression that is my dance. For me *spirit dance* is the ultimate form of human experience. *It does not have to be drug-induced. The music and the dance themselves are the 'drug'.* *Once the three portals of the human's being are in synch; once the music fills the heart and the mind and the soul of the individual, the body automatically takes over in a free form expression of the self. It's an incredible feeling that permeates every fiber of your being. You are being totally real allowing yourself to be human and dance; you come to a state that is total freedom within yourself; and what you end up experiencing is total aliveness of the human condition.* This is what I want people to know and understand. It is the Great Gift and the Great Medicine that we give to ourselves.

*The cost is *not* nothing; the cost is merely your commitment to be *you* *

En Español:

Bailar Como La Más Poderosa Medicina y Una Celebración de Su Ser

Si sabes de música reggae, que sepa cómo infecciosa es sobre tu alma, lo contagioso que es para bailar. Una vez que toma la decisión original, que le permita tener la libertad de dejarse llevar y mover su cuerpo, que ha comenzado el camino del placer que le llevará a muchos lugares hermosos. Como seres humanos, estamos hechos para bailar. En África hay un dicho, "Si puedes hablar, puedes cantar; si puedes caminar, puedes bailar." Bailar al ritmo de la música reggae es única, ya que no hay manera prescrita para hacerlo. No es como si estuvieras en un club latino y la salsa o merengue o bachata está jugando y hay más de una urgencia a bailar de una manera particular. Eso es lo que lo hace tan divertido Reggae. En realidad, nadie le importa cómo se baila.

Bob Marley es famoso por su danza del espíritu. Se permitió entrar en un estado de trance de la mente, y el espíritu de su alma se hizo cargo cuando bailó. Todos podemos bailar de una manera similar. Deja que la música entre en tu alma y bailar cómo se siente en ese momento. Creo que a través del proceso de la danza del espíritu - la curación es más posible tanto para el bailarín y aquellos a su alrededor; que es un vehículo eficaz para afectar contagiosa personas con buenos sentimientos positivos, y puede ser considerado como una forma efectiva de hacer realidad el objetivo que nos referimos a todos en los círculos del reggae como **UN AMOR ♥ UN CORAZÓN** –

He estado diciendo durante años mi forma de bailar es utilizar mi cuerpo como un instrumento e interpretar la música que escucho. Como percusionista, siempre estoy reforzar mis conocimientos de la música y esto a su vez afecta positivamente a la auto-expresión que es mi baile. Para mí danza del espíritu es la última forma de la experiencia humana. No tiene que ser inducida por fármacos. La música y la danza son ellos mismos la "droga". Una vez que los tres portales de bienestar de los humanos están en sincronía; una vez que la música llena el corazón y la mente y el alma del individuo, el cuerpo se hace cargo automáticamente en una forma de libre expresión de uno mismo. Es una sensación increíble que impregna cada fibra de su ser. Estás siendo totalmente real permitiéndose ser humano y la danza se llega a un estado que es la libertad total dentro de sí mismo; y lo que terminan experimentando es vitalidad total de la condición humana. Esto es lo que yo quiero que la gente sepa y comprenda. Es el Gran Don y la Gran Medicina que nos damos a nosotros mismos. *El costo no es nada; el costo no es más que su compromiso de ser usted --

Two Very Special People: Gladys Caquimbo & Ty Kennerson

So the reggae music's playing on stage and the people on the field are beginning to dance. As is my way, I can not refrain from joining in. The rhythmic down beat crashing on the drum and the persistent bass line pounded out so religiously, the lead guitar hardly more than a repetitive two finger pick just like the keyboardist, that staccato twosome of notes ad infinitum, this is the way the reggae comes to you, pulling you into its grip of wanting more and more and more. So I start moving my body with the music and slowly get more into it as the song develops. Sometimes you run into partners unexpectedly. It's kind of like your energy vibe pool intersects with another's and you're there dancing together. One might say that two auras encounter each other and agree to share moments in time together. This is how I met Gladys Caquimbo, through dance. After we had danced for awhile, we introduced ourselves to each other. She told me that her boyfriend "E" was the keyboard player (Elliott Rauch, now with *Xtra Ticket*, a *Grateful Dead* tribute band).   I invited them to my home in the parking lot later if they liked. Thus began the relationship of one of my dearest and closest of friends in life. It turned out that Gladys was very active in the reggae scene, involved with festivals and promotions of the music of several of these musicians.

Another great friendship was forged on this day. After the bands had played, there was one more duo that had yet to perform. They would not be playing on stage; they would be playing on the field in the middle of all the people. There would be no amplifiers needed; this was something you came up close to. To this day in my life, the power and the energy of the music I heard and received into my soul by these two individuals has not been surpassed. I can not describe in this hopelessly inadequate medium of word-making how much I was moved by this singer named "Ty" and this Niyabinghi drummer, Ras Joseph. Just one gifted voice and one beautiful Niyabinghi beat. This is music only to be listened to; it had nothing to do with dancing; this was the mecca of music I was seeking. All the other bands with all their instruments were great for the dancing; but this was totally for the Spirit ~

I had to meet each of them and share with them how much their music had affected me. Ty later stopped by *Peggy Sue* with some of his friends and that's how our friendship began.

68

One of the places that was really great to take the Peace Machine was the farmstead of Caymanian Denzil Dacres and Sister Care I. They would hold concerts and sponsor other musicians of the reggae community. He was one of my portrait assignments for an album he was producing. His group is known as *Dee Dread & The Zion Knights*. One had to enjoy the signs he had placed all around his property such as the two shown above with their messages of tough love; I felt like he had the right idea about communicating brotherly love within the framework of individual responsibility and that other venue operators would do well to initiate similar policies. *We must each of us try to be the best example that we can to others. Because that's the only thing that matters.*

Over the next few months and years as well, I would visit Ty and his friends at their Rasta enclave in Phoenix, AZ, and Gladys and her family in Mesa, AZ. I met Gladys' two wonderful daughters, Scarlett and Bianca, ages 10 and 8, respectively, in 1996. Gladys was one of those special people you meet in life; when they walk into a room, there was a *presence*, the social dynamics changed. A very attractive woman from Colombia, she had mastered the English language and was involved with social causes, in addition to her full time occupation as a hospice nurse. I became very good friends with her and her daughters, taking trips to Rocky Point, Mexico, a picturesque fishing village in Sonora. We were two of the biggest fans of reggae music that there could be and as such were accustomed to being seen dancing together at all of the reggae venues we attended. We were often mistaken as a couple; however, I had a relationship with a significant other and she became very seriously involved with a Hopi singer/songwriter, Casper. *"Casper Lomayesva is a Hopi/Diné singer who has created a sound that combines his native roots with the positive vibes of reggae music. Casper's music is filled with hope and power. The words are a reflection of his own philosophy on life, influenced not only by the sounds of crucial reggae music but of traditional Hopi culture."* (from: www.nativemusicrocks.com) He is a social activist for all people and became a concert favorite at reggae venues with his didactic and cogent reggae rap style of music. He produced several CD albums, the first and perhaps best known being: *Original Landlord*. His second album, *Sounds of Reality*, earned him a *NAME* award, equivalent to a Grammy for Native People. His third album, *Honor the People*, has received critical acclaim as well.
To learn more: www.4went.com/casper_lomadawa.html

My heart soared recently when I received, on Sept 12, 2010, a facebook message from Bianca, now 22, *"Hey, Dennis, it's so nice to see you on here. What an awesome trip life is! Its twists and turns...I want to tell you, I have a lot of positive memories from the years! The peggy sue, rocky point festivals..drum circles and ur instruments..The bad ass clubhouse u made! Your collages of art and photography! I hold all those memories dear to my heart!"* I have had no greater joy in life than to be remembered for the little things that mattered so much so many years ago. Thank you ever so much, Bianca. And I still carry with me the gift given to me on Oct 29, 1997, with these words recorded at the time from Scarlett: *"Dennis, you have an extraordinary life - you need to have this journal to keep track. It is from me and Bianca."* She handed me a lined-page diary with a magnificent photo of a lone wolf ambling towards the viewer in a snow covered world. Not a little too symbolic, eh? Very few entries were made in all those years; I keep it for the feel good memory and beautiful photo. I am reminded of the words of Carl Jung,
* *"One looks back with appreciation to the brilliant teachers, but with gratitude to those who touched our human feelings...warmth is the vital element for the growing plant and for the soul of the child."*

Extending The Motor Home Way of Living As A Viable, Symbiotic Alternative
What began as an RV way of life became much more. *Peggy Sue* was not just a recreational vehicle; it became my complete home environment. I had de-materialized from a "normal" two bedroom home with garage to a one room motor home complete with bathroom, fridge and stove, and an upstairs level that I hired a specialty welder, Vaughan Pruitt of Cliff's Welding in Mesa, AZ, to add on to the roof, connected to the downstairs via a 2'X2' tinted, hinged and removable sunroof. It had evolved quite a bit further than the original designers had intended. It was very comfortable to live in and to visit if you were so inclined. If I came to visit your home, effectively we were neighbors living side by side. It was a lot different than just visiting someone and leaving your home behind. The dynamics of interaction change, allowing for more personal involvement and continuity in the lives of all participants. At night, I

guarantee your privacy and am happy and comfortable (except for the excessive heat that is part and parcel of the Arizona experience) to return to my little oasis. Gladys and her family were just one of the friendship circles I shared this special relationship with. My friend Christel and her two daughters Roxy and Alexandra were another; my friend Kristie Edwards and her children, Zachary, Marina, Iesha, and Tarenah were another still, as was Sandra Andrews and her two daughters Melissa and Cindy. Dr. Sandra Andrews, as she can now be called after receiving her PhD in Education from Arizona State University, along with her very gifted graphic artist daughter Melissa, were the two computer whiz programmers who designed my web site in the summer of 2001 on www.floaters.org. For nine years, I could refer people to my website, *Studio D Mobile Photography*, until *floaters* had become totally re-designed by Sandra and ASU. Sandra allowed me to set up my video editing equipment in the downstairs room of her home in Mesa, AZ, after my home had been sold and for that I will always be grateful. I am indebted to Sandra for all the exposure I otherwise would not have had in sharing my vision and artwork to the world. Sandra's tireless efforts trying to develop and improve outreach programs for the disadvantaged and the needy deserve special mention. I have never met a more dedicated change agent for the cause of self-empowerment and improvement in the lives of others than Dr. Sandra Sutton Andrews – *Edtech research, nonprofit/social change/environmentalist --

Judith Campanaro: Artist & Healer

It's funny how you meet people in life. One day I was looking at a post card that an acquaintance of mine had received. I was quite taken by it; it was a reproduction of a painting. The colors were dramatically vibrant; it was a very interesting, Van Gogh-esque sunrise that really grabbed the imagination. I commented to the recipient of this missive how great this artwork was and she responded to me, "I know the person who painted that, she's a friend of mine; she's also a masseuse." 'Well, I need to call her for a massage.' I had always wanted to get a full body massage and felt that a woman's hands that were so gifted to produce such good art as this must be able to give quite a massage as well. Since she was an artist, I wanted to show her my appreciation for her artwork by surprising her with a 6 X 7cm copy transparency of that same piece of work. I photographed the post card full frame, placed the transparency in a protective clear plastic sleeve and attached a gold thread to it to hang as a mobile. When I got to my appointment and had a chance to meet Judi Campanaro for the first time in person, it was special from the first moment. Such a vivacious personality; she had a calming, peaceful aura about her. She was into aromatherapy and seemed to be tuned into the spiritual side of her being. She couldn't believe I showed up with a mobile of one of her pieces. She loved it. And I loved my massage. She was very professional and left me wanting more. A friendship developed and soon I was getting massages in exchange for photographing her portfolio of paintings.

She became one of those "friends for life" that we are fortunate enough to come in contact with in this world. When it was time for me to leave Arizona with Peggy Sue for the unchartered waters of Florida, Judi gifted me with the original painting of that postcard; it was entitled, *"Breaking Free"* -- In addition to her vast portfolio of paintings, Judi is a practitioner of the healing arts as well and instructor of same. From her website at: www.judithcampanaro.com, Judi writes, "My mission statement is *to facilitate empowerment through creative expression*. I am a firm believer that *art feeds the soul and empowers the psyche.* The more universal the thought, form and color, the more powerfully the work will speak to the harmony within each human being." In her book, *Art for the Soul: The Healing Magic of Creativity,*

"There is not a lot of empirical evidence as to why art heals. It is just a known fact. My concept is that making art brings us back to our center and in so doing, balance is restored to the soul...the act of creating brings you moments when you drop your cares and feed that part of you that needs nourishment from the beauty of the world around you."

The Promise

Both truly inspired and enlightening, *The Promise* represents one of Judi's most sublime works of art. When I think of Judi, the way she lives her life as a means for others to benefit, I think of the words of another selfless instrument of mankind: *"You are the lens in the beam. You can only receive, give, and possess the light as the lens does. If you seek yourself, you rob the lens of its transparency. You will know life and be acknowledged by it according to your degree of transparency, your capacity, that is, to vanish as an end, and remain purely as a means."* Dag Hammarskjöld

Dag Hammarskjöld: former Secretary-General of the United Nations, awarded the Nobel Peace Prize posthumously. John F. Kennedy said of him, "the greatest statesman of our century"

LOVE PEACE RESPECT ♡ *This Is* Jamaica *– Two Weeks With Empress Marcia Sinclair* ♛

One of the regulars I kept running into at my favorite reggae establishment, *Likle Montego Jamaican Café*, was Marcia (Mar-see-ya) Sinclair, a native Jamaican. I would spent a lot of time talking with her about my plans to visit Jamaica someday if for no other reason because I wanted to have that connection to the source of reggae music that had become such a big part of my life. One day Marcia had some news for me. She informed me that *Air Jamaica* was planning to begin direct flights from Phoenix, AZ, to Montego Bay, JA, beginning with an inaugural flight on June 15, 2000. She said they were going to make a big marketing push to get the word out, with press, free food, free T-shirts, etc. She told me she was definitely going and I should seriously think about it; it would be a great day to pick to go there. I didn't take too long to think about it. I had two weeks' vacation time coming to me, so I put in for June 15th - July 1st. Other friends of Marcia decided to make the trip as well, so now we were a foursome, more or less. And if all that was not the greatest news to look forward to, on the day of the flight Marcia tells me I can stay at the home of her parents, not to worry about renting a hotel room.

Thus began the hospitality of Marcia, her mother Ena and her father Wesley. But before we get to their home, we need to take a cab from Montego Bay to the parish of St. Mary. Introducing my first new friend in Jamaica, Denval Masters, our dedicated cabby. "Denny"- as everybody called him, had been involved in a relationship with Marcia in their past and now the two of them remained good friends. We practically had a member of the family as our chauffeur. Even though this connection existed, taking a cab everywhere you go can get expensive and so a good portion of our vacation money evaporated his way. I was videotaping my trip with a Sony 8mm camera as I intended to put together a personal documentary of my two week stay on the island. I remember we stopped at a quaint little open air café with hand-drawn menu. We had mannish water and curried goat for lunch and finished off the meal with a **rum and cream**. Jamaica is famous for their version of a rum and cream; it is a mixture, in the proportions that suit your palate, of a Nestle product, vanilla Supligen, a meal replacement drink, and the most famous of Jamaican rums, Wray and Nephew overproof white rum. This is *the gold standard* if you're visiting Jamaica and want to experience the Jamaican way. Any variation of the formula would just not be right. After an hour or so we reached Free Hill, St. Mary, by Pompano Way and the home of Marcia's parents with a sign in the yard, The Sinclairs. Like so many homes in Jamaica, the property had various fruit bearing trees on it. They had coconut palms, jackfruit and mango trees. They had ackee, almond, apple, avocado, cherry, and orange trees. Such fecundity I had never seen before.

The lot next door to them had a huge mango tree on it. At night, you could hear the cows (free roaming in Jamaica) gorging themselves on the luscious fruit. Marcia's mother was such a sweetheart. I would walk in the morning with her and her friends to greet the sunrise at the ocean a mile or two away. We would come to this lookout high up on an overhanging cliff with a breathtaking view of the crashing surf below. *This was Jamaica!* This is what I had hoped to see and experience. Another day with Marcia's Mom Ena was spent on their tract of land that they were farming in the hills of St. Mary. They had all sorts of vegetables in the ground and coconut, banana and plantain trees as well. I was a *Lucky Man*, as *Emerson, Lake and Palmer* so eloquently put it. [But, like I said before, *I don't believe in "luck" per se; I prefer to view "luck" as: 'when opportunity meets preparation.'* Aside from winning the lotto and random acts of Mother Nature, I can't think of anything that can occur simply by pure chance. There is usually an investment of one's will or energies towards (a) specific goal(s) that puts one in a position to attain certain positive or negative results; the actualization of which cannot be attributed to *luck*, but rather to the preparation *or lack thereof* towards those ends or results. Being deterministic here, we can also control some of this process by who we are and how we behave; thus, for me, a lot can be said for: *Character is Fate* -- we can to some extent control our own destiny. That's a powerful idea. If we accept this principle, we put ourselves behind the wheel of our journey; we do not make excuses, or rely on some other guidance, but just do what has to be done and take the credit or blame accordingly.]

ROOTS *Rock* *REGGAE*　　　　　**Dunn's River Falls • *Jamaica*　　　　*June • 2000***

It is easy to see why Jamaica is often referred to as the Paradise Island. The incredible variety of flowering plants and fruit-bearing trees will make a believer out of anyone. This uniquely shaped *"Burst of Red in a Sea of Greens"* stopped me in my tracks. It appears to be a variation of the many species of hibiscus found throughout the island.

One of the most common fruits in Jamaica and one of the most delicious in the world is the mango. When fully ripened with tinges of yellow and red, it is hard to resist. I didn't have to go far to find these young stringy mangoes; they were hanging from one of the many fruit trees on the property of Ena and Wesley Sinclair.   *"Ode to Chiaroscuro"*

I spent time with Wesley as well. You can't go to Jamaica and not come upon a game of dominoes. Wesley was pretty good at this Jamaican pastime, at the level of playing in tournaments in fact. But I was more interested in the lady he introduced me to at this tiny little bar next to the town hairdresser. Wesley would have his *rum and cream* and I would have an ice-cold *Guinness*. There seemed to be a chemistry between the lady bartender and yours truly. The bar was just feet from the ocean. I asked my new friend when was the last time she had gone down to the water and enjoyed herself down there. She said it had been too long. 'So why don't you and I go down there this afternoon?' "OK, I'll just shut the bar down for an hour or so, and we'll just come right back." That's how small this place was; nobody would miss it being closed for an hour. So we took a walk down to the ocean and spent some "quality time," just the two of us, nobody else in sight, a very private and special moment indeed.

My bartender lady friend thought it would be fun to turn this white boy's long hair into braids, so she had her friend, who owned the hair salon next door to the bar, do me the honors. It was fun for awhile but I think I looked a little silly because it was just not me and I couldn't quite get used to the idea; so, by the end of the day I was happy to revert back to my normal gringo style.

It takes much more than two weeks to get to know Jamaica. I had planned to visit Negril but there just wasn't enough time. This trip would be concentrated around Ocho Rios. One thing about Jamaica; it's the home of outdoor sound systems. People go into business by setting up a bunch of loudspeaker systems, corralling an area off, and charging admission. DJ's rule. Live music venues exist but DJ sound systems are what's happening. You can hardly go anywhere on the island and not hear a sound system booming in the distance or close by. If you like reggae music, you have reached Nirvana; such great selections of home grown *roots*, lovers *rock*, and dancehall *reggae* music, that you can't even imagine. One night, Marcia and Denny took her friends and me to a place called *Cool Out* - it was a café/bar nightclub but the sound system and the people were all outside. Very loud and very cool, people including myself dancing in the street as if a festival were going on; it's just the Jamaican way. And how many of the tourists who book their vacations at those exclusive resorts get to experience this real side of Jamaica? I'd be willing to bet it's close to zero %. Before we left the *Cool Out* my attention was distracted by a high pitched whistling sound that got louder and louder. A vendor was approaching us, pushing his cart to where we were and soon we were feasting on freshly steamed peanuts. *Yah mon!*

Ocho Rios. If you're looking for the greatest outdoor arts and crafts market of authentic Jamaican goods, you've come to the right place. I highly recommend this place. What I don't recommend is putting your video camera in front of somebody or their wares unless you are prepared to pay for the privilege. They are very serious about this. You want to take video, you pay. I was trying to capture footage for a documentary of sorts but was not prepared for this unknown surcharge. I spent a total of nearly $100 for the footage I insisted upon having. But it was worth it. The footage of the Rastaman with his dreads all the way to the ground; that was priceless. Since he was not greedy or pushy about it and said just give him whatever I felt, I thought about it for a minute. This man, who probably never cut his hair in his life, who was so committed to his life style and looked like he had next to nothing in the physical world; he deserved some respect. So I gave him $50. What he gave me was a lot. I wanted *money* to have nothing to do with it. But the facts of life are what they are; he needed it. He possessed nobility of soul. If you go to Jamaica, you need to go to *Dunn's River Falls*, especially if you like waterfalls. They'll take your picture with the falls as backdrop and you'll have a great time. If you're lucky and he's still alive, you might strike it rich with this old timer singing a rendition of *New York, New York*, one of the best musical experiences of my trip. It's funny how and when you encounter these musical gems. I went with Marcia's mother to a big family reunion way up in the country. It was for the consecration of a headstone for a matriarch of the family who had passed more than a year earlier. (It takes time to raise the money necessary to buy these stones.) There were all kinds of activity going on here. Three giant caldrons simmering their contents of mannish water, (goat's head soup), curried goat, and rice vied for space alongside large grills of roasting corn and barbecuing chicken. There were lots of kids running around so I thought this would be the perfect opportunity to share something special. Just like in the streets of Miami when I would magically produce a *Frisbee* from the holster I had sewn into the inside of my leather jacket and brought the adults together, I had an opportunity now to bring together a whole bunch of kids in the same way. Once the disc is in play, it's addictive to keep it going and lots more fun when you start to see that you actually have control of it. Every country I visit, I plant the seed of this *Freedom Frisbee* among the youth and after a good workout, one of them gets to keep it and continue the spirit going forward. (But it should be an authentic *Wham-O* or *Discraft Ultra-Star*, best at **175 gm**) The kids loved it as they always do and we tossed that thing for quite some time until I could determine who should take it away and leave them all on "auto-pilot." Remember, it is not just a flying disc; it is a tool to communicate and share with people, to tap into that exhilarating feeling of blessed freedom within our souls. Each person that allows himself/herself to fly it becomes thrilled by it. ***This I promise!*** *It should not be put away and forgotten.* -- I will observe the ritual until I can no longer breathe -- I was thirsty, so I went inside the house looking for relief. I met this old man inside and asked him what there was to drink. So he picked up his machete and started whacking away at this coconut with two or three strikes and, voilà, a delicious coco water. A unique and refreshing taste, not like what I tasted from our stores stateside. And then it happened again, another musical gem. This ten year old girl starts singing with all kinds of emotion, Mandy Moore's *Have A Little Faith In Me*. I recorded the whole song, just as I had the old man singing *New York, New York*. There's nothing I enjoy more than the chance encounter of a musical performance, whether solo or group, that fills your heart with hope for this world. Probably the most impressive of these musical opportunities was a group of youth in concert all playing steel drums. Ena had taken me to a church buffet and you could not help but be wowed to hear their precision and expert talent. I felt like, 'This is the footage my audience will see and hear as credits roll at the end of my video montage of sweet Jamaica!' And so it came to be.

Preparing To Set Sail From Arizona to Florida via the Bob Marley Peace Machine
It was not so easy to leave this island of paradise and beauty and return to Arizona and the job I had with Matheson Tri-Gas. I was a filler of industrial and medical gases including: O_2, Ar, N_2, CO_2, He, etc. I first worked for MTG in 1998, in Apache Junction, AZ. I had permission to park my motor home on the premises, and had a key to enter the building where I had access to a fridge, microwave, and phone. Also, with a simple shower head attached to a hose and the sink faucet in the bathroom, I could take showers because the concrete floor graded to a drain in the center of the room. This arrangement was a win-win for MTG. They had been getting broken into repeatedly and welders had been stolen from the showroom floor on more than one occasion. That all changed once they had a built-in security guard, the *Bob Marley RV*, parked there every night. I am indebted to Jeremy Malcolm, my supervisor for three years and a great human being, for accepting me for who I was and for giving me the trust that he did.

After my return from Jamaica, I was convinced that I needed to return to the island with the Peace Machine, do a tour of the entire island and write a book about the island, the culture, the people. My plan was to document extensively with photos and video and produce a comprehensive documentary of this cradle of reggae. When you make really big plans like this, you always have to be cognizant of that operating principle that you have no control over, namely, *"Life is what happens to us while we are making other plans."* I was putting a lot of passion and energy into the planning of this project. I felt that I probably had until the following summer to prepare carefully for all the things that would be required for this undertaking. I asked my welder friend Vaughan Pruitt to build a second level that could support several people at a time, complete with side rails and a 2'X2' opening for access into the motor home. I needed an upper deck to increase the living space and to have a platform for video-taping from a high vantage point. I also had a tent that would allow sleeping quarters upstairs if needed. The system worked out pretty well when it was put to the test with Gladys and her kids at Rocky Point *(Puerto Peñasco, MX)* one weekend. By the end of July, 2001, I was ready to leave my extended circle of social interaction and begin my journey. I would be making one more stop before setting out for Florida. I had a number of connections with the Native American community, none closer than with my Pima friends Yoli and Happy Bear. I thought it would be fitting to leave from their home. They had bestowed upon me a necklace of friendship made of beadwork and bone that I treasured and I wanted their images in my mind as I left the Great State of Arizona, home of so many *"original landlords"* (to borrow from Casper), the Indigenous Native Americans, pushed into government-designated *'corrals'* known as *"reservations."* This necklace and the eagle feather given to me by another Native brother became symbols of my bond to all indigenous people and the connection we all share with **The Great Mystery**.

Affirmative Kindness In Action -- *My Belief System Is Tested*

I was on the road by the first week of August, 2001. I had a great collection of music with me just like when I had taken my mega bike trip. But I was a lot more wary of the vehicle that was carrying my entire life with me, a 26 year-old Dodge camper that had seen its better days. You certainly have a different confidence level when you're aboard a brand new BMW and <u>you</u> are the 26 year old- *1974 trip*. I had replaced the engine twice so I was confident that *it* would not be the weak link in any failure scenario. Well, I had reason to be concerned. I had gotten as far as Oklahoma when my rear axle broke in two. I was stranded on the side of the road. And I would have to spend my saved money to fix it. I was not in walking distance to any establishment. I thought about hitchhiking to the next exit but there was a pick-up truck parked about 50 yards up on my side of the highway. I decided to find out if I could seek assistance there. When I got to the vehicle, the windows were down and a guy was sleeping on the seat with just his pants on, clutching a tire iron in his hands. It looked strange. I had second thoughts.

I hesitated against my better judgment and tapped on the passenger side door. Who awakened to me was someone I would have preferred never to have met. I began to feel that I was being tested, to see if I was worthy enough to continue with my journey; first my axle and now this. He kept that tire iron in his hand waving it around muttering some nonsensical gibberish and acting very weird. I thought maybe I had made a bad decision. When he seemed to calm down a little and I felt I could converse with him, I calmly told him of my predicament and asked him if he could help me to get a tow truck to pull me out. He says to me, *"Did I scare you? Are you afraid of me?"* as he's clutching his tire iron in one hand and smacking his other one with it. I say to him, *'I am afraid of no man.'* Those might not have been the words he wanted to hear because he was about to make a living hell out of the next couple hours of my life. You've got to picture this: a raggedy-ass pick-up being wheeled by a certifiable nut-job from hell. I think from here on in he was bent on convincing me that I should be fearful of him. Wearing only a pair of beat up and torn pants, no shirt and barefoot, he fires up his engine, never letting go of that tire iron in his hand. *It's at times like these that I draw on the scariest moments of my life with my father, believing that no one could be scarier than him on his worst day; therefore I should be able to handle this or any other crazy confrontation in my path. There's obviously a real danger in underestimating the circumstances in cases like these when it might be much healthier to adopt a **flight** response rather than an 'I can **fight** him with my mind' response.* I was desperate for assistance of any kind, threw caution to the wind and jumped into his asylum. He proceeded to push his petal to the metal going as fast as that truck could go, way, way past the speed limit and swerving all over the roadway. And he would not slow down. This went on for quite some time. <u>Not</u> a very good feeling- this powerlessness, this victimization. All I could think to myself was, what a big mistake I had just made! As we approached an overpass, he quickly and abruptly turned off the highway onto an unpaved dirt road going as fast as he could until we ended up probably in his living room, under the freeway with garbage strewn all over the place. I figured that here must be his digs. And he turns to me and says, *"I could do anything I want now and nobody would know the difference. Are you scared yet?!"* I'm thinking to myself, *'Holy f*kin shit! Is this* *the way my life is going to end?!* No f*kin way, I need to confront his ass right now; I can suffer one hit of that iron and I have an equal chance to kick *his* ass!' **But** I said to him, *'Look, if you're gonna fuckin do something, do it! I don't have time to fuck around with you!'* Not including the beating I received at the hands of the Hartford PD in 1976, the above scenario is probably the scariest situation I ever faced. "*Lucky*" for me, after a while, this character from another, *nonordinary reality* (as Don Juan would say) returned me to civilization and I was able to enter my world once again. *After some time thinking about this event over and over in my mind, I believe now that things did not escalate because I had refrained from a physical response as my first option and instead found myself using affirmative kindness* in its place; *kindness* is a powerful tool and can be a weapon and cure-all to heal the need.

Beginning Life Once Again With A New Challenge: Sometimes We Need To Change The Dream

My plan to ship Peggy Sue to Jamaica was stymied from the start. When I called the first shipping company, I learned that only recent model vehicles were permitted to enter their country and mine certainly did not qualify. My dream was not to be. I had spent a lot of my saved up money to get this far and now I needed to start working immediately. I found a labor pool, Tandem, at the intersection of 441 and Sheridan Rd. in Hollywood. I got sent out to Weston, FL, where a new high school that would be called *Cypress Bay* was being built. I befriended the foreman of all the labor crews on the site, a guy from Nicaragua, Jaime Cortez. I really wanted a full time job, not this day labor way of surviving from one day to the next. So, after awhile, I pleaded with Jaime to see if he could get me in with one of the contractors. He was friends with the sheetrockers and wall finishers, put in a good word for me, and I started working for E&M Contractors, a totally Latin construction outfit. I was the only non-Latino working for them. Only a few of them knew any English but that was just fine by me; I was trying to improve my Spanish. I got to be pretty good friends with Humberto Garcia *(Tico)* from Venezuela.

SOS *The Human Species: Are We Doomed To Extinction ? Will We Ever Stop Going To War?*

Can We Ever All Live Together In Peace?   PEACE ⧗ NOW

One day Humberto and I were carrying a heavy load of sheetrock from one building to the next and we overheard all this commotion from this worker who had a radio with him, "Man, somebody just crashed a plane into The World Trade Center in New York." My very first thought was, 'I don't think you can accidentally crash into the WTC.' And then we all hear about the second direct hit with another plane-- and that's when you know you're *under attack!* Now the fear is, 'How much more of this is going to happen? Will the White House or Capitol building be next?' I was worried about that sacred ground and the *Statue of Liberty* as the symbol of Freedom for all of the world's people. And then the first comforting thought comes across the radio, "They've grounded all flights in the country." Now we can't wait to finish the day's work so we can race home and glue ourselves to the non-stop coverage. It was pretty scary shit as we all know. And we all knew we would be at war. What's new? My whole life we have been at war. The wars just seem to dovetail into each other; ad infinitum: WW I, WW II, Korean War, Vietnam War, Iraqi War, the War in Afghanistan. Will it ever end? I think we humans are bent on our own self-destruction. Up to now we've managed to survive as a species. But the prognosis is not good. So many good minds know what to do but do not have enough power to sway the ones who do:
"The cause of War must be removed. Each nation's rights must be secure from violation. Above all, from the human mind must be erased all thoughts of War as a solution. Then and only then will War cease."
Haile **Selassie I**, H.I.M. - May 8, 1945, Declaration on VE Day, (Victory in Europe Day, end of WWII)
"Killing under the cloak of war is no different than murder." Albert **Einstein**
"Have we not come to an impasse in the modern world that we must love our enemies—or else?
The chain reaction of evil-hate begetting hate, wars producing more wars—must be broken, or else we shall be plunged into the dark abyss of annihilation." Martin Luther **King, Jr.**

80

The following is from, _Wisdomkeepers:_ _Meetings_ _With_ _Native_ _American_ _Spiritual_ _Elders_. Take a listen to the words of wisdom from Tadodaho Chief Leon Shenandoah Haudenosaunee, "Speaker of the House" of the fifty coequal "peace chiefs" comprising the Grand Council of the Six Nations Iroquois Confederacy in upper New York State, _("This confederacy was founded about 1000 A.D. by a prophet called the Peacemaker, who brought a 'Great Law of Peace' to the then warring Iroquois peoples.")_

October 25, 1985. **"We must stand together, the four sacred colors of man, as** the **one family** that we are in the interest of peace. We must abolish nuclear and conventional weapons of war. When warriors are leaders, you will have war. We must raise leaders of peace. _We must unite the religions of the world as the spiritual force strong enough to prevail in peace._ ☿ ✝ ☪ ✡ ☸ ✚ ☬ _It is no longer good enough to cry peace. We must act peace, live peace, and march in peace in alliance with the people of the world. We are the spiritual energy that is thousands of times stronger than nuclear energy. Our energy is the combined will of all people with the spirit of the Natural World, to be of one body, one heart, and one mind for peace. We propose, as a resolution of peace, that October 24th be designated as a Day of Peace, and a worldwide cease-fire take place in honor of our children and the Seventh Generation to come._ Day nay toh, Tadodaho Chief LSH." _Our Native brothers have a lot to teach us but we're not listening._ *We should be observing all of October as RELIGIONS UNITE MONTH until the goal of peace is actually achieved among all nations. That would be **True Synergy** on a global scale for **World Survival** – And most importantly, ***October 2**nd**, the birthday of Mahatma Gandhi, must always be observed and commemorated as the **International Day of Non-Violence:**

"An eye for an eye only ends up making the whole world blind." Mohandas Karamchand **Gandhi**

"Those who make peaceful revolution impossible will make violent revolution inevitable." **JFK**

"If you want to make peace with your enemy, you have to work with your enemy. Then he becomes your partner. Nelson **Mandela**

"When the power of love overcomes the love of power, the world will know peace." **Sri Chinmoy** Ghose

"Imagine all the people living life in peace. You may say I am a dreamer, but I'm not the only one. I hope someday you'll join us, and the world will be as one." John **Lennon** _If all nations treated each other peaceably with respect, we would realize world peace – the world would be as one. But the continued use of weapons of WAR to solve problems among nations precludes any such possibility. The military industrial complex is a self-perpetuating monster that will stop at nothing! JFK tried to abolish it and was assassinated for it. Humanity is at stake. The uniting of all religions to act in unison holds some promise- but there is more hope here:_ See p. 36

How To Turn A Loss Into A Gain – Venezuelan Culture & Hospitality

Humberto and I became pretty good friends. We teamed up when possible at the construction job in Weston. Unlike the other workers, his English was very good and he helped greatly with my Spanish.

He had a girlfriend In Venezuela and had been making plans to return to his country to be with her and her two kids. He called her every day with somebody else's cell phone and unknowingly (due to misinterpretation of the rate per minute the phone was being charged), ran up a phone bill of close to $1000. He came to me for a loan so I could help him pay it off. I really wasn't in any position to loan money to anyone nor did I like the idea of personal loans either, but I made an exception and gave him $400. When the weeks turned into months, I realized I probably would not see a return of the "loan."

It was fast becoming time for him to leave the US, so I made him a proposition. I said something like, 'Humberto, I know you're not going to pay back the $400 I loaned you and I don't want to be out the $400 either. So, to make it even, how about if I take a trip to your country and you cover my expenses for room and board for two weeks?' He thought this was a good idea and so I started planning to visit my first Latin American country. Maybe I would meet that Latin woman of my dreams and begin a relationship, who knows. I was excited to be visiting South America. (I was never one to lose sight of the fact that good things can happen _when preparation meets opportunity._ I prefer not to rely upon "luck")

The vacation would be from Christmas through the first week of January, 2002. Humberto lived in Maracaibo, a major city in the northwestern part of Venezuela. He took me to his mother's home where

I was introduced to his entire family. This was a well-to-do family. His Mom Virginia had her PhD in Social Work and is a professor with *La Facultad de Humanidades, Universidad del Zulia*. One of his brothers was also a teacher and played the family piano to perfection. Another brother was into electronics and was a computer savant. His sister was a lawyer. Only Humberto had not found a profession and was not sure what he was doing with his life. They had a maid and she cooked fantastic meals and you just couldn't imagine any better hospitality than what I was shown by all of them. I was thrilled to be there and realized that no amount of money could pay for all that I received from them. *(I couldn't help feeling that the decision I had made to come to this country was one of the best ones I had ever made.)* I photographed everything, determined to put together an album of my trip and send it to Humberto's Mom as a thank you for all their hospitality. It was almost Christmas and in preparation for this day the Venezuelans have a tradition of making *hallacas* at this time. It's a family enterprise. They are similar to the Mexican tamales. However, the food items which include a mixture of beef, pork, capers, raisins, olives, and boiled egg, are wrapped in cornmeal dough and then in plantain leaves bound with string.

Several members of the family including myself set up a production line since there are so many steps to putting these things together. I had the final position of tying the finished *hallaca* with string before boiling it. And oh, so good! -- just like the *ponche de crema*, an eggnog with rum made with condensed milk that was sure to follow. It was a great Christmas in a very loving household. I was blessed!

Hallacas tied and ready to cook

Chepina Josefina Barrios Nava ♡

Time to take a trip to the mountains. I met Humberto's fiancée and her two kids and we all planned a trip to El Tejar, Chiguara, about a 4-hour bus ride into the mountainous terrain south of Lake Maracaibo, the largest lake in South America and one of the oldest in the world according to fossil records.   His fiancée's mother and her extended family of brothers and sisters lived there with their mother. This was a large family of four brothers and four sisters, all in their 30's & 40's. I met *Chepina Josefina Barrios Nava*, 38 years old. I was immediately attracted to her. She had a great, playful personality and we shared a lot of conversation together. A very attractive woman, she was a physical education instructor at the local school. She would come up the hill to her home each day after school and I would be waiting for her so I could take off her shoes and give her a thorough massage. (I had taken a course in Reflexology from Judi Campanaro and knew how to give a good, therapeutic massage.) She loved it. Her sisters and mother started lining up, wanting some of that TLC I was dispensing, so I literally had my hands full each day. Chepina did most of the cleaning and cooking for the family and she was very dedicated to her ailing and very aged Mom. Her mother suffered greatly from varicose veins, was hardly ambulatory at all, and would just sit there day in and day out under the shade of her favorite tree on the property looking out into the valley below, reminding me of Samuel Beckett's play, *Waiting for Godot*, or waiting for her God to take her. She obviously missed her husband and companion who had long since passed and now was very much alone, even with all her children around her.

Chepina made the best tasting *arepas*, cornmeal pockets deep fried with cheese inside. We talked about our lives. I suggested she come to visit me in Florida. I would pay her way and she could stay with me. As a professional with property in her name (she was building her own home there at the time), she would be able to get a tourist visa with no problem. She thought this would be a good idea. The only problem I was having with her is that she was holding back emotionally. When I tried to kiss her on the mouth, she would turn away and let me kiss her on the cheek instead. She had talked about a relationship she had with some guy but said it was over. However, I felt that she was not completely over him and could not offer any degree of commitment to me. I felt like she really liked me but didn't know if she could really do this with me; that is, consider a relationship with this gringo in Florida. But at this point I was willing to accept things as they were. I returned to Florida hopeful but guarded about my involvement with this very special lady. And then Fate stepped in and changed everything.

Socaman Cliff Mayers & Wylefyah Band – *Bayside Amphitheater, Miami, FL* www.wylefyah.com

March 30, 2002. This was a very fateful day. I went to see my favorite music group, *Socaman Cliff Mayers & Wylefyah Band*, at Bayside Park in downtown Miami. A very talented Caribbean band playing Reggae, Soca, and Calypso music with members from Jamaica, Grand Cayman and Miami, they often appeared at Bayside's amphitheater near to the water's edge. Quite the picturesque setting. The free concert program that Miami sponsors here is a big people favorite. And the two types of music that bring overflowing crowds to this venue are Reggae and Latin music. Some days I danced to the music in front of the band, other days I just sat on the tiered concrete seating provided. This day I was an observer. I was watching this Latin woman dance with long black hair and big dark sunglasses. She had a black dress on cut above the knees and was barefoot, dancing quite well. After awhile, she caught my eyes trained on her and beckoned me down to the dance floor with her forefinger. So I get up, walk down the bench seats to the dance floor. A friend of hers says to me, "She doesn't speak any English; she wants you to kiss her, and she wants me to take a picture of you two kissing." I'm thinking to myself, 'This is progressing quite well. A Latin woman who is a total stranger wants me to kiss her. How cool is that?' So, without hesitation, I put my arms around her and planted my mouth to hers. *(Something I couldn't accomplish with Chepina in one week's time!)* And as I started to break away from her, I felt her come back to me for another go round, which I didn't respond to. I couldn't believe it!

The band started playing some reggae music and I let loose. I'm a totally free form dancer and reggae music is what I live to dance to. I went off. She couldn't believe this Americano so into his groove. And when they started playing some calypso music, *she* really started to shine on the dance floor. So we had something in common; we both loved to dance. After the band finished their set, she grabbed me by the arm as if to say, "He's with me; he's mine." It gave me pause that this woman was so aggressive, so forward with the kissing and now with conducting me to where she was sitting. I dismissed these early cues out of hand preferring to think that maybe this was the opportunity of a lifetime I had been waiting for. Finally, a Latin woman comes into my life when I'm not even looking for anybody; just minding my business listening to music. I should have paid more attention to the second thoughts I was having.

One needs to cultivate and utilize one's inner voice to promote self-preservation – soliloquy for survival -

We left together and I introduced her to *Peggy Sue*. She didn't run away; so I guess I passed the litmus test (didn't think I was too weird). It was quite a bit for her to take in, having recently come from South America. (Actually, it was quite a challenge no matter where you were from.) Turned out we had a couple more things in common. She had just arrived from Rosario, Argentina, in August of 2001. She had just gotten out of a 14-year relationship with a boyfriend. I had just arrived to Miami in August of 2001 as well and had come out of a 14-year relationship to Jennifer Rebholz. She introduced herself as Lolita (but I found out later that her name was Monica). She preferred to be called Lolita, so that's what I and everybody else called her. She took me to meet her friends in Miami Beach from her hometown in Rosario. They were very gracious, friendly folks and to this day we remain friends, Beatriz and Hugo De Vito and their two sons Kenneth and Dylan. I also got to meet her really good friends from Mar del Plata in Argentina, Laura Buccico and Luis Fioritto and daughters Maria Ines and Maria Emiliay. Our relationship had begun. She was living in South Miami around Caribbean Boulevard working as a caretaker for the elderly and I was living on the premises of the Cypress Bay jobsite in Weston.

Follow The Signs When They Are Presented To You – Men: Think With Your Higher Head

I made the long and expensive trip from Weston to Perrine every weekend to see Lolita. After a few weeks of this, we decided to put our energies together and rented an apartment by the bay, at 34th and Biscayne Boulevard. She got a job locally and started bicycling to work. I would meet her two or three blocks from home with fresh flowers every Friday or Saturday and walk her home. I was pretty excited about our new relationship and wanted to share the news with my best friend Gladys. I was hoping that the two favorite people in my life could become friends. I called Gladys, introduced her and the two of them began to talk, and continued to do so for quite some time. After about 15-20 minutes, Lolita hands me the phone, and I was anxious to hear what Gladys had to say. And to my shock and alarm, she says, *"Congratulations, Dennis, you're going to be a father!"* Why 'alarm' and 'shock' that your woman is going to have a baby? How about if you had a vasectomy about a year before! So I tell Gladys I don't know anything about her being pregnant and I'll have to give her a call back. Then I turn to you know who and ask her, *'Is it true. Are you pregnant?...Is it true...are you?'* (Of course I'm speaking in Spanish as Lolita knows no English.) She wouldn't answer me. I wouldn't relent, *'Que es la verdad? Es verdad, si o no? Necessito saber la verdad'.* Finally, she shakes her head affirmatively. Then I tell her I had a vasectomy a year before, so who's baby is it? Another round of interrogation until I get an answer.

This went on for some time and finally she took it back, saying she made it up. *'Why did you make it up?'* Her answer really pissed me off and began to open my eyes up to just exactly who this woman was and how far she would go to defraud the truth. She answered me this, *"I lied to Gladys because I saw how close the two of you were and I wanted to make her jealous."* I couldn't f*king believe it! So I got right back on the phone to Gladys and told her this. She was livid. She said she didn't want anything further to do with her, that as of that moment forward, she had "scratched" her out of her life. *"You and I will remain friends, but I don't want anything to do with her!"* This was terrible news and it started to make me wake up about the woman I had chosen to be with. She obviously had some deep seated

84

issues relating to jealousy (*celos enfermisos*, the jealousy sickness) and what had just transpired was a foreboding omen that I refused to act upon or do something about. *(I had actually arranged to fly back to Arizona but I cancelled that flight at the last minute, preferring not to end the relationship.)* And I would pay a very dear price for that inaction. I would call this the *first crisis* in our relationship.

Lulu At The Hitching Post (Lucille DesRoches & Bob Glemboski)

We planned to attend my sister Lucille's wedding in October of 2002. We would have to take a bus from Miami to Hartford. Anybody who's ever taken a bus ride for more than a 1000 miles knows that it's not a very pleasant experience. You don't really get to sleep; you're constantly awakened and moved right along. It was time for my family to meet Lolita and for her to get to know my family. She met Michael first who picked us up at the bus station and then he drove us to Dad's house where she met the infamous Leo the Lip and his wife Christine. Lucille was about to marry a great guy, Bob Glemboski, a man who, from all accounts of my family members was a tremendous person for Lulu. I was happy that she had found a loving, caring, dedicated man in her life. And if that wasn't enough (which it was), he was a successful engineer as well. So, everybody was happy for Lucille and Bob. My sister had a very elegant wedding and everyone had gotten an opportunity to meet my fiancée. Lolita was now a member of the family. We spent time at my mother's house in Wethersfield with her husband John Bukowski, where Lolita had an opportunity to bond with the other half of my parentage. She was in store for lots of good cooking and baked perfections. Inevitably, we needed to make the joyride back and so we did.

Peggy Sue Moves On

After Cypress Bay High School had been completed came the inevitable lay-offs. I took a course to be a security guard and got licensed but ended up doing work in some medical facility instead. After 9/11, work was not as plentiful. A lot of companies were getting reluctant to hire. A universal hiring freeze seemed to be in the wind. I had given up a good paying job with benefits in Arizona believing I could chart my life as a photo-journalist in Jamaica and now I found myself unemployed with no prospect to fulfill that dream/lofty goal. I called MTG but they had no openings. Every couple of months I would check back to see when they might be accepting applications once again. One day while arriving at the medical facility that I worked at, my brakes failed. Serious damage had been done to my front end and parts could not be found in wrecking yards or by computer or by any means possible. I called a tow company and had *Peggy Sue* towed to the street in front of our apartment building. I was with the driver in his tow cab, Gilberto, Cubano, as he spoke to me in Spanish saying how much he liked my ride and how some day he and his wife would love to have something like this. He told me how he had spent some real time in prison for selling marijuana and how his life had been set back. *Peggy Sue* remained there on the street for about two weeks until one morning I came out and found it placarded by Miami Police. I was informed that if the vehicle was not moved within 24 hours, they would have it moved and I would pay for the expense. So I called Gilberto and told him that today was his lucky day and he didn't have to wait any more for that dream to come true. No money exchanged. A motor home complete with a radically redecorated interior, perfect for a Rasta man or similarly-minded individual, with an awesome sound system, and the energy of peace, love, and understanding from six years of irie souls enjoying its ramparts. In the act of giving, one doth receive. I was thinking now of Paul Simon's great song, "*She Moves On*" (from _The Rhythm of the Saints_, 1990, with guitar arrangement by Cameroonian

guitarist Vincent Nguini). So long, *Peggy Sue*. Everything must evolve ↺ -- *we can't stand still* -- ⤳ ∞

Chapter 22: *Struggling To Survive, A Marriage & Love Triangle -- Surprise Visit*

Good-byes are never easy, but one must move on. So now I would have to learn the bus system. My job was not close; it took two buses about 45 minutes to get to work. I would have to make the adjustment. It was December just before Christmas, 2002. A knock came to our apartment door.

I open the door and can't believe my eyes! *'Tommy! What the hell ?* (as we give each other a big hug) How'd you find this place? I can't believe you're here.' *"Hey, Den, come on outside, I want to show you something."* Lolita and Tom greet and we all three truck downstairs. We exit the building and he walks us over to the street where Peggy Sue used to park, and says to me, *"I heard you lost your RV and needed some wheels, so I brought this down for ya."* 'WHAT!! I CAN'T F*KIN BELIEVE YOU!'

And now we are the owners of a 1987 Nissan Stanza 4-door sedan, a car he had purchased new and maintained religiously and was in great shape! How the hell do you like that?! Check it out; *what goes around comes around, both bad and good. It's that* Karma principle from Buddha Teaching (Dharma) [Hinduism and Buddhism]. My brother Tom or as I liked to call him, *TomCat Kid*, had put the car on an Amtrak train and had it shipped to Miami (Tom was a Supervisor for Amtrak). That was really special. And that's the way Tom was, totally unselfish and giving, personifying loving kindness and compassion. He had only one night to spend with us before catching a train ride back to Connecticut, so we took him to Bayside which had been transformed into a festival of Christmas celebration with the world's tallest Christmas tree (so they were claiming). We shared some grub and grog and talked about our lives until the *Z's* won us over. Thank you, Tom. You're the greatest. And soon it was time to part ways once again. And as you may know, good-byes are never easy. We jumped into that little Nissan and to the train station we went. I forgot what it was like to drive a *'normal'* vehicle and pay so little to go so far. Tommy really boosted our QOL, our quality of life. We could go shopping, visit Bayside or our friends in Miami Beach so much more cheaply and efficiently. We were back in the game.

Hard Times Lead To Windfall & Re-Employment

Over the next 5 or 6 months, we struggled to make ends meet. I wasn't getting any help from Lolita for the rent or any other expenses because she was sending all her money to her daughter and mother back home in Argentina. It was a theme that would play out for our entire relationship; what I made was for us; what she made was for her and hers. I always felt a sense of abandonment towards our relationship by her. When I would talk to her about this; how difficult it was for me to provide for everything with such a small income, she would say that where she came from, the man takes care of everything. I tried to reason with her that in this day and age it takes two to make it happen in a relationship, two who are a part of providing for each other. I would question her, 'Where is the <u>we</u> in our relationship; you never say <u>we</u>.' These were further *cues* that things were just not right in our relationship. (I was reminded of Charles Horton Cooley's *"<u>The</u> <u>Looking</u> <u>Glass</u> <u>Self</u>" – pay attention to the cues in your environment*)

Observe – Observe – Observe

At about this time, I received a letter in the mail from my father. He had made a very big decision. He said in his letter that he wanted to disburse his inheritance to his eight children. He said he wanted to be alive and see what each person would do with his estate rather than pass on not knowing. He had only one requirement; that we use the money for something good; that we not waste it away. So I held this check for $10,000 in my hands, thinking, *'Cool beans! I can do so much with this!* Thanks, Dad, you're a life safer!' I decided that I wouldn't touch this gift until I could put it towards the purchase of a home for us. I'm not sure how much time passed from the receipt of this windfall when another good piece of news was headed my way. I received a phone call from Arizona; Matheson Tri-Gas had called to tell me I could have my old job back; they needed a filler for their new operations in Phoenix. But I had to get there as soon as possible. After brainstorming the possible actions I could take, I decided to fly back to Phoenix, begin once again with MTG, and search for a mobile home that would be in the budget I had at my disposal. Then I could return to Miami for Lolita, ship our possessions via UPS, and drive our little blue Nissan with all of our personals across country. When I arrived in Phoenix and reported to

MTG, their offer had changed. They informed me that a day or two after they had offered me back my job, a company-wide employment freeze of all MTG facilities nationwide had been instituted. They could not hire me back as an employee; but if I wanted to work as a sub-contractor with no benefits (medical, vacation, 401K), they could hire me on that basis, of course not at the rate they had quoted me in Miami. One has one's doubts about the inner workings of corporate America; I had already seen what Rockford Corporation was capable of doing. I had to take what I could get. I was not about to look this gift horse in the mouth, even though it was suspected of having *hoof-in-mouth* disease. *(This was August of 2003. By March of 2004, I was re-hired with full benefits and it became a moot point.)*

A New Home, Car & Marriage In Apache Junction, Arizona

Thanks to my friend Christel Reuther, I had a home to stay in while I searched for a mobile home to buy. She helped me look at homes and one in particular seemed promising. I put $5000 down (1/4) and moved into the Raindance Mobile Home Park on Tomahawk Road in Apache Junction, close by and in view of the Superstition Mountains, famous for lost gold treasures of some old time prospectors. I picked out an engagement diamond ring and returned to Miami for Lolita. I shipped the bulk of our possessions via UPS to our new mobile home address. That little Nissan Stanza from my brother Tommy made it across country without a hitch. We were most grateful. I worked out a trade with my mechanic, my Acoustat speaker system and Hafler amplifier for his 1988 Toyota Celica. Now Lolita had a little red sports car of her own. She got a job working as a cashier in a *gasolinera*, a mini-mart with attached gas pumps. She still couldn't speak English but understood enough to enable the basic transactions required of her in this capacity. She was good with numbers and very detail-oriented.

Everything seemed to be going well and we began making plans to marry on Valentine's Day, 2004.

Then I get the shocking news from my sister Lucille that Dad had passed away on January 5, 2004, following the onset of sepsis from a gall bladder infection. Only a couple of weeks earlier I had been on the phone with him inviting him to the wedding, fully expecting him to make it. Life happens; plans change. *"You can't always get what you want but if you try some time, you just might find, you get what you need."* *(Rolling Stones)* We really wanted him to be at the wedding but he just couldn't make it. But he gave us what we really needed, a home of our own. Thanks, Dad. **R.I.P.** Lenny D. Denny D

I introduced Lolita to my very good friends Terry and Patricia Wright of Cave Creek, AZ. Terry piloted commercial business jets for a living and Pat ran their two restaurants, *Emire's*. She wore all the hats: cook, baker, hostess and was the indefatigable spirit and personality of this chic, specialty eatery. We had run into them at a famous watering hole in Scottsdale, AZ -- *Greasewood Flat*, and when we told them we were making plans to tie the knot, they insisted on having the occasion at their home, a beautiful horse property in the sparsely populated outskirts of the town of Cave Creek. We wanted the date to be Valentine's Day but Terry's boss wanted to be flown to Canada with his girlfriend. So we moved it up to the following Saturday. Pat was the perfect hostess and created the most beautiful setting for our special day. Lots of great people and family and stories around the campfires. Two of the best friends one could ever have, Terry and Pat Wright, the pride of Texas and South Dakota.

Close To The Breaking Point: I Maneuver My Way Out of Hell (MTG: Matheson Tri-Gas)

(Phoenix MTG) I was living in Apache Junction. The MTG plant in Phoenix was 33 miles away. The summers in the Phoenix latitude of Arizona are brutal. They keep records for how many days consecutively there are in excess of 100 degrees, and the record is not far from 100 in a row! My new supervisor in Phoenix was not like the all-American personality Jeremy Malcolm I had at MTG's Apache Junction location, a supervisor who showed a great deal of empathy in his capacity as employee advocate for his workers. No, this was a hard-driven man, exacting unrealistic expectations of his employees and causing them one by one to seek employment elsewhere. I was expected to fill cylinders

all day with the various gases, then load four trucks all night for all of the drivers. I was putting in 10, 12 or even 14 hour days to get all this done; it was too much for any one person to do. I had the good fortune to meet and befriend David Andrew, the man in charge of regional operations for MTG. After confiding in him all that I was going through and all that was going on with this Phoenix operation, I put in for a transfer to Florida, since David Andrew had come from the Southeast region as head honcho. It took two years to materialize, but a transfer finally came through. It was February, 2006, and I was more than ready to roll back to Florida with a 'life-saving' transfer to work at the Ft. Lauderdale filling plant.

Mark Myhr Saves The Day

My father's wife Christine passed away only about 6 months after he did, from cancer. She was outlived by her daughter from another relationship and by her son, our brother Mark. They would inherit the proceeds from the sale of Dad's home, and that didn't sit well with all of Dad's children. It's times like these that make you realize what a person is made of, what their principles are and exactly what priorities they hold near and dear to their own self. Mark Myhr (DeRoche) did not hesitate. He divided his half of the proceeds among all of his siblings, even though he hardly knew them, having lived most of his life clear across the country in California. I was reminded of Mark's actions when I came across the following passages, attributed to Confucius in the _Book of Changes_ or the _I Ching_:

In Appendix I, Chapter XXVI, "the good fortune attached to the subject's not seeking to enjoy his revenues in his own family shows how talents and virtue are nourished."

In Appendix II, Chapter XXXVII, "As wind comes first from fire, so does transforming influence emanate from the family."

In Appendix II, Chapter XLI, "The aim of the superior man is simply to be increasing what others have; --that and nothing else."

I think these three statements eminently describe the actions of Mark DeRoche Myhr. Thank you Mark, my brother -- _And speaking of "threes" - congratulations on placing 3rd in your age group during the Tri Santa Cruz International Distance Triathlon 2015 and for finishing 458 out of 1700 participants in the Big Kahuna Triathlon aka IRONMAN 70.3 SANTA CRUZ held Sept. 13, 2015 - I now pronounce you Super-Jock of the DeRoche and Myhr clans! Folks, that's a 1.2 mile ocean swim, a 56 mile bike ride and a half marathon 13.1 mile run!! And he did it in 5:38:43 **at age 43**!_   _(40:31)_   _(2:40:10)_   _(2:08:36)_
(5:29:17 + T-times)

Problems In The Bedroom & In The Pocket Book

Lolita was hungry to experience as many famous places as North America had to offer. The problem was, we really couldn't afford taking plane flights, renting cars, paying for hotels and restaurants and all the other expenses incurred on these adventures without running up more and more credit card debt. We went to Kauai, Hawaii, for our honeymoon for two weeks, Las Vegas for a week, and to San Francisco for a week. In addition to those outlays, we both travelled to Rosario, Argentina, for two weeks (plane flight for two=$1500). So, financially, a hole was being dug, and it didn't feel very good.

It was time for me to make that cross country voyage one more time. Lolita would not follow for eight more months. She _"didn't want to give up her job"_ as assistant manager of the mini-mart; so I would be going solo. Our relationship had cooled down during the last year of our time together in Arizona. I had unsettling feelings that she might be seeing another man. She began asking me to sleep in our spare bedroom, preferring to have the queen-size bed all to herself, dismissing out of hand my suggestion of her involvement in any extra-marital affair. These misgivings were to prove all too accurate as I would learn further on in our relationship. I would call this the _second crisis_ in our relationship.

"Flight of The Eagle" -- Thinking of Krishnamurti And The Responsibilities Of Freedom –
& The Wisdom of Charles Darwin

Jiddu Krishnamurti preached freedom, setting man free from his cages and fears, *"You have to be your own teacher and your own disciple. You have to question everything that man has accepted as valuable, as necessary."* dd: It is only when you truly start thinking what your life requires and are willing to put the necessary energy towards its actualization that you find yourself in control and can accomplish so much more with a clear vision of the process towards those goals. I had just freed myself from the *cage* of the Phoenix plant operations and the *fears* of my marital relationship and was ready to re-establish my life, single if necessary, once again. *I have come to view adaptability and flexibility as two of my biggest strengths.* And Charles Darwin would agree: *"It is not the strongest of the species that survives, nor the most intelligent that survives. It is the one that is most adaptable to change."*

I was ready *"to fly like an eagle"* -- I rented a U-Haul, loaded it up with most of our belongings, and towed the Nissan behind, saying *'enough! of this hot hell on earth,'* longing for a more normal climate once again that did not go practically a year without rain. I was fortunate that MTG kicked in for a relocation allowance, something I had to negotiate. Of course my supervisor wanted no part of that decision, but that was par for the course for him. David Andrew and my new southeast regional manager Ian Freedman made it happen. I had an orientation meeting with Ian Freedman and a walk-through of the Miami plant operations with Doug Mitchell, former ops manager turned sales manager. The Miami plant was a much more professionally-run operation. It was a much larger facility dealing with a much larger customer base. It felt so good to be in new surroundings *with no Simon Legree!*

MTG - Fort Lauderdale, Florida

I was needed at the much smaller Ft. Lauderdale facility to replace a filler position they had lost. I reported to Kim Strniste, the plant manager, a veteran of this gas filling business who hailed from Massachusetts. He was an ex-biker like myself, though of Harley ilk - but at least we had a little bit in common. He was one of those individuals that commanded your respect immediately- not because of his bald-headed, 6' 1" muscled frame totally covered in tattoos, kind of like Mr. Clean's outcast twin, but because he had a comprehensive knowledge of the business and a no-nonsense, let's-just-get-it-done attitude that was firm but fair. You had to like that. He wasn't there to overwork you; he just wanted to get a job done, and the drivers would be loading their own trucks, *not the filler!* So I was much happier in Florida than I could ever be in Arizona. I reported directly to the store manager, Tony Di Bruno, another supervisor who commanded your respect but from a much lower altitude and stouter position. Tony was very knowledgeable in the welding business, hailed from Pennsylvania, and knew the entire operation inside-out. He had been a filler and knew every aspect of my position and was kind of the resident troubleshooter-mechanic on premises for the pumping apparatus and all other physical plant requirements. Both he and Kim were versed in the MTG manual of protocols and procedures and educated me further in the knowledge of such. I liked to think of the three of us as the "boys of the North" making it happen for the "people of the South." We were all very good at what we were there for. [I would like to thank Mark Walker for supporting me in my efforts to make a difference at MTG.]

Back To Mobile Home Living

Thanks to my brother Mark Myhr, I had enough funds to purchase another mobile home, this time in Seminole Park, in Hollywood, FL. The mobile home park was within the confines of the Seminole Indian Reservation and within walking distance from the famous *Hard Rock Hotel & Casino* in Hollywood where the troubled Anna Nicole Smith met her demise. The home needed a lot of repair and remodeling to make it livable; so I put every available hour and dollar towards its refurbishment. By the time Lolita finally made it to the property, I had installed a new pine laminate floor throughout the home, replaced the badly damaged ceiling and installed a new air conditioner and king size bed. She arrived in October of 2006, eight months after my arrival to Florida in February. I was feeling the pressure of the computer age and finally purchased my first PC in November, 2006, which I continue to be using at this time, an HP Pavilion dv6000 laptop. I put myself through a crash course to become computer literate with my

Russian friend Vilen Polyakovich from the Geek Squad at Circuit City and am happy to report that I feel very comfortable with the level of proficiency that I have acquired. You never know who becomes your friend in life. Take Vilen. I would pay him for one hour of his going rate to come to my home and school me, but he would stretch that hour into two and three at no additional charge. When I was down and out and had no funds and malware had messed up everything, he took my laptop to his home and fixed it at no charge. This is a genuinely caring individual. Thank you Vilen P for putting me on the electronic map, and for hooking me into cyberspace. I could now communicate with friends and family via e-mails and just in general realize an improved quality of life to survive in our fast-paced techno world.

We were not done squandering money we didn't have. Lolita wanted to see New York City, Niagara Falls and Washington, DC. So those trips were planned and actualized. In addition, we visited the *Georgia Aquarium* in Atlanta, GA, the world's largest with over 8 million gallons. I highly recommend this venue for the Wow factor, especially if you want to experience our seas' worlds intimately.

Credit card debt was now around $15K. I decided to put an end to this abuse. There would be no more trips. <u>There</u> <u>would</u> <u>be</u> <u>no</u> <u>more</u> <u>use</u> <u>of</u> <u>credit</u>. *It was time to pay off all this debt:* **MyTCA.org:**
(It took 5 years, from 2009 – 2014, to pay off $15K debt through this organization– referred to by **B** *of* **A**)
(Finally I could now begin to repay the $5K still due for my 2010 legal battle vs Fisher and Zeuner.)

As I had done in Arizona, I enrolled and paid for Lolita's membership in a health club. A former, very successful body builder, she would frequent LA Fitness twice or three times weekly -- essentially to swim laps, as she was an excellent swimmer. She started talking about a guy she had met there as if he were only an acquaintance, a guy named Greg. He turned out to be the guy she had met in Arizona and lived with during the months she had stayed behind. *(From her own confession to me after our divorce; he followed her out to Florida where his mother lives and stayed with her.)* The bedroom tells a lot.

You can look how well your relationship is progressing or regressing to some extent by how well things are going in the bedroom. And things for us had been steadily declining, for obvious reasons as it turned out. More and more, we became two separate individuals living in the same home, rarely doing anything together anymore. Lolita hardly ever cooked. I wasn't much better and so our eating habits revolved around weekly pizza on Fridays and weekly spaghetti on Sundays and fend for yourself otherwise. *(Oh, well, one is not always so fortunate to have that great cook in the kitchen. 'Can opener, please.')*

Eddie DesRoches Comes To Town

On the 1st or 2nd of July, 2007, I received a call from my long lost nephew Eddie DesRoches, son of my brother Richard. He was calling from the road somewhere in his trip across the U.S. from California, where he was working and living, to ask me if I could do him a favor. He was on his way to Miami to meet up with his wife from Colombia, Diana, and her son Sebastian who were due to arrive from Bogotá on the night of the 3rd. He realized he would not be able to make it to the airport on time and asked if I could go to the airport and meet her and take them to my home where he would arrive later that night or the next day. I told him no problem, don't worry about anything, I'll take care of it. I met Diana and her son very late that night. Their plane was delayed and international customs is no joke. I think we got to our home around 2:00 AM in the morning. Lolita poked her head out to acknowledge our guests and they retired to the room that had been prepared for their arrival. Eddie arrived the next morning with his trusty GPS navigator and a long overdue reunion of the two of us finally came to pass. I hadn't seen Eddie since he was a young kid, so to see him as a grown man and now married was like meeting someone for the first time. I think we hit it off real well. Where I was a fledgling neophyte with my computer, Eddie was a maestro, he really knew computers inside and out. He downloaded a bunch of stuff to improve the options I would have with my laptop. We made plans for the 4th of July. We would all go to Hollywood Beach for the day *(except Lolita who preferred not to share her day with the rest of us)* and then head out to Bayside to watch the fireworks at night on the water. It was a beautiful day, I would even call it a perfect day enjoying each other's company and all that Florida had to offer....

until we returned home (it was around 10:30 PM) ---

Marriage Irretrievable: The Death Knell Sounds

After a few trips unloading our beach gear, Lolita appeared at the door of our bedroom and motioned me to her in a loud whisper. She was upset that I had not gone to her as soon as we had arrived. I told her it was late and I didn't want to wake her. Then she says to me in a menacing tone, *"Tu eres calentón por ella!"* *("You have the hots for her!")* She is accusing me of having desires for my nephew's wife who I had just met the day before. I answered her, *'Tu eres loca?!'* *('Are you crazy?!')* And immediately she explodes in a full blown rage, attacking my face with both fists clenched as a man would attack another man. I had all I could do to raise my arms to block her incoming blows to my head, all the while yelling at her, *'Tu eres demasiado loca, no puedo vivir más contigo!'* *('You are too crazy, I can't live with you anymore!')* My nephew Eddie and his wife Diana were totally shocked by my wife's attack and decided to leave us alone until an hour or two later that night. It was a disastrous ending to an otherwise perfect day. I knew it was time to begin the process of divorce. I refuse to live with a woman who is prone to such violent and psychotic episodes. I catered to my father's mental illness his whole life; I wasn't about to start all over with another case of the same. I wanted a woman of peace and joy to spend my life in harmony with, growing together in love unending, *real love*. And I would insist upon it. *Nothing else mattered as much for my life.* [I have since learned to appreciate the *Transcendental Way of Zen*, p.116]

WANTON WEDNESDAY *September_19_2007* ‡

The Death Knell Sounds Again   Alan Watts – SUICIDE: https://www.youtube.com/watch?v=f_HkQ4-x4P4

Two and a half months later I received **the worst phone call of my entire life**. My sister Lucille was on the other end all choked up, and began, ever so slowly…I knew from her tone before she uttered even one more word after, "Den…," that someone had passed away-- you just know those phone calls when you get them. I figured my Mom's husband John who wasn't doing so well. She says "No." So I say, 'Mom?'- again, "No" and before I could continue this macabre guessing game, she says, *"Tom!"* I f*kin screamed!! **'WHAAAAAAAAAAAAAAAAAAAAAATTTTTTTTT!!!!!!!!!!!'** I lost it! I couldn't f*king believe it!!! 'What happened, a car accident???!!!' "The police found him hanging in the woods by his house." **Then I really lost it --** *I was destroyed!* Why in the f*king world did this guy, of all the people I know, do this?? Our youngest and favorite brother Tom who got along with everybody, had a wonderful wife and three really good kids and a beautiful home in Hebron, CT --- *how the hell was this even possible???*

That's the nature of suicide. There is no telling **why** or **how** sometimes, it's such a devastating crush on the senses, it's a loss that hits so deep and so hard that you're left reeling in an emotional fog of hurt and numbness for the longest time. As I'm writing this, we just passed the three year marker from that fateful day. It is still fresh and raw on the emotions. I called his wife Tina on the 19th to try to console her further and in the process console myself a little more. Tom was two days shy of his 51st birthday when he ended his suffering; he left a very detailed statement to each of his family members. It seemed to have been written with the calmest detachment from what he was about to do. He had dramatically surprised us and arrived in Miami at our doorstep in December of 2002, and now with even more drama five years later done the opposite and left us forever, **a huge shock and surprise to everyone ---**

I truly believe that each of us reserves the right to choose how we leave this world but what I have a real problem with is if we waste our life away prematurely, extinguishing our flame when there is so much life to be lived. If we are suffering mentally-emotionally, *there are many remedies available* that should be taken advantage of before such an ultimate and final decision is even given *any* consideration; *e.g.: the most powerful, transformative psychotherapeutic medicine ayahuasca also brings spiritual enlightenment.*(55)
* *"The art of living well and the art of dying well are one."* Epicurus

The Physical & Emotional Abuse Continues

In July, 2008, and not without some reservation, against my better judgment, I chanced to take Lolita to the home of my Haitian friend, Luis Alphonse, who was having some friends over to celebrate the arrival of his mother-in-law from Jamaica. I was talking with my friend's daughter for several minutes while Lolita was sitting close by on the other side of the table. When Lolita got up, I joined her and we started walking alongside the pool area. She reached up and dug her fingernails which were like knives deep into my neck until I started bleeding. Once again, irrational jealousy popped its ugly head in full view of an unbelieving public. My friend was speechless as was I. We picked up our things and left. That was the last social event I would attend with this violently aggressive woman, who had such deep-seated psychological and emotional baggage that no other outcome but a poisoned relationship could be the end result. I tried my best; I treated Lolita like a queen and tried to take her to all the places she dreamed of, even though we couldn't afford it. We certainly had some good times but we certainly could not continue on in life as we had been. I was looking for peace and harmony in my life, not confrontation and physical violence. I kept thinking of, *"Quien busca halla." ("Who seeks shall find.")* *One must always pay attention to that inner voice and follow one's heart. (soliloquy for survival & instinct)* Sometimes emotional abuse is as damaging or more so than physical abuse. When the first anniversary of my brother's suicide approached, we were not doing so well. When the actual day arrived, 9/19/08, we had an argument about something and as I was opening the door to leave the house, with vile in her voice, she says to me, *"Mátate hoy!" ("Kill yourself today!")* From that day forward, I had conducted myself as a single person in a dead marriage. Some things are forgivable; others are deal-breakers.

Chapter 23: I Chart My Own Course For A New Life -- Colombian Culture & Hospitality

A few months later, in December, Lolita left for a month's vacation to Argentina, due to return in the middle of January, 2009. I decided to take my own trip, to celebrate my birthday in Colombia. I made plans to visit Eddie and Diana in Tuluá, a small city southwest of Bogotá and northeast of Cali. I now considered myself single in my heart and was open to any new relationship that might come to pass. I was planning to begin the divorce process with money from my tax refund after my return from Colombia. Diana had talked about a friend she had who she thought I might like. So I was looking forward to meeting her. No one had informed me as I made my plans that she had moved to Panama, so I was surprised to not find her there when I arrived in Tuluá. But I had the opportunity to meet Diana's cousin *Claudia Lorenlai Quintero*, a very special lady who is also one of my best friends in life.

I had already been introduced to the culture of Colombia to a large extent by all the years in friendship with Gladys Caquimbo. Gladys' ability in the kitchen was legendary. I don't remember the names of a lot of the dishes she prepared; but if you were lucky enough to sit down at the table of Gladys, you were in for a memorable feast. Nobody can cook a fish, head and all, like the Queen of Cuisine, Ms. GQC, and her *sancocho* was always out of this world. I was blessed to share in such culinary exceptionalism.

In addition to Gladys' expertise in the kitchen, she was also involved with social causes. One of the events that Gladys put on was held at the famous Baseline Mansion in Phoenix, AZ. Her goal was to bring together as many different cultures as possible to share the music, arts and crafts, and food of the various ethnic backgrounds. She called it: *"Uni-Fest: A Multi-Cultural Awakening"*

She invited a group of her Colombian *gente* who put on a spectacular show complete with traditional costumes who told the story of the *campesino* with song and poetry. It was heartfelt. The musicians and singers were very moving. This was the culture of Colombia and I never saw it better represented than on this day, even after having visited the country in person. Gladys put on a truly good show!

Now in Colombia, the time for my birthday- January 11th had arrived. *I always have to give a shout out to Mary J. Blige who shares this day with me and hope that my niece Heather DesRoches also is enjoying her day as well.* I had the great pleasure to meet Diana's sister Dora and cousin, Claudia Lorenlai Quintero, and both the mothers of Diana and Lorenlai, all of whom shared the same home *(next page)*. I did a photo shoot of Lorenlai and her best friend Yurany Gue. They took me to a beautiful park, El Parque de la Guadua Tuluá, "Guillermo Ponce de León Paris" which was a dream setting for a photographer with its botanical gardens. This was the beauty of Colombia, a natural paradise to behold.

It was time to prepare for the party. We spent most of the day procuring provisions and getting everything ready. I met lots of people and had a tremendous day filled with special memories.

We enjoyed asado de carne punta de anca con papas cocinada y platano maduro asado. And of course, when in Colombia, one must have Cristal Aguardiente, a licorice tasting aperitif like ouzo or sambuca.

I can't remember a birthday party where I had so much fun! I really needed this time for all the suffering I had been going through in my marriage. And the best part was just about to begin.

I had brought my conga that has been in my life for over 25 years and all of my percussion instruments with me to share with the people, along with my lap top loaded with hundreds of music selections from the Latin and Reggae worlds. One of my favorite musicians in life is Carlos Vives, and his album, *Clasicos de la Provincia*, was the one I loved to play my conga to most of all; especially the song, '*La Gota Fría*.'

I love playing my conga more than anything in the world and I love to dance more than anything in the world as well, they are equally consuming experiences allowing the individual *to be totally real, totally free, and totally alive!* You just know this is what you should be doing and you want to share it with everybody else. I sometimes feel like a universal messenger with the mission to *spread the joy* to all! [My thanks to the Greek musician of the New Age genre, *Iasos*, and his album, Inter-Dimensional Music: Spread the Joy! *I was overwhelmed by the breathtaking sunrise at the top of Haleakalā, House of the Sun, over 10,000 feet high in Maui in 1979 as this music was being played, literally sending my soul into a higher dimensional realm. I had just completed a pilgrimage to the top of this sacred volcano that had once given birth to this Hawaiian island so many years ago- truly one of the best moments of my life!*]

We played Latin dance music well into the night with a house full of family and friends. It was special; an unforgettable experience in my heart and soul. *Gracias a toda mi gente! Viva Colombia!*

Tuluá, Colombia

Fresh grapes in market town Tuluá and a bamboo forest in El Parque de la Guadua Tuluá

Kindness and Compassion   *(the most important words in this book)*

The biggest takeaway from my readings of Buddha Teaching is that we humans come to that place within ourselves and AWAKEN to the knowledge that *lovingkindness* (sic), (also known as *metta*), *and compassion for others is the way* to relate to one another and the best way to maintain a cohesive community.   Just think if the majority of humans would embody this powerful way of communication and the *kind* of *world* we would be living in. Also, related to this concept is the 2nd of the Five Precepts Supporting Our Relationships, (from Steve Armstrong in *Voices of Insight*), which parallels the Christian teaching 'Turn the other cheek,' when he writes "Opening our heart to acknowledge the pain, fear, and confusion conditioned in others takes a steadfast fearlessness, and it takes practice…*As we become familiar with the ways of our heart, our conscience awakens us to the effect of our actions on others. Exercising restraint of behavior that causes painful feelings in others requires discipline of commitment as well as energy.*" *"Kindness is the language which the deaf can hear and the blind can see."*- M. Twain **Humility is the goal, eliminating ego is the solution and kindness is the result. dd*   (You can count on this metamorphosis and I can say this from personal experience – it is the key to a better existence-- I came off my high horse (R-90S) and went the Bob Marley way, "Me feet is me only carriage.") I have come to view my years riding motorcycles as a self-imposed discipline, a training ground that instilled qualities in me of the warrior – to find the courage to fight for my convictions and to persevere to the very end. I would not be the person I am today if I hadn't trained so hard throughout all those years.*

Time For An Arrest & Restraining Order *(sometimes the kindest action seems like the harshest)*
Back in Florida meant back to the reality that there was some unfinished business between Lolita and myself, our divorce. On February 11, 2009, events at our home pushed me into filing mode. Lolita finally realized that I was about to go forward with the process and started with some very aggressive and hostile behavior. We were living in separate rooms at opposite ends of the mobile home. She would be waiting for me in the kitchen when I got up at 5:00 AM and would get up in my face and taunt me and give me little smacks to the head, evidently trying to bait me into retaliation against her. The frequency and intensity of this abuse continued to escalate. *I had gone to the police to let them know that a real potential for violence seemed imminent between us and wanted to know what my options were as I refused to be physically abusive or violent towards her.* They told me without hesitation to call them immediately the next time she attacked me. On 2-11-09, she came into my room and hit me very hard across the top of my head and began punching me all about my body. When I reached for my cell phone, she wrestled to take it away from me, but I managed to bring up the #1 listing in my phone, the Seminole Police Dept., *that I had programmed to call easily in such an event as this*. They arrived to our home in just a few minutes, isolated and questioned both of us and arrested her for spousal abuse. I decided it wouldn't account for much if she were to return right back at our residence after bonding out of jail, so I went the next day to the Broward Courthouse and filed for a restraining order to keep her out of the residence. It was granted for 30 days and eventually extended for 80 more days. Across the street from the court-house was a brightly colored late model Scion advertising divorces for only $399, www.DivorceYes.com. I hired Alexandra Rodriguez as my attorney and began the process toward my end goal of freedom from the prison I had put myself into. It would take 10 long months to accomplish.

Dominican Culture & Hospitality
The stress of daily confrontation was over and I could begin to heal. I'm not an avid bar person but I felt I deserved a drink and decided to check out the food as well at *Cumbala*, a Mexican Restaurant in walking distance from my home. I met the nicest bartender/waitress and began to practice my Spanish as she did not speak English. A very attractive woman from the Dominican Republic, Yibell Alegria was working to support her four children in Santo Domingo and we immediately developed a rapport which eventually turned into friendship for each other.   I would order my usual, a *quesadilla con pollo*, and a *Negra Modelo*, a delicious dark style beer as the name says and in my opinion the best Mexican beer

and one of the world's finest brews as well. I shared with Yibell my woes of marriage and of the divorce process that I was pursuing. I shared with her as well my hope to visit another country and meet a Latin woman who had never been to the USA. I've seen too many people come to this country and adapt to some of the bad habits of our society; i.e., they become materialistic and lose that sense of value for what they have as being sufficient in life. I was looking for someone who was happy with a simpler way of life and would not fall into the trap of the insatiable. *(Lao Tzu:* **"To know that you have enough is to be rich.")** When Yibell asked me what type of woman I preferred, I told her a Caribbean Indian woman, a Taína, is who appealed to me most. She told me her cousin, Rosa Alvania, was such a person and was actually staying in her home in Santo Domingo taking care of her home and her kids; and that she was single with a daughter Milennis, 10 years of age. I asked her for her phone #, and looked forward to giving her a call... T h e n   c a m e   a n   i n v i t a t i o n . . .

Yibell called me one day and invited me to a birthday party for her cousin Ashley who was turning two years old. It was an opportunity to get to know her family and experience Dominican hospitality. After I had parked my car across the street from the home of Yibell's grandparents Dominga and Pedro where the party was, I exited my car and before I could reach the other side of the street, I see this very attractive woman coming towards me with a big smile on her face, and one of the warmest human beings I had ever met; and she welcomed me to her parents' home and told me she was Rosa Albania's cousin Zoraida, an aunt of the birthday girl. She ushered me into the home to meet her mother and father and all the other folks outside in the back yard where all the cooking and barbecuing was going on. It was a fantastic day sampling all the traditional island food choices including pavo, pollo, ensalada de papa, arroz con gandules, yuca, tostones y chicharrónes. Went down so nice with the magnum of Sutter Home Moscato I had brought to share. Dominican people are very warm and friendly with a zest for life, especially with their wonderful music and dance contributions to the world, *Bachata* and

Merengue. I was falling in love with their culture ♡ and it felt like I had finally found my heart's home.

At some point in the festivities I mentioned to Yibell that I had my conga with me in the trunk of my car. She told me excitedly to bring it right away. I usually like to be ready when I go to a party. I usually have my conga and percussion instruments and my laptop full of music with me; but only if the opportunity or vibe is just right will they materialize, like the Frisbee from my leather jacket in days gone by. So I was going to play for the people. *There is nothing better than this!* To share with those whom you love all the love that is *in you.* I opened up my percussion bag and handed out instruments, playing each one in my way, as sort of an introduction to that instrument, and giving it to whomever seemed game to play it. I then patched my HP into their large boom box system, pulled up some of my favorite songs from the Dominican superstars Antony Santos and Aventura and began assailing my conga with all the passion and emotion of my being, totally at one with the music. Now everybody was around the music and really enjoying themselves. I cued up two of my favorites, Kat DeLuna's *"Whine Up"* with Jamaican superstar Elephant Man and *"Run the Show"* with Busta Rhymes & Don Omar. Then it was time for Frank Reyes, Zacarías Ferreíra, Raulín Rodríguez and Omega *"El Fuerte."* This was a very good day!

Rosa Alvania Gomez Ortega

On June 4, 2009, I had my first communication with Rosa Alvania; we had a wonderful conversation together. We started a chat line on the internet and in short time had grown fond of each other. Everybody has a history that they bring into a new relationship; sometimes the past can even overwhelm the present. I was to learn of recent events that had taken place in the lives of Rosa and Milennis. Rosa had been the victim of physical and emotional abuse at the hands of her longtime boyfriend. Now she was single with her non-biological daughter Milennis that Rosa had raised since she was a baby, and in all ways was the very caring and loving mother of. Rosa had suffered some very personal traumatic events recently in her life including the loss of her father only six months earlier. You don't ask up front when you meet someone, *"Say, how much baggage do you have?"* You go with your gut and your heart, although vetting is a good idea early on in the relationship. I found a heart full of love and caring for everyone's life that she touched and that was one giant green flag for me! Remember that goal in life that I referred to earlier? To find *at all costs* that *real love* that my heart had been searching for all these years. *(Thank you, Jody Watley, for immortalizing those words.)* I decided I would go to Santo Domingo and meet her in person. I traveled to the Dominican Republic from July 24-28. We had a great time together and I knew this was a special woman who had come into my life. She was such a dedicated *tia* to Yibell's four children, two daughters and two sons: Tiuska, Yanelly, Steven and Rosbel. Her relationship with these two older girls and two younger boys was very close. She cooked and cleaned and even washed clothes by hand! She was someone special, and little by little, she took over my whole world. We shared some special memories during my five days in her country and I was already planning my next trip for her upcoming birthday, September 21st -- the same birth date as our brother Tom.

• I thought forevermore that the day *21 September* would always be an unwelcomed reminder of my brother's auto-erasure- *because of it being his birthday*. But now I am in love with a woman who has the same birthday as him and find that I can celebrate this special day once again. This brought me a very good feeling. I will take the opportunity on this special day each September to honor all the good and positive things that my brother Tom stood for and for the exemplary life that he indeed did lead. One of the best artist-photographers I have ever known. A commemorative retrospective of his life's work beautifully compiled by our brother Paul DesRoches is available and can be seen here:

https://www.mypublisher.com/index/?e=OHm3Q8zJl3RIhSCZZo-

IHNEPOQOrmEbB&showForm=true   *9-21-56 → 9-19-07*

Tom DesRoches "Beaming"

> ## Gratitude
>
> "Gratitude unlocks the fullness of life.
>
> It turns what we have into enough, and more.
>
> It turns denial into acceptance, chaos to order, confusion to clarity.
>
> It can turn a meal into a feast, a house into a home, a stranger into a friend."
>
> Melody Beattie

Las Flores de **La República Dominicana**

Nonis y Cajuiles (frutas medicinales)

Playing for the People   *Barrio El Brisal, Santo Domingo 9.20.09*

We decided to celebrate Rosa's birthday a day before her actual birth date, reserving the 21st for a day at the river. It turned out to be a fortuitous arrangement. We had the party at her mother's home where we danced and played music the whole night through.

There is nothing I enjoy more than playing for the people, especially loved ones. This was my first opportunity in this country to celebrate with music and dancing the birthday of a loved one. Playing percussion instruments gives an individual the chance to passionately live through each of the great moments of the songs being showcased. And all can join in, harnessing the energy of each person in One Love Unity. I always have a bag full of percussion instruments and they are always eagerly picked up and played by the folks in attendance. It was a great evening of family and friends with many memories to be had for all. This is what it's all about for me. Celebrating life with family and friends. It seems to me that if we use are brains too much and lose touch with the basic ties to our humanity, we give up too much that our soul craves and demands and the price for not satisfying these basic needs can be catastrophic. So why not stay close to what is so sacred at your very core?   *"We know what we are, but know not what we may be"*   Shakespeare

"High on the Hog" - On our way to spend the day at the river we came upon a feast alongside the road – it was the best ever!   *Santo Domingo, Dom. Rep.   9. 21. 2009*

If there's any truth to the saying, *"The way to a man's heart is through his stomach,"* this bowl of *sancocho* would go a long way to prove it; it was the best I had ever had. It was the first time Rosa had prepared it for me.   *"Sancocho del Cielo"*

Ten days after I had returned from my trip, I lost my job following an explosion of an oxygen cylinder I was filling. I could have been killed. It went off like a concussion grenade; I couldn't hear normally for a very long time. I had accidentally filled a cylinder that was *out of date* that had corrosion on its interior wall *(it was later determined)* and the cylinder exploded to about 20 feet away *(not in my direction)*. Because it should not have been filled and I had placed my life in jeopardy, I was terminated for negligence. MTG has a zero tolerance safety policy and admittedly I was responsible for this violation. After more than ten years with MTG, in a very poor employment market, I found myself out of work. I lost my job and I had all but legally lost my marriage; *but I was in love and that is very powerful medicine. I had a lot to be positive about and I was determined to remain proactive.* The only upside to not being employed was that now I could spend two weeks visiting Rosa instead of the couple of days I had left vacation time that I had planned. We had a great time together. I went to where she grew up *en el campo* outside of *La Vega* (where Michael Jackson and Lisa Marie Presley were secretly married in May of 1994), met all her friends and family, and we started dreaming of a life together. For her birthday, I surprised her with a cake that had my favorite photo of her (that I had taken the first time I went to see her) reproduced in computer-generated *glaseado comestible*, edible frosting. It was a carrot cake with cream cheese frosting and oh so good! I had two other big surprises for her; a Dell laptop with internal camera so we could communicate via live video broadcast, and a heart-shaped diamond ring. She was very happy. *(Relish the great moments you encounter because there are no guarantees.)*

November 25th- A Special Day: International Day for the Elimination of Violence Against Women
My divorce date was at hand, scheduled for November 25th, the day before Thanksgiving. I would have a lot to be thankful for on this Turkey Day. Isn't it ironic that **November 25th**, since 1981, has been designated *International Day for the Elimination of Violence Against Women* and it was Lolita's violence against me that brought an end to us? And isn't it also ironic that there is a connection for the choice of that date with the Dominican Republic, where Rosa Alvania resides? That was the date of the brutal assassination in **1960** of three *Mirabal* sisters, political activist-martyrs in the Dominican Republic, ordered by Rafael Trujillo, dictator, who received his own karmic retribution a year later.
[A *must see* 2001 film of this story, *In the Time of the Butterflies*, starring Salma Hayek as *Minerva*, one of the sisters, and Edward James Olmos as the Dictator Rafael Leonidas Trujillo is highly recommended.]

I offered our mobile home and our 1999 Chrysler van in the divorce proceedings. She wanted more. She wanted half of my 401K *and alimony- **that*** never happened! I only had $14,000 in my fund from savings and investments. She got half of that as well. With my half, I paid off the van's loan balance of $3600, and paid another $1000 for my Fiancé Visa, ($500 to Immigration and $500 to paralegal), paid off a couple of debts, and *I was left with one thousand greenbacks for my retirement!* I had no place to live and could not afford an apartment as I was already paying $600 a month for Rosa's apartment, phone, internet and other essentials such as food, her daughter's schooling, and numerous medical expenses. There's one more item that needs to be shared, Lolita's confession. The last time we spoke together right after the divorce became final, Lolita shocked me with two admissions. I guess she didn't want to carry the guilt of her actions any longer. She told me that the guy named Greg who she had said she met at the gym was really a guy she had met in Arizona when we were out there together and that they lived together during those eight months before moving out here to Florida (he currently lives with his mother not far from the mobile home address). When I asked her, 'Why? Was I not good enough for you? Wasn't my love enough for you?' She actually told me this, "One man is not enough for me; I always have one other man in my life." I should have paid more attention to definition #2 for *lolita* in Dictionary.com: *nymphet.* The only other thing I could think of, and I'm probably a lot closer to the truth than I realize, is that this was her way of getting back at her father. She told me so many stories about all of his philandering and all of the pain and suffering that she witnessed her mother go through on his account- that this was her way of getting even with him. I didn't have to be played like this; I had been shown various *signs* and *cues*. *Don't ignore the signs and cues!* And, once again, *think with your higher head! *I think susceptibility to relationships like these corresponds directly to the degree of emotional health and stability of the involved partners; if I had been more secure emotionally and confident in my affairs with women, I wouldn't have subjected myself to the various toxic environments I found myself in*; first with Joanne and then with Lolita; *I wouldn't have ignored or dismissed the signs and cues. Live and learn or be doomed to repeat the error of your ways! *Very Important to Understand This!*

*Homeless Once Again: *An **Opportunity** to Eliminate Ego & Realize A More Humble Me*
So, I started living out of my car and would do so for the next five months. Not an easy way to go.
One of the reasons I was able to live under these conditions is because I had learned to survive in the Peggy Sue era quite well in the street. But this was a lot more uncomfortable. I had a couple of helping hands. On the weekends I would visit the home of my fiancée's cousin Zoraida Mercedes and her family, and at least could get cleaned up and be re-constituted as a human being. She has gone out of her way to accept me as a member of the family and for that I am truly grateful. She is married to Alejandro, a workaholic mechanic who, interestingly enough, specializes working on his namesake, *Mercedes*. They have a son Alejandro, 21, who works with his Dad and they have a daughter Sorangi, 16, in high school. These are the great folks whose home I would visit on the weekends to reinstate my being human. Before the year would end, they would play a far greater role in my life, unbeknownst to me at the time. As I sit here writing my story, I am in their home and have been since my release on August 6, 2010. Thanks to their unbounded love and acceptance, they have agreed to keep me in their home while under house arrest during this long case process. I was truly blessed to have my fate cross paths with this loving family from *Moca, La República Dominicana*.
The other helping hand that came to my aid was Willy Ventura, owner of *All American Trailers,* in Ft. Lauderdale. He allowed me to park on his property so I didn't have to worry about the police, parking illegally somewhere. He also allowed me to use his company facilities, and that was a big bonus. And then he went one step further; he allowed me to sleep in the yachts that were boarded within his fenced property. This relationship lasted all the way up until I was able to rent a room in a former neighbor's home. He was instrumental in my survival during my time of need and I thank him for that.*: *Although it is truly difficult to live the life of a homeless person, it is truly rewarding the better person you can be- the most valuable Buddha teaching that has profoundly changed my life is 'the elimination of ego' to achieve humility; this formula will bring a person back to their core self from which we all derive; i.e., to lovingkindness --*
A Very Ugly Chapter In My Life That Caused Me To Write This Book
During the time living out of my car, I was contacted on three separate occasions by my former neighbor, Mary Fisher, with offers to rent a room in her mobile home. She first contacted me sometime in January, asking me for $300 per month to rent a room in her home. I told her I couldn't afford to pay two rents; I was already sending $600 per month to my fiancée in the Dominican Republic. About a month later, she offered for $200 per month to rent her property. I told her I just didn't have that much in my budget to put towards a second rent. A month or so later she made a final offer: if I would pay $100 towards the water and electricity, and help out around the house, she would accept that.
I decided to accept her offer and called her on April 9, 2010 to confirm and move in as I was planning to attend the wedding of Zoraida's sister Alicia the very next day, April 10th • The very first thing I did to help her out was the day after the wedding. Her car had not been running for some time, so I was determined to get it going for her. It turned out she needed a new battery. I bought the highest grade battery for her Taurus, paying close to $100. In addition she received $100 for the room as agreed. I offered to paint her home, a major undertaking because heavy repairs to the fascia of the right side of her home all along its length were required after serious hurricane damage that had never been repaired properly. This took three weeks alone to repair. In addition, before painting could commence,

103

I needed to locate and repair the three leaks I found on her roof that were causing water damage inside the home. I spent approximately $300 on a new 8' ladder and on the various painting and repair supplies that were required. I needed to complete all repairs in her kitchen and hallway and make sure that the water damage had halted and the roof was repaired properly. Another worker had installed sheet rock along the whole side of her kitchen very badly and it needed serious repair. To fix and paint all of the interior took five days. It took until about the middle of July to complete all the major repairs and to do the pressure washing and painting of the home. So I had fulfilled my agreement with Mary. Almost immediately upon taking occupancy in Mary Fisher's home, she began to complain that the $100 she had asked of me was not enough. It was a classic case of "bait and switch." She baited me to rent a room for a low price and then insisted that it was just not possible for her to pay all her expenses by herself; that two people sharing a home together should be paying 50/50. She was ignoring all the work I was doing for her as my part of the agreement to offset this token rent amount. So, we did not get along very well. Generally, I would walk away from her when her tone got ugly about our financial arrangement and that would make her furious. She typically would call her son Billy and complain to him about me. In addition to the work I performed outlined above, I can account for numerous trips I made taking Mary Fisher to her rehab appointments for her ankle: to a Pembroke Pines rehab facility, to an orthopedic specialist adjacent to Washington Memorial Hospital, to her doctor at the 4700 Sheridan medical facility in Hollywood, and the time I took her to Johnson Memorial ER after she had fallen and fractured her left ankle, staying with her all day in the hospital. I treated Mary Fisher like my own mother. I physically carried her into and out of her car when she was not able to do so and attended to all of her needs as required of a habilitating, walker-bound patient.

Anatomy of A Frame

On Monday, July 26, 2010, Mary and I shared some words with each other, and as usual, she got her phone and called her son Billy. She went to her usual spot outside on her porch that was separated from the inside of her home by a sliding glass door. After she had closed the door behind her, I went over to the side of that glass door that had been painted by her so nobody could see inside. I heard part of her conversation, saying to her son, *"I just want him out of here!"* She had never asked or told me to leave her property; if she had, I would have gladly vacated the premises. I decided to take my laptop to McDonald's where I could connect to their Wi-Fi, and search Craig's list for a rental. I found one I really liked and sent an e-mail to communicate my interest (my attorney has a copy, internet-dated, of this e-mail). I returned to my rented room and several hours later came a knock at my door, "Hey, Dennis, Billy". I opened the door and Billy Fisher steps into the room and comes nose to nose with me, his muscle behind him in the hallway. *"You're done here. You need to get your stuff out of here right now!"* To which I say, *'You can't forcibly throw me out of here. I have an arrangement with your mother and I have rights* (I had been living there for 3½ months). *We need to involve the Police. Call the Police and let's do this by the book.'* To which he responds in a very ominous and threatening tone, *"You don't want to mess with ME! I have 50 people who work for me—you DO NOT WANT TO MESS WITH ME!"* To which his accomplice, David Zeuner, says, *"Billy, let's do this the way I said, let's do this the way I said."* [Turned out to be very important words – because it points to the fabrication they are about to perpetrate.] Billy Fisher backed up and I closed the door and locked it. **There was no contact by any individuals involved.** * *This is the moment that I should have called the Police, not leaving it to them. I immediately began packing my things, putting everything on the bed. I was not going to submit to their threats and intimidation but I no longer felt comfortable living there and no matter what the police were going to say, I had decided to vacate the premises. The Seminole Police Department is a five minute walk from her mobile home and from the one across the street where I used to live. I thought that the presence of the police was going to be a good thing but I didn't count on the wickedness of these two con artists. They falsified police reports saying I attacked one of them with a screwdriver. When the very young and obviously inexperienced female officer **Robinson, badge 179** told me of their story about the attack on them; it didn't matter what I had to say. She tells me I attacked the one and the other was a witness to it. *(*There was a minor, self-inflicted scrape on Zeuner's arm- made to look like I had attacked him.)* I protest how one can be witness to the other if they arrived together in the same vehicle and as vigilantes conspired to perpetrate this fabricated scenario of events. Billy Fisher, originally from New Jersey, according to his mother Mary, inherited *Fisher Films* from his father; his job is staging scenarios for television for either HBO or Showtime. He had no problem staging this scenario, hijacking the legal system and perjuring himself along with his friend as to what transpired on July 26, 2010, the day he tried to force me out of home.   The title of this episode he is peddling needs to be:

'All-Mighty' Shorts Producer Stages Felony Assault to Rid Mother of Tenant

William Fisher and David Zeuner acted above the law. They should not be allowed to get away with their criminal behavior. By writing this book I have done my part to make them accountable. *Bullies need to be held to the fire - their lies, threats and intimidations shown for what they are.* **This is justice.** *Stand Up For What's Right! Never let injustice go unchallenged -- If someone frames you- don't let them get away with it- it may be a long hard road but you must go there and see justice done.*

I had never even seen the screwdriver they claimed I used on them until I saw what appeared to be the tip of one protruding from an evidence bag after I had begged the officer to gather what they had for fingerprints. It had a long blade like the one Mary always kept on her barbeque grill by the stairs entering my side of the mobile home. I offered to take a polygraph but was ignored. I NEVER FELT SO HELPLESS OR VICTIMIZED IN MY LIFE! [Since June 29, 1976] I've always devoted myself to be an agent for peace and non-violence and now I am in handcuffs with all liberty lost! I'm facing a very serious charge for a manufactured scenario that two criminal thugs professionally conned the law into believing happened. This has to go down the right way and I am exonerated and found NOT GUILTY. If these criminal thugs, these two professional con artists get away with this travesty, this staged assault scenario, and I am found guilty for something I didn't do, I will be crushed as a human being, my faith in the system lost forever. I have given the most I could in this world to be the best person and citizen I can be. *I can not and will not allow these perpetrators to be successful.* I have always been an agent for peace and positivity for others around me. My four years as a Social Worker with the City of Hartford, CT, from 1972-1976, and one year as Psychiatric Social Worker at St. Luke's Hospital in Phoenix, AZ, during the period 1978-80 with the School of Social Work at Arizona State University should attest for something. The legal system is being held hostage by two thugs who are flat out liars whose modus operandi is: LIES, THREATS AND INTIMIDATION. They cannot be allowed to win over the modus operandi I choose: PEACE, LOVE AND UNDERSTANDING. I have been on this planet for 62 years as of this writing, always on the right side of the law, always defending righteousness and helping my fellow man to help himself. How insane would I have to be to give up my entire life's work and begin at 62 to resort to armed physical battery on another human being? It's totally out of the question, obviously.

In my Mission Statement to the world I referred to my heroes in life; namely, Mahatma Gandhi, Nelson Mandela and Bob Marley. Those are the individuals who I look up to and try in some small way to emulate. This is too big to lose to a couple of punks who wish to get away with murder, character assassination that is, and who feel that they have successfully hoodwinked the system and gotten away with this hoax. I need to have faith in the system, however flawed it may be, believing that the TRUTH will win out and I will be exonerated. This time will be different; there will be no plea bargain here.

ONE THING IS FOR SURE: YOU ARE NOT INNOCENT UNTIL PROVEN GUILTY – YOU ARE GUILTY (UPON BEING ARRESTED) UNTIL *PROVEN/VOTED* INNOCENT – YOU ARE AS AN INMATE AND TREATED LIKE A CRIMINAL. The law states that the burden of proof test is that: "THERE IS A PREPONDERANCE OF EVIDENCE BEYOND A REASONABLE DOUBT" -- I WOULD SUBMIT TO THE COURT THAT WHAT WE HAVE HERE IS A PREPONDERANCE OF DOUBT BEYOND REASONABLE EVIDENCE. THE FACTS DON'T LIE.

I am thinking of the book: _El Poder Infinito De Su Mente_ by Lauro Trevisan. (_The Infinite Power of One's Mind_) The author speaks about how our thoughts are everything. Positive thoughts become, lead to positive results/actions. I'm trying to apply that principle now more than ever before. The TRUTH must prevail; the TRUTH will set you free. You have to believe in something!

The title for this book could have been "**Under House Arrest**" or "**6 Months' Freedom Stolen**" because almost every page has been written with a GPS monitor attached to my left ankle as a Defendant in the custody of the Broward County Sheriff's Dept. in FL, and the case has taken six months of my life. The two events of great injustice in my life from 1976 and 2010 were the main catalysts for this writing and needed to be told. But I prefer to present a positive theme as the guide to my life's journey. I wanted to share with the world the story of my life as viewed via the operating principle, _**to be totally real is to be totally free is to be totally alive**_, a concept I arrived at after analyzing my life's experiences and seeing that there was a common denominator in each of those that had been taken to its highest commitment (I refer to them as _all-consuming experiences_)- whether it be motorcycling, dancing, playing my drum or as participant in the primal forces of Nature. TBT Real → TBT Free → TBT Alive

I also believe that if any one of the three conditions is lacking 100% commitment, neither of the other two can be experienced at the totally-in 100%; e.g., if you are not totally free to experience dancing, you cannot feel the total aliveness that you might otherwise enjoy. They are interdependent variables. As well, they represent three distinct philosophical perspectives that when viewed together operate synergistically in harmony with each other.

To Be Totally Real   Is To Be Totally Free   Is To Be Totally Alive

To Be Totally Real ... as exhibited by the philosophy of **Jean-Paul Sartre** –

living in the present moment, an existentialist point of view, a way of life _'that stresses the individual's unique position as a self-determining agent responsible for the authenticity of his or her own choices.'_ For me personally, 'to be totally real' is to be totally honest with each and every individual action or pursuit toward each undertaking, goal or endeavor.
* There is nothing more totally real or more totally wrong than WAR – the blood spilled by men against themselves. And it represents the red flag that has been raised for all of humanity to take notice that WAR is not the way to solve the differences among members of an "advanced" species. *_In truth_, **Homo sapiens** _has not been able to advance as a species past the barbaric stage of 'kill or be killed,' giving to war the power to reign forever supreme._
"The Real You" – Alan Watts   https://www.youtube.com/watch?v=mMRrCYPxD0I

Is To Be Totally Free ... as in the teachings of **Jiddu Krishnamurti** instructing

us _"to be free from all the stupidities of one's life. To be free from them is only possible in becoming aware of one's relationships, not only with human beings, but with nature, with everything."_ For me personally, the action of being totally 'real' creates the resultant state of 'total freedom within oneself,' allowing for the capacity to act or conduct our lives in unison with the goals that we have set, giving us the right to proceed unencumbered by worrisome second-guessing. But with total freedom comes total responsibility for oneself.
* Freedom is golden and the most valuable of human prizes. "Give It Away & It Will Come Back" – Alan Watts   https://www.youtube.com/watch?v=CXq_mVU8nyc

Is To Be Totally Alive ... as the wisdom of **Buddha** shows us, *"The secret of health for both mind and body is not to mourn for the past, worry about the future, or anticipate troubles, but to live in the present moment wisely and earnestly."* For me personally, the highest level of a human's aliveness can only be reached by being totally honest and real about one's actions, thus gaining within oneself a state of total freedom *(which could not be the case with any compromises of the truth)*, and this freedom to act allows one to continually re-invest in *self* and push the envelope of one's sentient being *to know and feel* to the pinnacle of 'being-ness,' remaining perennially in the state of *'being here and now.'* The best example I would give here is the act of 'spirit dance.' (pp. 66-67) For some, as The Buddha Teaching imparts, Dharma, the highest state of aliveness and the knowing of ourselves completely can only be reached through practiced meditation.
* Our planet Earth is totally alive with green, the very symbol of life.
"Live Fully Now" – Alan Watts https://www.youtube.com/watch?v=HdqVF7-8wng

* * * The colors chosen to separate the above three interdependent premises *(for ease of understanding and symbolic significance)*: red, gold and green, serendipitously mimic those associated with Ethiopia and the Rastafarian way of life. I chose them with the utmost respect due to this country and to the Rastafarian religion. Without the Rastafari movement, there would not have been any reggae music and that would be a great tragedy.

Chapter 24: *Final Thoughts & Reflections* – *We Are The Architects of Our Own Destiny &: Change Agents Making A Difference Re-Shaping Our World* – *A Tribute To Whistleblowers*
The legal system we have in our country, the U.S.A., like all other legal systems of the world, is not perfect. I used to think it was the best system in the world and that things just couldn't go so wrong if you did right by your fellow man but that is not the case. Officers can make very serious mistakes and arrest the wrong person and, as in my case, set the real criminals free. Then you have double indemnity; first by the officer arresting you for something they think you did but did not do, and secondly by the prison and court components of our system which accept as fact that grand error and at each successive level in the legal system come to view your case with their own set of damaging blinders to not see or know the real facts. And as we all are aware, the ultimate failure of this process has sometimes resulted in the ultimate sacrifice of the innocent in his or her own execution, legally murdered at the hands of the State via capital punishment- a shameful cancer on our American culture.
*I think Michael Moore is the best example of "STAND UP FOR WHAT'S RIGHT! & Do It With Kindness"
Inspired by the social critic and activist Michael Moore's powerful documentaries, the Academy Award winning Bowling for Columbine (2002), Fahrenheit 9/11 (2004), my personal favorite Sicko (2007), and 'the most subversive movie Michael Moore has ever made,' WHERE TO INVADE NEXT (2016), I am in my small way trying to do something to effect positive change vis-à-vis the status quo, the way things are with our criminal justice system; i.e., the police and the court system. We're not going to get anywhere in this world if we don't try to make a difference. We're still the most war-mongering nation that continues to reject out of hand the modus operandi of PEACE which our Native Wisdomkeepers have tried to hand down to us, just as Mahatma Gandhi and Nelson Mandela and Martin Luther King, Jr. among others have tried with their legacies. *But there is hope.* How great is it that an African American only one generation removed from his Kenyan roots could win two terms as President of the U.S.A. That was truly remarkable. And the progress he has achieved as the first President to finally bring about universal healthcare in our country is nothing less than a miracle! Kudos to a seminal change agent for that. *But his legacy could have been greater than this -- *"the anti-whistleblowers' president."* Very sad.

From the *RootsAction Initiative*, "Since Obama's inauguration seven years ago, his administration **has prosecuted more whistleblowers than all other presidents combined** – doing huge damage to civil liberties and the public's right to know." (from January, 2016, www.RootsAction.org)

Barack Obama studied and carried on the tradition of *Saul Alinsky* as a Chicago-based community organizer focused on improving the living conditions of poor communities. Alinsky (1/30/09 - 6/12/72) was famous for his grass roots organizing and political activism. His book *Rules for Radicals* has often been used as a primer for those seeking to effect change on a mass scale. I have also admired Saul Alinsky's teachings, wanting to take power away from the HAVES and to give power to the HAVE-NOTS. I was personally very moved by Barack Obama's *Hope and Change* platform and campaign –*however* -- I have had strong misgivings since the President was elected. I have the following grave concerns:

Beware § The Greatest Injustice For All of Us May Be Our Subjugation to the National Security State -Unwillingly- With or Without Our Knowledge or Consent – Marking the End of Our Constitutionally Protected Privacy Rights Including the Right of Dissent and Free Speech - Obama has upheld the invasions of our privacy by the NSA and referred to Snowden as no more than a wayward hacker - Wrong*!!* History may judge our country very harshly as we witness the wrongful condemnation of *Edward Snowden* as traitor when indeed he has shown himself to be a patriot of the highest order risking his own personal life and freedoms to expose our government for its totally invasive operations to control the lives of each and every one of us. It is difficult for me to write these words but I no longer look at reality with blinders on. I am also appalled to see the life of WikiLeaks whistleblower *Bradley (Chelsea) Manning* torn apart and jailed for simply leaking the truth about horrendous crimes that were being committed by the American side during the Iraq war. In his defense Manning said, "I am prepared to go to prison for life or even be executed." *What happened to our Constitution and Bill of Rights?* The message is clear: *you do not have the right of free speech when it's inconveniently or disgracefully putting the government in a bad light.* The iconic Pentagon Papers' whistleblower who helped bring down the Nixon administration, *Daniel Ellsberg*, says it best, *"It is only the person who reveals the criminal activity who is prosecuted for it."* The brilliant documentary by *Brave New Films*' founder and president *Robert Greenwald* is most illuminating for showing that *whistleblowers are the pioneers of change*; indeed, that *they are heroes for standing up for what was the right thing to do.* The documentary, *War on Whistleblowers: Free Press and The National Security State* serves as a landmark exposé and primer for those who would have the courage to uncover the truth for the betterment of society. The documentary states, "The more powerful the national security state becomes, the more we need whistleblowers. The national security state is a self-licking ice cream cone -- it is there to protect its own interests." [Our world's most recent victory from whistleblowers- the *Panama Papers*] Like the title of Barack Obama's book, I too had "the audacity of hope" and was proud to vote for him twice but I am very upset and disillusioned that his platform of *Hope and Change* was subverted. **Obama promised the most transparent administration in history**, *"The way to make government responsible is to hold it accountable, make it transparent, so the American people can know exactly what decisions are being made and whether their interests are being well served."* But the redacted 28 pages missing from the 2002 *9/11 Commission Report* still have not been released as we head into the 2016 presidential election between Hillary Clinton and Donald Trump. What has been documented is the Obama Administration's relentless use of the Espionage Act to go after journalists to silence or intimidate them: *Daniel Ellsberg*, *"In 2011 there were 92 million classification decisions (content deemed "classified") which is four times as many classification decisions as George W. Bush. That's not increased transparency of course, that's closing the curtains."* Bill Keller, Op-Ed Columnist, The New York Times, *"They (the Obama administration) have indicted more people for violating secrecy than all of the previous administrations put together."* And finally, this comment from *Thomas Drake*, the former NSA official accused of leaking classified information and for which the government tried to send him away to prison for the rest of his life, "It is extremely dangerous in America right now to be right as a whistleblower when the government is so wrong. So speaking truth to power is now a criminal act…it really criminalizes the news gathering process." *An excellent historical perspective on all this: http://www.theguardian.com/us-news/2016/may/22/how-pentagon-punished-nsa-whistleblowers

Also: *Bravehearts: Whistle Blowing In The Age of Snowden* - by Mark Hertsgaard

Judge Andrew P. Napolitano gives us a lot to think about as well in this historic rant: https://www.youtube.com/watch?v=SB3RPpN9Mlo *(Sadly, Bernie Sanders is not the 2016 Dem nominee.)*

I wonder what the writers of our Constitution would have to say about the United States of America today? And what can we say about our American democracy now- or to be more to the point, about democracy itself at this stage of our history and at this stage of the Grand Experiment? Has not the USA transformed completely into an oligarchy? *Trump for* **President⁉** *Are you kidding me⁉* - The *American Dream* Dinesh D'Souza talks about in <u>What's</u> <u>So</u> <u>Great</u> <u>About</u> <u>America</u> may be turning into the *American Nightmare (If it comes to pass, it will be a calamity for us and the world-- a sad world legacy):* "As an immigrant *I think what's so great about America* is here is a country where *the individual is the architect of his or her own destiny.* In most countries in the world, your destiny is to some degree given to you; your decisions in life, what to become, what to believe, where to live, who to love, who to marry. In other countries these decisions are made by parents or by the society. You have choice but the choice is within confined parameters. I think life in America by contrast, *the individual is in the driver's seat of his own life* and that's a very exhilarating idea. And it's the reason why America is so appealing, especially to young people all over the world." *Free speech* is also an appeal of America but as we have seen with the whistleblowers above- even in America we do not have the absolute right of free speech. I am obviously very thankful that *for the moment* we do have *some freedom of speech* in this country and that's a very big deal. Forever an advocate of the concept that your character in many ways plays a role in your fate, that what you stand for and fight for have a direct correlation to the results that define your destiny, I submit these pages. We must stand together against the injustices of our system, especially when violating our basic freedoms for the truth. *As the Italian sculptor *Davide Dormino* said at the unveiling of his commemorative piece in Berlin on May 5, 2015, speaking of Edward Snowden, Julian Assange and Bradley (Chelsea) Manning, *"They've lost their freedom for the truth, so they remind us how important it is to know the truth. The statue pays homage to the three who said **no!** to war, to the lies that lead us to war and to the intrusion into private life that helps to perpetuate war."*
Unfortunately, *complacency* as an operating principle is alive and well in defining our bureaucratic systems and our lives personally if we allow ourselves to do nothing. The struggle continues and it is in our best interest to continually stand up for what is right and if necessary to fight for our freedoms, our liberty and our civil rights. *And fighting with a pen is better and more humane than fighting with a gun.*
"Mankind are more disposed to suffer, while evils are sufferable, than to right themselves by abolishing the forms to which they are accustomed." Thomas Jefferson

Amendment 1   The Bill of Rights, U.S. Constitution

Congress shall make no law respecting an establishment of religion, or prohibiting the free exercise thereof; or abridging the freedom of speech, or of the press; or the right of the people peaceably to assemble, and to petition the Government for a redress of grievances.

The U.S. government (Goliath) threatened to fine **Yahoo** (David) $250,000 a day if it refused to hand over to the National Security Administration user data from online services (2007). And it was set to double the fine every week that Yahoo refused to comply. *Yahoo* objected that the request was unconstitutional and a violation of the <u>Fourth</u> <u>Amendment</u>. Edward Snowden's revelations showed that

the NSA (also *known as the All-Seeing and All-Knowing Agency*) was in fact collecting information from U.S. citizens on a massive scale without a warrant via the PRISM Program (a warrantless wiretapping program) which is a clear overreach in government surveillance.
[Condensed from: www.theguardian.com by Dominic Rushe, September 12, 2014]

Amendment 4

The right of the people to be secure in their persons, houses, papers, and effects, against unreasonable searches and seizures, shall not be violated, and no Warrants shall issue, but upon probable cause, supported by Oath or affirmation, and in particular describing the place to be searched, and the persons or things to be seized.

* *These Amendments are the heart and soul of our Bill of Rights and must not be trampled upon!!*
"DON'T   TREAD   ON   ME!"   *Now in Feb 2016 we are facing the FBI battling Apple to force them to create a backdoor to their iPhone 5 (intentionally weakening the digital security of Apple's products) 'in order to access the San Bernardino terrorist's phone' for data. At stake: "Whether national security can dictate how Silicon Valley writes computer code. Code is protected by America's free speech law."* **Tim Cook says 'No'. TC: "We must get this right. History has shown us that sacrificing our right to privacy can have dire consequences. This is a defense of civil liberties. This case is about the future."**
Dilemma: Where does digital security end *(what are the limits of encryption)* and national security begin?
* It's great to see that Facebook and Twitter are backing Apple in this phone encryption battle with the FBI.
Warning: ***"Those Who Sacrifice Liberty For Security Deserve Neither."*** **Ben Franklin**
*An internet rights activist group **Fight for the Future** makes it clear what the FBI is going for. From this group's campaign director Evan Greer, "Governments have been frothing at the mouth hoping for an opportunity to pressure companies like Apple into building backdoors into their products to enable more sweeping surveillance."* ***An awful lot is at stake here**- I just hope Apple stands strong and prevails for the privacy rights of us all. [As of 3.28.2016, the US government has dropped its court case against Apple and the cold war has resumed.]

An Analysis of Survival Skills

"Believe nothing, no matter where you read it or who has said it, not even if I have said it, unless it agrees with your own reason and your own common sense." Buddha
I was the child of a bipolar father. I was forced to see and know life through the lens of this illness.
I think the key to my survival lay in the fact that at a very young age, witnessing the antics of my Dad, I realized that I needed to protect myself in some way, draw myself into my own little world, for *(what I would later learn to term)* my own emotional and psychological integrity and health, for my own protection and refuge. I had to believe in myself, become self-reliant and create a kind of separate reality, to borrow from Don Juan. I couldn't go along with his itinerary for my life although I had to keep him believing that I was.   This seemed to work pretty well in developing confidence in myself. *Marcus Garvey: "If you have no confidence in self, you are twice defeated in the Race of Life. With confidence, you have won even before you have started."*   And I need now to tap into that same strategy of confidence in order to survive the current crisis I find myself in.   Correlative thinking exists in the psychological literature re: self-control and persistence, from *Daniel Goleman's "Emotional Intelligence: Why it can matter more than IQ"*: "What factors are at play, for example, when people of high IQ flounder and those of modest IQ do surprisingly well? I would argue that the difference quite often lies in the abilities called here ***emotional intelligence,*** which include self-control, zeal and persistence, and the ability to motivate oneself." Goleman explores *"what hazards await those who, in growing to maturity, fail to master the emotional realm--how deficiencies in emotional intelligence heighten a spectrum of risks, from depression to a life of violence to eating disorders and drug abuse."* Maybe I mustered enough self-control and persistence and had enough self-motivation to make it out alive, although barely so, emotionally and psychologically speaking. Then there was this effective strategy:

Steve Jobs advised in his 2005 Stanford graduation speech, *"Remembering that you're going to die is the best way I know to avoid the trap of thinking you have something to lose. You are already naked; there is no reason to not follow your heart. Have the courage to follow your heart and intuition; they somehow already know what you truly want to become. Everything else is secondary."*

Another author speaks about the power of *accepting oneself* as a strategy for *making it* in this world:
It came to me as a positive confirmation of my early strategies in life *to survive* when I visited Judi Campanaro's blog at: http://www.couragetobeme.blogspot.com   She was commenting on a book she was reading, *"Voices of Insight"* edited by Sharon Salzberg, a compilation of teachers of Buddhism in the West: in his chapter *Sacred Friendship*, *Steven Smith* speaks about acceptance of oneself and life as it is:
"The staggering range of joys and sorrows all beings experience is the way of the world. It is natural law, the truth of things as they are. Just as the nature of the physical world is turbulent systems with the ever-changing conditions of wind, water, heat, and earth, so too our inner environment is a turbulent system. We are ever challenged with changing fortunes of gain and loss, pleasure and pain, praise and blame, fame and disrepute. *Spiritual friendships show the way of the wise; with wisdom and lovingkindness one can skillfully navigate through these systems with equanimity."*

"It is acceptance of oneself, and life as it is, that is the secret of navigational success."

A Mother's Love and Example

I think another key to my survival was my mother. She never gave up trying to do the right thing for her seven rivalrous ducklings, essentially a single parent for most of our lives. Putting herself through hairdressing school gave us all a lot more confidence as to what could be accomplished when you put your mind to it. It gave us pride to see her achieve that very meaningful and productive goal and wean us off of public assistance. Over the years she has sent me numerous uplifting, motivational cards for the various occasions. My favorite card ever, a Carlton Card, I received in January, 2000, on my 52nd birthday and is most worthy to share with the world. My mother wrote, "Dear Dennis, May you enjoy another Birthday, Good health and a wonderful future, Happy, Happy Birthday!!" What follows were the words on that card which I had framed as an 8X10: *"Life's Instructions, Son, from Me to You.*
If I had just a moment to tell you all I know, and then to wish you well, I would tell you…"

Don't miss a day of your life.	there may not be.
Find ways to make each day matter--	There are happy endings in life,
to you, to another, to the world.	but not always,
Develop, listen to, nurture,	and some are easier to understand
and trust your instincts.	than others.
You will compete in life,	We are all part of something
but life is not a competition--	bigger than life,
it is a gift to be shared.	and although I don't know
You are enough as an individual person.	for sure what it is,
You'll meet many special people in life.	I am grateful to have shared
There may be one special person,	so much of life with you.

Thanks Mom for giving me life, for bringing me forth into this world. I'm sorry for all the pain and suffering I may have inadvertently caused you and I forgive you for all the pain and suffering that you have inadvertently caused me. We have both grown to be better people because we have both chosen righteousness as our path- you in your own way and me in my own way as well; and the example each of us shows to others becomes our own separate legacy. We have shared a lot of good memories between us and hopefully we can look forward to share more of the same. *The most important consideration of all is that all of our actions derive solely from the source of lovingkindness and compassion -*

What It Is To Live

Before I let you go, I want to leave you with some very special words; they sort of represent the way I have chosen to live my life, and the one experience above all others that exemplifies its meaning would have to be as witness and partaker of the *total eclipse of the sun* in 1972. Cue up Pink Floyd's "Eclipse"

Joseph Campbell provides a helpful guide to all of us as we plot our journey through life, *"Follow your bliss."* Campbell arrived at this from his spiritual studies of Hindu religion within which the language of Sanskrit defines *Ananda*, one of the three components of transcendence, as rapture or bliss.

"Life is not about the amount of breaths you take, life is about the moments that take your breath away." (*Vicki Corona* - "Tahitian Choreographies")

My friend Andy Gumkowski is fond *(as I am as well)* of these words from *Hunter S. Thompson*:

"Life should not be a journey to the grave with the intention of arriving safely in a pretty and well-preserved body, but rather to skid in broadside in a cloud of smoke, thoroughly used up, totally worn out, and loudly proclaiming 'WOW'! What a Ride!"

*On this same subject is the wisdom of *Jiddu Krishnamurti* from a talk given in London on March 16, 1969, (from *"The Flight of the Eagle"* - 1972):

Question: "What do you want us people here in the world to do?"

Krishnamurti: "I don't want anything. That's first. Second: live, live in this world. This world is so marvelously beautiful. It's our world, our earth to live upon, but we do not live, we are narrow, we are separate, we are anxious, we are frightened human beings, and therefore we do not live, we have no relationship, we are isolated, despairing human beings. *We do not know what it means to live in that ecstatic, blissful sense. I say one can live that way only when one knows how to be free from all the stupidities of one's life.* To be free from them is only possible in becoming aware of one's relationships, not only with human beings, but with nature, with everything."

Message from *Hopi Elders*, Oraibi, Arizona -- *(We Need to Heed the Messages of Indigenous Wisdom)*

"We have been telling people that this is the 11th hour. Now you must go back and tell the people that THIS is **the hour**. Things to be considered... Where are you living? What are you doing? What are your relationships? Where is your water? Know your garden. **Create your community. Be good to each other. And do not look outside yourself for the leader.** This could be a good time *(baby's foot on mother's womb)*. **There is a river now flowing very fast.** It is so great and swift that there are those who will be afraid. They will try to hold on to the shore. They will feel they are being torn apart and will suffer greatly. Know the river has its destination. **The elders say we must let go of the shore, push off into the middle of the river, keep our eyes open, and our heads above water.** See who is in there with you and celebrate. **At this time in history, we are to take nothing personally; least of all, ourselves. For the moment that we do, our spiritual growth and journey comes to a halt. The time of the lone wolf is over.** Gather yourselves! Banish the word 'struggle' from your attitude and your vocabulary.

All that *we* do must be done in a sacred manner and in celebration ---
WE -- YES, *WE!* **ME YOU** WE ARE THE ONES WE'VE BEEN WAITING FOR"

Source: (highly recommended to watch) -- [YouTube Video]: "Hopi message from Elders: We are the ones we've been waiting for" http://www.youtube.com/watch?v=KrPDQeNo52M
The Hopis have the word KOYAANISQATSI (ko.yaa.nis.qatsi), defined by the 1982 Godfrey Reggio movie essay of the same name as: 1. crazy life. 2. life in turmoil. 3. life out of balance. 4. life disintegrating. 5. a state of life *(US NOW!)* that calls for another way of living.

"I believe that unarmed truth and unconditional love will have the final word in reality."

Martin Luther King, Jr. 👑 *He truly was a king - for change - and a martyr for human rights and equality~*

I owe an enormous debt of gratitude to my sister Lucille, affectionately known as Lulu. She is the one person who had everything to do with my release from custody in the Florida justice system. I call her my angel sister Lucille because without her assistance I might be doing hard time with all my liberties and freedom nonexistent due to my lack of funds to provide for my own defense.

We should all be so fortunate in life to have someone who can be there for us in times of dire need.

Thanks to her I have been able to write my life's story and possibly provide a guide of do's and don'ts to others, to make a difference in the lives of one or two more out there. Thank You

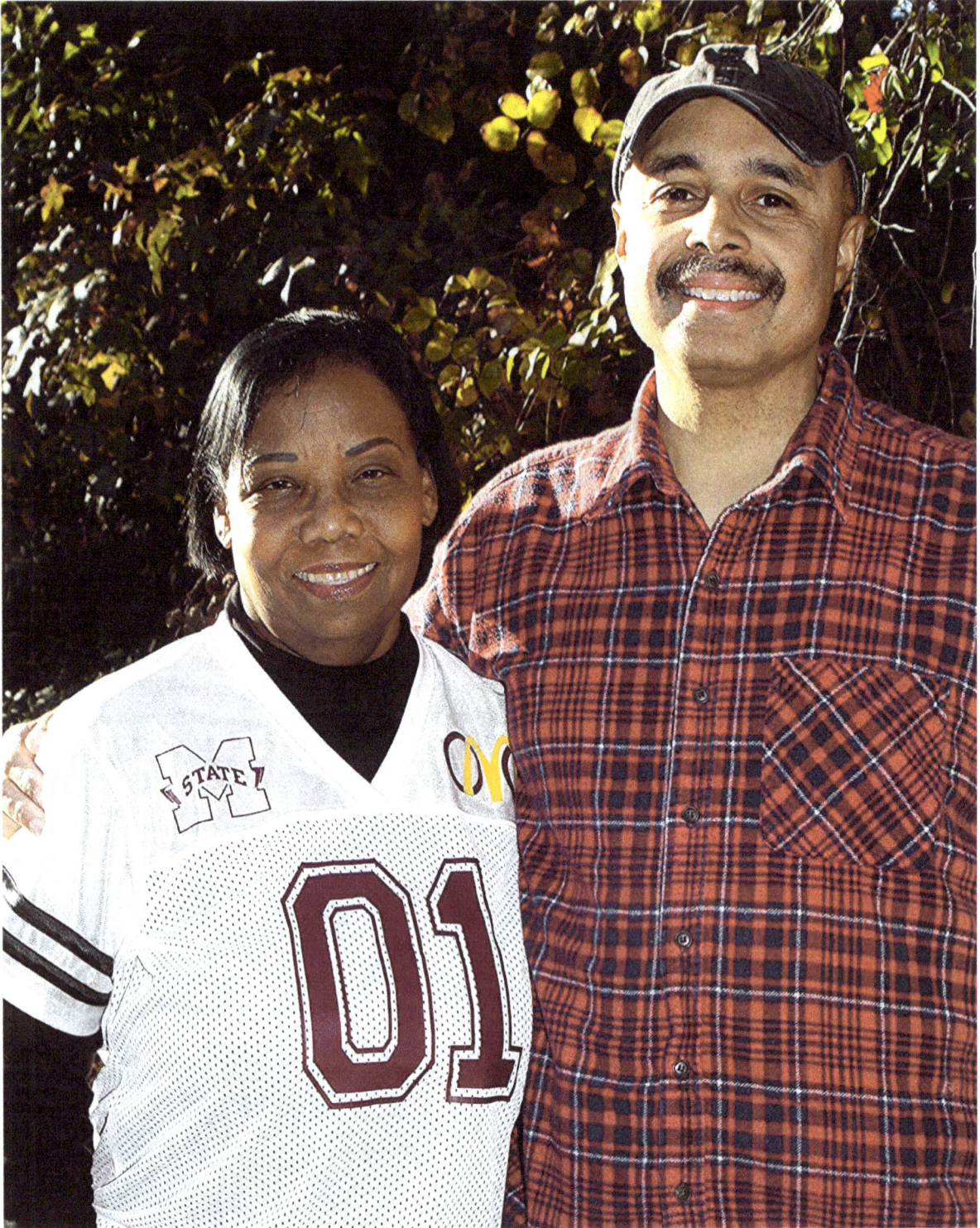

"Trinidad Pride & Joy" Sherral Baker **#1** – with husband Tony • November, 2014

Sherral Baker – a life defined by lovingkindness and compassion to others

Addendum: Margarita Isabel Reyes Martinez (11/2013 - 7/2014) & One More USA Tour
A lot has changed as I insert this new chapter of my life for this book's second edition. I had spent ten months living with Rosa Alvania in Santo Domingo from March, 2011, until January of 2012. My return to Miami Gardens, Florida was difficult as I could not afford an apartment and needed to resume my status as "homeless" until nine months later when my brother Michael gifted me with our Dad's 1990 Pontiac Transport Minivan. This became my last home on wheels and lifted me out of the perilous streets of Miami until September of 2013 when I sold it for an airline ticket to Medellin, Colombia. For personal reasons between us the relationship between Rosa Albania and myself had come to an end. I accepted an invitation from my friend Sergio Cuartas Velazquez to rent an apartment he had in the pueblo of Ayapel-Cordoba. It was an eight hour bus ride north of Medellin and presented itself as a time capsule of the past, almost like a town that had been forgotten. The trip to this remote pueblo gave me the opportunity to experience the stunning beauty of the verdant mountains and lush valleys of Colombia. This is truly a most beautiful country. My soul was uplifted immediately to share such a space in time as this. I realized that this was a country that I could very comfortably call my home. But in order to obtain resident status I would need to be gainfully employed or married to a Colombian woman. As my 90-day visa was nearing its expiration date of December 12, 2013, I made plans to visit Maracaibo, Venezuela to surprise the friends I had made twelve years earlier and to pass the holidays with them and then I could re-enter Colombia with a new visa. Then Fate stepped in once again and I crossed paths with a beautiful Colombian woman, una India del tribo Zenú, at Ayapel's famous restaurant *Donde Jorge* belonging to an acquaintance of mine, Jorge Emiliano Pérez Lozano. I had the good fortune to meet Margarita Isabel Reyes Martinez and a serious relationship soon developed between us. I travelled to Panama instead of Venezuela to extend my visa and we began living together, the two of us with her precious six year old daughter Eliana, Margarita's pride and joy. We were to-gether for eight months until circumstances presented themselves requiring an end to the relationship.

Margarita Reyes Martinez e hija Eliana Duque Reyes   Ayapel, Colombia   Nov - 2013

I needed to return to the US for emergency surgery to have my gall bladder and kidney stones removed. I spent the next four months in Richmond, VA, living with my brother Paul and his wife Karen who most graciously offered their home for what turned out to be a very lengthy stay of convalescence. These were some of the best months of my life. Getting to know my brother once again on a deeply personal level was exhilarating for my soul as we shared many things together that we could not have had the opportunity to do otherwise. I am forever grateful to my brother Paul and his wife Karen.

With the help of my brother Paul I purchased a 1999 Chrysler Town & Country minivan and set out to visit the USA and many of my friends along the way, some of whom I had not seen for many years. I stopped first in Mississippi to see my good friend Sherral Baker and her husband Tony, then proceeded to Mesa, AZ to see my friends Sandra Andrews and Gladys Caquimbo. While in Mesa I borrowed my 28X40" print of the *Grateful Dead* from the Millet House Gallery to have it scanned for a digital file *(one of the two most important images in this book on pp. 56-57)*, then headed to California where I visited with Kristie Edwards, Judi Campanaro, and my long lost brother Mark DeRoche Myhr whom I had only seen once when he was a few months old *and now is a successful engineer at the age of 43!* I proceeded to Lower Lake in northern CA and spent a month with my friends Terri Larsen and Peter Shifman and my new friend Loren Wolf *(awesome sculptress)*, then to Boise, Idaho, to visit with Jim Cochell and his wife Joanne. A lot of great times with some very amazing people. I finally had the opportunity in Provo, Utah, to meet with Jon D. Green, the professor emeritus from BYU who wrote the Preface to this book. Then I proceeded to Florida and visited lastly with Zoraida and Alejandro Mercedes and Hector Emilio Fernandez before saying good-bye once again to the USA and returning to the Dominican Republic. I had 'parked' my "international conga" in Alcarrizos, Santo Domingo three years earlier and was anxious to reunite with my one true love that has been with me since 1985. When I reunited with my drum and the percussion instruments I had brought with me, it was time to celebrate at the home of my friends Augustin and Yendry Peluche—with their parents and brothers and sisters. It was a ritual to remember! The sounds of Zacarías y Santos, Raulín y Reyes, Vargas y Martínez and many more can still be heard round and round in my brain, such is the richness of song from *Los Bachateros!*

One Final Consideration: "To Be Or Not To Be" In A Relationship

All my life I have strived for the best relationship possible in marriage but have been repeatedly unsuccessful. I now have been exposed to "The Transcendental Way of Zen" which eschews the concepts of *relationship* and *marriage* in preference for *relatedness* and *friendliness* and I find that I am a lot happier person in life because of this fundamental change. To wit: *"First meditate, be blissful, then much love will happen of its own accord. Then being with others is beautiful and being alone is also beautiful. Then it is simple, too. You don't depend on others and you don't make others dependent on you. Then it is always a friendship, a friendliness. It never becomes a relationship, it is always a relatedness. You relate, but you don't create a marriage."* Marriage is clearly not for everyone and after several attempts to achieve happiness within its realm, I for one must admit that it can not be for me.

*I would like to share once again what I consider to be **the most important words of this book**: (+ p.95)*

The power of one's will combined with the power of love and kindness is truly monumental. We need to bring these forces together actively at the conscious level, make them part of our way of life, the way that we relate to one another for the good of all.   Dennis DeRoche

Good things come to those who wait but not to those who sit on their laurels and do nothing. Keep on doing and being the best that you can knowing that many good things will come to you. Pay your dues and be prepared to enjoy the fruits of your labors. **Because Karma is a beautiful thing.** ☺

Moraliza Valenzuela Ramirez   Yuly Tejeda Soto   Rosario Encarnación Furcal

"Tres Mujeres de La Amabilidad y La Compasión para Los Demas"

La Caleta-Boca Chica, Santo Domingo, La República Dominicana • 31-7-2016

"Cuando se tiene Amor en su corazón y Respeto para los demás, tendrá la Paz."
"When you have Love in your heart and Respect for others, you will have Peace." dd

"En cada acto de nuestra vida debemos de sembrar amor."
"In every act of our lives we must sow love."   Oxalc

"Debes tener siempre fría la cabeza, caliente el corazón y larga la mano."
"One must always keep a cool head, warm heart and compassionate hand."
Confucius

Aztec Drum

"WHAT YOU LEAVE BEHIND IS NOT WHAT IS
ENGRAVED IN STONE MONUMENTS,

BUT WHAT IS WOVEN INTO THE
LIVES OF OTHERS"

PERICLES – Greek Statesman: 495-429 BC

118

Sacred Aztec Rhythms
Navajo Reservation
Northern Arizona

"I see you."

Epilogue: In Tribute to Quetzalcoatl

Not since the spellbinding enthrallment I had experienced as witness to the purest Niyabinghi beat accompanying the vocals of Ty Kennerson had I partaken in such a powerful performance of drumming as the sacred rhythms being pounded out by this Aztec master and soul keeper of his culture's tradition. He was the percussion component of a visiting Aztec dance troupe from Los Angeles performing way up in northern Arizona on the Navajo Reservation.

For someone such as myself, drummer and percussionist for most of my life, this opportunity granted me to capture these images and experience these sounds up close and personal was a treat and a gift and something I will always treasure. I am so happy I chose to be a disciple of the drum; I cannot derive greater pleasure than to receive into my being such as I experienced on this day, the sacred beating of drums passed down from centuries of generations of Aztec culture, so proud and great a civilization that the Aztec empire was for all of its domination in Mesoamerica. And the spirit of the *Aztec god of the arts, of learning and knowledge Quetzalcoatl* was sure to have been here as well. Experiences such as these *woven into the lives of others* as this one was for me eminently qualify as "threshold moments" to live for and live through. I hope I have been able to weave a few threads of my own into the souls of a few more out there.

James Cameron's AVATAR was a monumental leap forward in movie-making for all of its techno-logical achievements and as well for its timely messaging for us humans as caretakers of our earth, suggesting that our stewardship leaves much to be desired. Indeed our civilization itself is in the crosshairs as we continue the nonstop raping of our planet for its natural resources at all costs for its obtainment. At some point, there will be no more. At some point we will reach the *unobtainable*. I was most affected by Cameron's magnanimous look at what the indigenous have to offer in our world. He rightfully suggests that we must *see the other side* to understand and fully appreciate one another's worlds. When the outsider can say to his indigenous brother "I see you," a basis for moving forward is established and we can then have a much more compelling interest to preserve each other's world. What is observable is that we are living in the same world but act as if there are two, the world of *them* and the world of *us*. It's as if the dominant culture is taking a condescending view towards his indigenous brother (as the mining company boss Parker Selfridge did of the Na'Vi of Pandora) which is WRONG. *We are all the same even as we are different* and we each have a great influence upon one another. And we can learn so much more about each other and our mutual future if we would allow ourselves to do so. And we must agree that some grounds are sacred, there is no *eminent domain*. *August 9th – International Day of the World's Indigenous Peoples

"We are all the same even as we are different"
****Four Sacred Colors of Humankind: Red + Yellow + Black + White = One Human Race
 "RACISM"   *DOES   NOT*   EXIST – HATRED FOR ONE'S ETHNICITY DOES – WE MUST STOP USING THE WORDS *"RACIST"* & *"RACISM"* – And stop insulting our own intelligence! **You can't have racism if there is only ONE Human Race!** The word 'racism' is used to mean, generally speaking, the hatred of a group of people who have a different color of skin or different culture than our own - but that's not 'racism' - *it is 'hatred for some other person's/group's ethnicity'.* So that person or group of people are practicing hatred of another's ethnicity or background or simply showing intolerance for another person's color of skin. There should be a new word(s) invented to replace the misnomers 'racist' and 'racism,' like 'ethnicite' or the practice of 'ethnicizing' or 'anti-blackism'/'whiteism' – practiced by 'melanites' - those who cannot accept the dark-

skinned pigmentation of others or its lack thereof- **because the word 'racist' itself perpetuates segregation**, is a word that is emotionally charged with hatred and prejudice and only makes matters worse among us *when in all reality we do not belong to different races* -- **we are all of the _same_ human species** - known scientifically as: **species Homo sapiens**. There are not 'Black Homo sapiens' or 'White Homo sapiens' or 'Asian Homo sapiens' or 'Indigenous Homo sapiens' --- *there are no sub-species* – we are all equally the same- **THERE IS ONLY THE ONE HUMAN RACE OF HOMO SAPIENS** & WE HAPPEN TO COME IN **FOUR SACRED COLORS**:

RED YELLOW **BLACK** WHITE – *With Many Ethnic Backgrounds* – **Hello!**
Wake Up World To A New Vision – **_How It Is_** – & Let's All Make This Work Together!!

*"To truly know the Black man and the Red man and the Yellow man and the White man is to love the WHOLE that is US" -- dd * * Xenophobia is an insidious disease – the enemy among us!*

ONE HUMAN RACE -- ONE BLOOD -- ONE WORLD
THE BROTHERHOOD & SISTERHOOD OF HUMANKIND
O   N   e

* **Read:** Robert Sussman's "The Myth of Race: The Troubling Persistence of an Unscientific Idea"
http://www.amazon.com/Myth-Race-Troubling-Persistence-Unscientific/dp/0674417313/ref=sr_1_1?s=books&ie=UTF8&qid=1428414429&sr=1-1&keywords=robert+sussman+the+myth+of+race

"Biological races do not exist--and never have. This view is shared by all scientists who study variation in human populations.
Yet racial prejudice and intolerance based on myth of race remain deeply ingrained in Western society. In his powerful examination of a persistent, false, and poisonous idea, Robert Sussman explores how race emerged as a social construct from early biblical justification to the pseudoscientific studies of today."

o—o o—o   o—o   o—o   o—o   o—o   o—o   o—o   o—o   o—o   o—o   o—o   o—o   o—o   o—o   o—o

Brazil ♨ 477   **Honduras** ♨ 111   **Colombia** ♨ 77   **Peru** ♨ 67   **Mexico** ♨ 43

Martyrs from 2002-2014   **HOW**   **MANY**   **MORE**   **?   ?   ?**
NOW! We must address the continuing injustices being wrought upon our planet –
The Continuing Rape, Violation and Destruction of Our Most Precious World Treasure –
The AMAZON RAINFOREST & The GENOCIDE/ETHNOCIDE of Its Indigenous People
* A real-life AVATAR is being played out in the Amazon Rainforest of Brazil, Ecuador, Peru, and Colombia. And *after nearly 30 years of Texaco and Chevron drilling for oil in Ecuador,* (1964-1992),

their legacy is appalling. ☣ Known as **'Chevron's Chernobyl in the Amazon,'** Texaco, now part of

Chevron since 2001, "dumped billions of gallons of toxic waste water into the rivers and streams resulting in widespread devastation of the rainforest ecosystem and local indigenous communities – one of the worst environmental disasters in history. They left behind 350 wells and 1000 open-

air unlined waste pits filled with crude and toxic sludge." ☠ *Amazon Watch*

Loggers and state-backed oil and mining projects are attacking the Amazon in full force. Pre-eminent activists are being murdered. Two leaders who tried to make a presence at the Lima

Climate Change Conference COP20 held from Dec 1-14-2014 were executed: anti-logging activist Edwin Chota and anti-mining campaigner José Isidro Tendetza Antún. Peru ranks fourth in the repression of environmental activists (67 have been murdered from 2002-2014). [During this same period, 477 environmental activists lost their lives in Brazil, 111 in Honduras, 77 in Colombia, and 43 in Mexico- according to the NGO Global Witness Report *How Many More?* "All of them are victims of an ongoing colonial genocide and cruel exploitation of native populations that began with the Age of Exploration and continues to this day." Global Witness in conjunction with the UN Human Rights Council is calling on governments and the international community to monitor, investigate and punish these crimes.] Honduran activist and winner of the 2015 Global Environmental Prize, Berta Cáceras: *"They follow me. They threaten to kill me, to kidnap me, they threaten my family. That is what we face."* A member of the indigenous Tolupán in Honduras, *"We aren't going to give up the struggle to keep our natural resources clean and in the hands of the community. There are those who want easy money by tearing up the land, contaminating the water. We have been here respecting the earth that gives us food and we intend to stay here fighting for our right to feed ourselves."* The report states, "The true authors of these crimes- a powerful nexus of corporate and state interests- are escaping unpunished."

OUR Rainforest is under full frontal assault!   And it is all state-sponsored. We are losing the Amazon. *** Go to: www.amazonwatch.org to see what you can do. **Let's not let these injustices go unchallenged**. We have these great events such as the People's Climate March of Sept 21, 2014 in New York City (attended by Amazon Watch) where 400,000 participated and just two days later the United Nations Climate Summit and a week later in Peru, the COP20, the Lima Climate Change Conference, all to coalesce world discussion into action- but heads of state to a person in the Amazon continue the doomsday march into destruction of our most grandiose gift to mankind. I don't know if we can save our precious Amazon- there are so many bent upon exploiting and destroying it for personal gain with no thought to indigenous life, whether it be the flora, the fauna or the people themselves.   Nothing seems to make any difference as long as there are ores to be mined, oil to be drilled for, trees to cut down or rivers to be dammed- as long as the myopic greed of people in power continue to subjugate the innocent masses of people struggling to eke out a self-sufficient way of life in harmony with Nature as they have done for countless generations and whose only desire is to continue doing so.

ETHNOCIDE

"The President of Brazil Dilma Rousseff says the dams (such as the Belo Monte Dam over the Xingu River, the third largest hydroelectric dam in the world with a planned capacity of 11,233 MW) provide cheap electricity, *but the cost is paid here in the destruction of the environment and the destruction of people's lives.* [15,000 square km of Brazilian rainforest, the forced displacement of 40,000 people, including 25,000 indigenous people from 40 ethnic groups] **Indigenous peoples** of the forests **have long called for** *a shift in our collective consciousness, a different world view that celebrates our interdependence on a living, thriving Earth."* [1] *(emphases added)*
Jonathan Watts – The Guardian 12.16.2014

[1]Just as the Hopi emphasize, koyaanisqatsi • *"a state of life that calls for another way of living"*

Many years ago while walking my hometown city streets of Hartford, Connecticut, I came upon a placard on a telephone pole and wrote down immediately the words I found to make them part of my philosophy of life:

"There is a destiny that makes us brothers; none goes his way alone –
All that we send into the lives of others comes back into our own."

Edwin Markham

Gratitude & Acknowledgments

Very special thanks go out to my lifetime friends of the heart, mind and soul- Judith Campanaro and Carlos Hernández Chávez, who have always been there for me as comrade collaborators throughout my professional life, just as my friends Chuck Horvath and Peter Potaski have been during my earlier, formative years. Each one of these special friendships has added immeasurably to my personal life and has been instrumental in my evolvement as a human being. I am blessed to have been a part of their lives.

As well, I am forever indebted to the scholarly contribution I have received from Jon D. Green, Professor Emeritus of Brigham Young University, for his forthright dissection of this biography. His thorough examination of my life's story with literary referencing is most appreciated and also very instructive for the reader. *In addition, email correspondence with Jon inspired the title of this book.*

The tutelage and inspiration of Dr. Sandra Sutton Andrews, a guru of cyber-space and hero of bridging the digital divide for accessibility to all people including the impoverished and disadvantaged in life, has been instrumental to my evolution as a change agent activist and for that I am both fortunate and grateful. Because of Sandra and her daughter Melissa, a presence on the Net was established for my photographic works within an artists' forum at the formerly active site: www.floaters.org *(6/2001-10/2010)* A new and improved version is being developed for release.

Sandra Sutton Andrews: *Educational Technology Researcher, Nonprofit Technology Volunteer*

I thank my ex-wife Jennifer Rebholz for her contribution to this book and for all she has given to my life as I could not have accomplished as much in my journey without her. And special thanks go out to my brothers Michael and Paul DesRoches who have contributed so very much to my life- and to my brother Mark DeRoche Myhr who made such a big difference in my life during my time of need.

And I must not forget my friend and V.I.P. socio-political activist Terri Larsen, a true advocate of righteous causes. Our country and our world need more people like her bringing causes and issues to conscious awareness--sharing the knowledge and staying politically involved. As she has said to me, *"It will take all of us to make true change, just keep fighting the good fight, bro!"* *Public Access TV, Radio & the Internet* • Facebook: **SSS Multimedia**   Email: **info@sssmultimedia.com**

SSS ≈ SENDING SMOKE SIGNALS ♨ ≈ ≈ ≈ ≈ ≈ ≈ ≈

When I was at my lowest and found myself living in the streets of Miami, I was fortunate to encounter two very caring souls who I refer to as fellow soldiers in *The Army of Righteousness*, souls who have stepped up to be positive change agents for the good of others and who have lent me a helping hand and a way out of the downtrodden morass I found myself mired in. *Thank you, Sherral Baker for your lovingkindness and compassion.* Many thanks also go out to Shelley Stephenson for being there as a true friend as well during my time of deepest need. I am truly blessed to have received so much from each of you and I treasure the exceptionalism you both have shown to me as human beings from your friendship and support. *And thanks to **McD's (Marc O'Ferrall, OMG)** & **Dunkin D's** for Wi-Fi hook-ups. If it were not for these free internet connections, I as a homeless person could not have written this book - nor could I have if it weren't for **Capital One** giving me the credit to finance this project - as I am the world's worst fund-raiser -- *it is interesting that things come to you in life when you are ready to have them - "a la kairos."*

Many special thanks as well go out to my life-long friends Wayne and Gail Ryznar who have always been there for me through thick and thin and to JoEllyn Hyska, a dedicated social activist who personifies kindness and compassion. And, finally, thanks to supporters Yuly Tejeda, Rosario Encarnación & Moraliza Valenzuela *(Dom Rep)*, Elizabeth Matos, Clayton E. Long, and Conny Kasse for their contributions and aid to my cause. I am most grateful to all those mentioned . . . & :

☀ I am truly thankful and blessed for all those who have had a positive role in my life. ✌ to all

INDEX

125

Reviews

A life journey interwoven with a philosophical ideology, June 29, 2013

By Paul R. Desroches Sr. "Virginia Ragtopper" :

This review is from, **To Be Totally Real Is To Be Totally Free Is To Be Totally Alive: Never Let Injustice Go Unchallenged** (Paperback):

While I rarely give 5 stars to books I've consumed, this non-fiction work reeks of real and meaningful stuff. Dennis DeRoche is unabashedly honest and disarming in his explication of unfortunate events which have had momentous effect on his life. More important, however, is that throughout his unusual presentation of personal history accompanied by actual photographs of people, places, and cultural venues that have been instrumental in his journey is a positivism and a hopefulness and a confidence that emerges which offers real insight as to how the world might evolve as a better place. Intelligently written, with many references to personal relationships (as with Timothy Leary, for example) DeRoche lays out his journey through life as a kind of didactic expression of salient lessons learned from his many varied experiences. Reading between the words, it offers guideposts for all of us to find peace in our lives, and dares to posit that there is a reason to believe that men can live together in harmony, by adopting principles espoused by inspirational minds like Haile Selassie, Bob Marley, along with many other luminescent minds in history. Bring an open mind to this unusual presentation of ideas and personal history, and you may be surprised at what you end up reflecting about. This author dares to be different, but seeks the same ideals as most of us……fulfillment in life, peace within oneself, peace among mankind, and meaning through honesty, trust, and hopefulness.
Recommended!

"'The Truth Will Set You Free' is the captivating legacy of a unique individual who faces the challenges of life with fearless tenacity. Not only does DeRoche pay homage to those who have touched his soul, but he presents a candid and intimate view of his journey to freedom. Bursting with life, his story is both inspirational and empowering. A memorable read that will keep you turning pages to the very end."   Judith Campanaro, LHMC, AT
         Author of "Art For The Soul, The Healing Magic of Creativity"

Preliminary Book Reaction/Feedback (pre-publication)

10/28/2010   "I absolutely love Chapter 3 on. I think you have a wonderful voice, articulate and inciteful and ironic and often humorous. Evidence of a classical biopic are evident."   Dave DesRoches

11/2/2010   "It's great. Congratulations." Sandra Sutton Andrews, PhD
Director, Research & Design, Applied Technologies Institute, Arizona State University

3/7/2011   "Congrats on achieving this…you have always had strong emotive force coursing through your gray matter, and the ability to organize your life experiences in a tome such as this is remarkable."   Paul DesRoches

3/9/2011   "Crazy, Lobo! What a captivating piece of work. So much to learn from your life, man! I'm honored to have been a part of it and hope that sometime not far from now we'll meet again. The book is awesome reading--honest as I haven't read before. Thank you. What else can I say, my brother? Coyote."   Carlos Hernández Chávez

3/27/2011   "Job well done Dennis. I love the analysis of survival section—surprised and honored that you quoted my blog—I love the Hopi u-tube. I love the book. You're amazing-please be careful on your journey. I wish you all the best."   Judith Campanaro

3/27/2011   "The book should be a movie."   Michael DesRoches

8/11/2011   "I am looking through your transcript. It is awesome."
          Dee Gans   stayingwell@comcast.net

11/1/11   "Everything looks GREAT!!!!! Good luck with your publishing efforts!"
                                                    Jennifer Rebholz

K   I   N   D   N   E   S   S   I   S   T   H   E   K   E   Y
24 HOURS of KINDNESS
https://www.facebook.com/thekindnesscenter/videos/10153700578607370/?pnref=story.unseen-section

Tribute to Wayne W. Dyer – for helping us with understanding *forgiveness* and *blame*:

Forgiveness • "The willingness to forgive is a sign of spiritual and emotional maturity. It is one of the great virtues to which we all should aspire. Imagine a world filled with individuals willing both to apologize and to accept an apology. Is there any problem that could not be solved among people who possessed the humility and largeness of spirit and soul to do either –or both- when needed."

Blame • "All blame is a waste of time. No matter how much fault you find with another, and regardless of how much you blame him, it will not change you. The only thing blame does is to keep the focus off you when you are looking for external reasons to explain your unhappiness or frustration. You may succeed in making another feel guilty about something by blaming him, but won't succeed in changing whatever it is about you that is making you unhappy."

≈   ≈   ≈   ≈   ≈   ≈   ≈   ≈   ≈   ≈   ≈

The Moment of A Lifetime   (Fate and Destiny have been working overtime for this surprise-)
How does one begin to put into words the most incredible experience of one's life? I will try. I had just terminated a relationship with a woman in La Caleta, Boca Chica on March 1st, 2016. I had allowed myself once again to become victim of a *chapiadora* and knew when to cut my losses.   I decided to visit my favorite spot at the ocean about a ten minutes' walk away with a close view of the big waves crashing on the volcanic surf-line. It's always an awesome experience to partake in the forces of Mother Nature and today was no different. The sun was not far above the horizon and in a few minutes more would be engulfed by our spinning marble. I was there for about 40 minutes with nobody else in sight and then in one shining moment of Fate my solitude was broken like---
"Hola! Soy Estefani." (as if to say, *"I'm the one you've been waiting for!"*) A beautiful African-Caribbean woman *(India Amazona)* plops down beside me on the stone wall in front of the crashing waves. She came to me like an apparition out of thin air- like a mermaid from the very sea in front of me! Our chemistry was immediate and beautiful and she has turned out to be the biggest love of my life that I had been searching for--for so many years! She is the miracle of my life, my very own

129

Black Magic Woman as Santana was so apt to name another. I finally met someone on this island who truly cares for and loves me for me. Age does not have to be a barrier in relationships. *"Age is a state of mind- if you don't mind, it doesn't matter."* What's real is the love that pours out of two human beings for each other- it is a beautiful experience and we are blessed to share our lives together. Once again I am being forced to choose between 'a relationship' or 'relatedness.' The *Transcendental Way of Zen (p.116)* has made its mark upon me and I have come to view this path as a higher level of consciousness to manifest one's love for another. But *a relationship it is*- and <u>relatedness</u> is what we share of our lives together. I have never wavered from my desire to cultivate a relationship with an Indigenous or African woman and I am now blessed with the life of *Estefani Rosario Mansweta - a woman of both Indigenous and African heritage-*
"Seek and ye shall find"   *The Power of Love is the Magic it holds in its Giving to others –*

Fani Rosario Mansweta y yo "Amor á Kairos" La Caleta, Boca Chica 2 Marzo 2016

130

Para El Mundo Hispánico –

El momento de su vida - *Suerte y el Destino han sido trabajando horas extras para este sorpresa-*
¿Cómo se empieza a poner en palabras la experiencia más increíble de la vida de uno? Intentaré. Acababa resuelto una relación con una mujer en La Caleta, Boca Chica el 1 de marzo de 2016. Me había permitido volver a ser víctima de una *chapiadora* y sabía cuándo cortar por lo sano. Decidí visitar mi lugar favorito en el océano a unos diez minutos a pie y ofrece una vista cercana de las grandes olas rompiendo en la volcánica línea de la resaca. Siempre es una experiencia impresionante para participar en las fuerzas de la madre naturaleza y hoy no fue diferente. El sol no estaba muy por encima del horizonte y en unos pocos minutos más podría verse envuelto por nuestro mármol hilatura. Yo estaba allí durante unos 40 minutos con nadie más a la vista y luego en un momento brillante del destino mi soledad se rompió como -- *"Hola! Soy Estefani!"* (Como si fuera a decir: *"Yo soy ella que usted ha estado esperando!"*) Una mujer afro-caribeña hermosa *(India Amazona)* se deja caer a mi lado en la pared de piedra delante de las olas. Ella vino a mí como una aparición de la nada, como una sirena desde el mar frente a mí. Nuestra química fue inmediata y hermoso y que ha resultado ser el más grande amor de mi vida que yo había estado buscando - por tantos años! Ella es el milagro de mi vida, mi propia mujer negra de la magia como Santana era tan apto para nombrar a otra. Finalmente me encontré con alguien en esta isla que realmente cuida y me quiere para mí. La edad no tiene por qué ser una barrera en las relaciones. "La edad es un estado de la mente, si no le importa, no importa." Lo que es real es el amor que brota de dos seres humanos de entre sí -- es una experiencia hermosa y tenemos la suerte de compartir nuestras vidas juntos. Una vez más estoy siendo obligado a elegir entre "una relación" o "un estado de relacionados." *La manera trascendental del Zen (p.116)* ha dejado su huella en mí y yo he venido para ver esta ruta como un nivel superior de conciencia para manifestar el amor por el otro. *Pero una relación lo es-* y el estado de relacionados es lo que tenemos de nuestras vidas juntos. Nunca he dudado de mi deseo de cultivar una relación con una mujer indígena o africana y ahora estoy bendecido con la vida de Estefani Rosario Mansweta quien es india y africana – *Que Fortuna!*

"Quien busca halla."

El Poder del Amor es la Magia que posee en su Dar a los demás

≋   ≋   ≋   ≋   ≋   ≋   ≋   ≋   ≋   ≋   ≋   ≋   ≋   ≋   ≋   ≋   ≋

* Me gustaría compartir lo que considero que son las palabras más importantes de este libro :

El poder de la voluntad de uno combinado con el poder del amor y la bondad es verdaderamente monumental. Es necesario hacer llegar estas fuerzas conjuntamente de forma activa en el nivel consciente, hacerlos parte de nuestra forma de vida, la forma en que nos relacionamos unos con otros por el bien de todos.   Dennis DeRoche

Las cosas buenas vienen a aquellos que esperan, pero no a los que habitan en los laureles y no hacer nada. Sigue haciendo y siendo lo mejor que se puede saber que hay muchas cosas buenas vendrán a ti. Pagar sus cuotas y estar preparado para disfrutar de los frutos de tu trabajo.

Debido a que el Karma es una cosa hermosa. ☺

www.ingramcontent.com/pod-product-compliance
Lightning Source LLC
Chambersburg PA
CBHW050644150426
42813CB00054B/1175